# The Last Snake Man

# THE
# LAST
# SNAKE MAN

Austin J Stevens

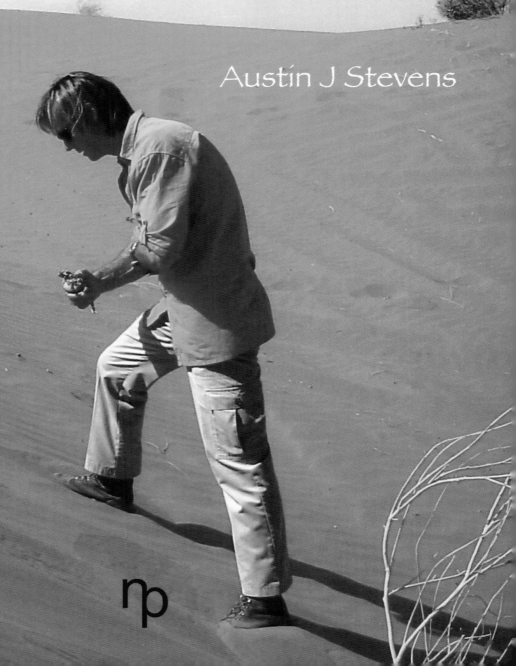

np

# Contents

**Credits & Acknowledgements**
The author wishes to thank Linda Hattenbach for the cover picture photohraphy, together with additional pictures of the author travelling. The following people are also warmly thanked for the assistance they have given the author and occasional photographs used; Graham Booth, Gillian Burke, Keith Brust, Steven Cassidy, Becca Cecil-Wright, Duncan Chard, Simon Christopher, Robin Cox, Michael Davies, Natalie Dunmore, Rob Franklin, Andrew Graham Brown, Andy Hawley, Laura Hervey, Bernin Isaac, Frank Krausse, William Lamar, James Leigh, Rory McGuinness, Bruce Means, Matt Oldfield, James Pursey, Neil Rettig, Ian Salvage, Warwick Sloss, Richard Sprawson, Toby Strong, Andrew Thompson, Mathew Thompson, Amy Twomey, John Waters, Steve Webb and Romulus Whitaker.

The Last Snake Man by Austin J. Stevens
ISBN13 9780953656462
© Austin J. Stevens 2007, all rights reserved
First Published in May 2007 by Noir Publishing, 10 Spinney Grove, Hereford, HR1 1AY.
Copyright © Noir Publishing 2007

British Library Cataloguing in Publication Data:
A catalogue record for this book is available from the British Library

The publisher wishes to thank Sally Andrews and Bob Hughes for additional assistance with this volume.

For further information on Noir Publishing titles and Distribution please visit www.noirpublishing.co.uk

For Barbara

# CHAPTER ONE

# For My Country

Nothing we had been taught, not all the hours, days and months of training, none of it, could fully prepare us for that first, sudden staccato of murderous sound. Not all the lectures, not all the priming and realistic rehearsals. It was as though time had suddenly stopped, and all movement strained under the effect, as the brain fought sluggishly to convey the impulses necessary to initiate the movement desired of the limbs. It was the most terrifying moment of my life !

But I was not alone and in front of me I saw hunched bodies shrouded in camouflage and adorned in natural foliage hurled unceremoniously sideways and at full stretch, as the staccato of sound was suddenly dwarfed by the overpowering thunder of a detonated Claymore mine. And it was, for me, without doubt, as I am sure it was for the others, the most terrifying moment of my life !

Off to my right, and slightly ahead of my position, the familiar thick-set figure of Jan Petser lurched backwards, almost losing his footing, as though struck by an invisible fist and suddenly crimson colour washed his neck — but he did not fall. Instead he forced his body forward and down towards the sandy floor, his left index finger tight around the trigger of his R1 military assault rifle — and copper-cased death spewed from the barrel. This blurred, split-second vision terminated the dream-like unreality, and my brain was suddenly free of the slow, sluggish effects and I followed Petser's example, emptying the contents of my first magazine in a second, as I dived for the earth, but to the opposite side, away from Petser.

As I pressed down hard on the magazine release, the container dropped into my waiting hand and I flipped it over smoothly to insert the attached refill and within seconds this too was empty and the smell of cordite and gelignite burned my nostrils and eyes. Again and again I released the magazines, flipped them round and repeated the motion, while the butt of the machine in my hand hammered into my shoulder until the pain was almost unbearable. Each of the ten men in the section carried sixty magazines of twenty rounds each and each one was doing now as Petser and I were - and the sound of it was terrifying !

From across the bush, someway off to the left of my position, I was suddenly aware of the over-riding, continuous staccato of the LMG (light machine gun). Our cover team of three men was directing a steady hail of bullets from the seemingly endless lengths of connected metallic belts. Operating from slightly higher ground, this machine was saturating the surrounding thick bush with rounds, probing and infiltrating every metre of space from where the attack had come. On the field radio, David Steenkamp was screaming "Kontak! Kontak!" and repeating our position over and over again. His body and face were flattened into the sandy earth, with his free hand clamped firmly over his head.

Though it is impossible at the time to gauge the force behind an ambush attack, all encounters are reacted to with the same retaliation strategy; concentrated return fire in all directions, followed by an immediate "follow up" operation under cover of the LMG's.

Now, from somewhere in the bush behind me, came the explosive release of two rocket grenades, launched from the barrels of assault rifles, and their streams of white smoke rose high into the cloud studded sky, to return to earth a hundred metres ahead with explosive force. This usually

*The one metre long Angolan dwarf python is considered one of the rarest snake species in the world*

meant that the attacking force had been pin-pointed and now all fire was trained in this direction, while barely centimetres over our heads the streaming blanket of tracers from the LMG covered us with unrelenting rhythm.

"BEWEEEEGGG!" ("Move!") screamed the sergeant, now for the first time raising himself from his position. "BEWEEEEGGG! SPREI UIT EN VOLG OP!" ("Move into follow-up!"). And there was a sudden decrease in firepower as camouflaged bodies miraculously appeared from the undergrowth to form a rickety line off to the right of the LMG position. Lunging for our positions in the line, our hearts pounding in our chests, we moved together, at all possible speed through the thick bush, bent low, rifles held high while, from behind, the LMG never missed a beat, covering our advance.

The advance line was divided into two sections of three or four men each. While one group moved ahead, the other remained low and gave covering fire. Following this, the firing line would then advance ahead of the first line, while they in turn supplied the covering fire. And as the line advanced, so the LMG team, at all times stationed off to the side of the advancing line, would move alongside, the machine gun now suspended at waist height, the heavy duty barrel glowing red from the friction of seemingly endless rounds fed through from the loaded metal belts.

*A youthful Austin during his time serving with the South African Defence Force.*

Run, zig-zag, drop down and fire! Up again. Run, zig-zag, drop down and fire! Until your chest is heaving with the effort and your legs tremble and stagger with exhaustion. Six months of intensive training was now being put to the extreme test. Fitness played a major role in the infantry and from day one we had been pushed to the extreme, with every imaginable exercise routine invented; running, jumping, carrying loads, climbing and a further host of aerobic type, basic training exercises. We had complained, grumbled and dodged wherever possible, never truly believing that we would ever be faced with any real need for it.

After six months of it we smirked, scoffed and were arrogant. That we were being foolish, we only suddenly realised the day the order came to mobilise. Suddenly our cosy, almost home-like bungalows, safely stationed on the outskirts of the Transvaal town of Middleburg, were exchanged for drafty tents, two thousand kilometres to the north, in a strange, unfamiliar land, somewhere, it was rumoured, close to the Angolan border !

So quickly had we been moved, first by train, then by plane, and finally by truck, that we did not even know in what direction we were headed. It was all "Hush hush", and rumours spread like wildfire and the sergeants and corporals gleefully kept us in suspense with lots of knowing "Tut tuts" and the traditional Afrikaans' "Nou gaan julle kak" ("Now you're going to shit") routines. Deep depression settled over us all as wives, lovers and familiar things were left behind and the Hercules troop carrier lifted into the night sky, destination unknown !

Since then, life had become very different and very important, as the reality of its frailty was brought crashing home to us with our first confrontation with bullet-riddled and mutilated bodies !

Landing at the air base Grootfontein, after hours of restless, broken and uncomfortable sleep in the cold metal body of the carrier, we were ushered hastily and unsympathetically to a waiting convoy of Bedford trucks which immediately started up and left the air strip one by one, as they were loaded full of men and equipment. Belching diesel smoke as they went, the trucks carried us for some eight hours non stop, before being met by a squadron of armoured vehicles which then escorted us the final distance.

Dumb-struck and feeling sorry for ourselves, we gazed out the back of the canvas covered Bedfords as the unfamiliar land outside rushed by. Mostly consisting of endless stretches of Mopane bush, there was little to cheer us and the dust churned by the tyres billowed up, causing us to cough and choke. Later, after being met by the escort of armoured vehicles, the trucks spread out more, keeping just within sight of each other as the surrounding bush grew thicker and taller and the sand below looser. We were warned to keep low, with rifles at the ready, with "one up the spout" and the safety catches off ! Tired, exhausted, hungry and filthy as we were, we now became apprehensive as well. Were we really in danger, or was it the usual army training attitude of "act as if the situation is real"?

However, it was real and, though as yet none of us knew exactly where, we suspected enough to guess that this was the front line area of South West Africa (Namibia), where South Africa deployed its forces to engage the enemy, SWAPO insurgents (South West African People's Organisation) trained and armed by Russians in Angola, Zambia and other African countries further north. Determined to rid Namibia of South African rule, they came not in waves, but in specialised, highly trained small groups; terrorist trained, programmed to trek southwards, fully armed with AK47 assault rifles, ammunition and an assortment of other sophisticated Russian and Chinese-made explosive devices. Their mission; to infiltrate and destroy places and installations of strategic importance to the South African government.

*Austin with his ten man infantry section in Angola*

The first Europeans to venture into the interior of South West Africa were explorers, later to be followed by gun runners and liqueur dealers who traded their goods for livestock from the local tribes. In 1878 the British annexed the Guano Islands along the coast and the harbour of Walvis Bay. In 1883 the German trader, Luderitz, acquired huge areas of land from the Nama Hottentots in the south of the country around what is today known as Luderitz Bay. A year later the German government placed the area under their protection and, by 1884, the Germans were well established over the entire land, except for British Walvis Bay and the Guano Islands.

During the First World War, South African troops successfully invaded the German occupied South West Africa and the country was placed under South African administrative control by the League of Nations.

By the year 1959, the first stirrings of African nationalism began its sweep across the continent. In South West Africa, the OPO (Owambo People's Organisation), under the leadership of Sam Nujoma, seized on social grievances for the purposes of agitation. (As indeed was happening in white ruled countries throughout the north). These movements soon became militant, which quickly escalated into violence, and Tanzania, under the Marxist regime of President Julius Nyerere, became the launching pad from which many African nationalist movements launched subversion back into their own lands. It was from here that the renamed OPO, (now SWAPO: South West Africa People's Organisation), backed by Soviet weaponry and indoctrinated my Marxist ideals, launched their offensive against the South African administration in power, the police, and, eventually, the defence force.

In the early years it had been the duty of the police force to patrol and secure the fifteen hundred kilometre length of the Namibian border (dividing Namibia from Angola and Zambia in the north), but as the pressure increased and infiltration by guerilla squads became more prolific (towards the end of the 1960's), the army took over the full operation, and so continued the bush war which would persist for another twenty years.

One of the numerous "pets" from Austin's early years - a venomous tree snake

Arriving finally, and without incident, at our new home to be, (for what turned out to be the following six months), we were immediately hurled headlong into further, and more specialised training; close-combat bush tactics, camouflage, personnel and anti-personnel landmine identification and disarming, tracking and assault techniques under fire, to name but a few. Only after some days of this concentrated training were we finally informed of our exact location on the map. The region was known as Kavango, which is divided from Angola by the Okavango river, and our training camp was some kilometres west of the pan-handle zone known as the Caprivi Strip, the most north-easterly part of this land called Namibia. We were two thousand kilometres from home, many of us away for the first time.

We were unhappy and nervous. This was the big league now and we felt out of our depth. There were lectures every day and the more we learned the more nervous we became. According to the officers in charge, the enemy was better trained than us, more experienced, fearless, and invisible! It was little wonder that after each such lecture there was near panic amongst us newcomers. Literally we were being thrown in at the deep end and it was now, one week later, while on a routine foot patrol that we made our first contact with the enemy and it still remains to this day, the most frightening moment of my life!

An African puff adder moving through lichen

Suddenly, there came a terrified scream from one of the leading team, and he fell to the ground still screaming. It was Chris Viljoen, better known as "Whitey" for his head of snowy white hair. He was hit in the leg, but from the resounding performance he was delivering, his life seemed not to be in immediate danger. However, this incident spurred another round of rifle rockets to be launched from the rear team and once more the staccato of machine gun fire was drowned by the combined explosions to the front. There was dust, sweat, running, wheezing, smoke and explosions and, through all of it not one of the enemy had yet been sighted! They were to all intents and purposes invisible in the bush and obviously more experienced than us.

Then, from above, came the sound that we all secretly had been praying for; the thunderous roar of powerful jet motors and great blades of spinning steel. Low over the trees they came, two helicopters spaced some distance apart, like giant birds of prey flying so low that their down-draft tore at our clothes and hurled a vortex of wind across the bush, bending the trees in its wake. As we gazed up at their approach, relief in our hearts, the two great machines thundered over our position and from their open sides suddenly came to life the murderous beat of the twin-mounted 50mm Browning machine guns – and all hell broke loose

for our attackers, now certainly running for their lives!

Constant radio communication with the choppers, guided us on the ground where, at full tilt, we advanced in a ragged line, all except Petser, who was still bleeding from the Claymore shrapnel that had lodged otherwise harmlessly beneath the fleshy skin of his neck, and Whitey, who continued to hurl abuse at the enemy he had not yet seen, whilst the medics attempted unsuccessfully to render him calm.

Steenkamp's radio message had saved the day, his broadcast co-ordinates being accurate to the metre. Green smoke grenades were ignited and within minutes a third chopper was landing within a clearing, in answer to Steenkamp's call for "Casevac" (casualty evacuation). Within a minute another chopper arrived which poured a fresh platoon of thirty men, with Bushmen trackers who melted into the bush. These were seasoned men, experienced in the art of bush war and, once they reached our advance team, we dropped back. The follow-up was in their expert hands now and we were retired by chopper back to base for de-briefing.

It was our first contact and, though we had not even seen the enemy, we had advanced, made ground and had reacted as we had been trained to. By the volume of fire we had been subjected to, it was obvious the enemy had been in some force, possibly a dozen men or more. We would soon know, as the progress of the follow-up operation crackled over the field radios.

Landing minutes later at base camp, we became immediately aware of the change of attitude. Helping hands were everywhere, carrying our kit and even our rifles. Even our base commander, Captain Brandt, (the sour old bastard), even he was now suddenly respectful. So it was in the army, and probably still is today, you are nothing until you have proved yourself. And we had proved ourselves that day and survived to speak of it. Silently, our dusty, sweat-streaked bodies still shaking with the aftershock of what we had just experienced, our hearts still revving from the adrenaline in our veins, we gathered together before our commanding officers. There was a new pride in our stance. We may not yet have been veterans, but we were certainly no longer the new boys on the block.

Raising his hand now, the captain signalled for us to bow our heads in prayer, for such is the way of the Afrikaaner, a strong supporter of the Lord's word and way. So, together and in silence, the entire group removed their cloth caps and bowed their heads in prayer, believers and non-believers alike. For whatever may be, one thing was for certain: we had just faced death that day, death in its most frightening form – on the battle field of man's war, and not one of us was yet nineteen years of age.

But not all times on the border were bad times. There were many good times, and the few occasions that we were actually faced with direct enemy contact were far out - numbered by more pleasant engagements. However, there was always a certain reserve, as one really did not know what the immediate future would bring.

With a name like Austin James Stevens, it was quite obvious that, if not directly British, I was at least of English background and it was somewhat of a mystery as to how exactly I came to be placed in an Afrikaans regiment. However, by the time the army discovered the mistake and suggested that I should be transferred to an English regiment, I had already firmly established myself with bed, position and friends. Thus, at my request, and

seeing as I was fluent in the Afrikaans language, I was allowed to stay.

My British background, in fact, stemmed from my father's side, as his father (my grandfather) was from Bristol, England. He had sailed to Africa and finally settled in South Africa, where he met and married an Afrikaans woman. From this marriage came three sons, one of whom was to be my father, Stanley Stevens, who later, too, met and fell in love with an Afrikaans woman, Mercia, my mother. In the late months of the year 1950, I was, in Africa, christened with the name of my grandfather. Six years were to pass before I was to be presented with a brother.

In childhood I was fortunate as we lived on the outskirts of town where much open ground and virgin bushveld still remained. This was encroached upon steadily as the years passed, but I was afforded some years to roam, study and appreciate the nature of Africa, be it at that time on so small a scale. It was here at the tender age of twelve years, that I made my first contact with the fascinating world of herpetology – reptiles and amphibians and, once bitten, (not literally yet!) the fever was never to leave me.

On the day I brought home my first "pet" snake my parents reacted as most would– with some horror! My father promptly chopped off the head of the luckless serpent, thereby sealing my resolve to pursue the subject with even greater determination! The battle raged throughout my high school days, and beyond. Neither of my parents had any inclination towards nature, in any of its diverse forms. I was to be trained as a lawyer or a doctor; nature did not figure anywhere in such plans. However, school records soon disclosed what I already knew, but what my parents refused to accept. My grades were not of the standard required for the needs of doctor or lawyer. Besides, I was too distracted to consider such study seriously as I spent most of my free time roaming and exploring the wonders of nature that I seemed to discover and re-discover everyday in the bush.

This, of course, supplied my parents with a strategic argument in their favour and I lived constantly under the threat of "boarding school" (my greatest fear) or, at least, the total expulsion of all my snakes and snake cages that I had by now, through much argument and tantrum, accumulated in my room. However, as is with most situations, there are usually more sides than one to view. So, when I brought home a poor school report card, I was traditionally threatened with the options and the matter was usually closed with my father promising to have all my snakes removed the very next day by the local snake park. However, friends and relations visited our home, they were quick to comment on my "snake career" and would insist on a show and talk on my interesting subject. At this time my father would preen visibly, as he explained to all how he helped to build some of the better cages and how adept his son was in the knowledge and handling of these housed serpents. Naturally the line was drawn when first I approached the subject of venomous species, but, by the time it was confirmed that I had indeed a number of these in stock, all my father did was further astound his friends with stories of my handling of these most feared of creatures!

Naturally, however, when one day I returned from a snake-catching expedition with a swollen hand, the result of a burrowing viper bite, a fresh argument was roused and the "war" intensified somewhat. For a time I truly thought that my parents had reached their limit of toleration. But what I had not suspected, was that by this time, they too, had come to terms with the matter, realising that obviously it was more than a passing

A South African berg adder

As its name suggests, the Madagascar day gecko is unusual amongst geckos as it is a diurnal species

An unusually patterned Namib Desert horned adder

phase for me. Thus, though naturally my safety was of prime importance to my parents, they reluctantly accepted the situation, deciding that encouragement would serve more good than condemnation. So it came about, once it was established that my life was in no danger, that my father once more still further astounded his friends with the next exciting episode of his son's adventures with the "death dealing" serpents!

Being a boy at school meant of course that I was much restricted from furthering my practical knowledge of nature and the creatures that lived wild in the bush. Though I spent every available minute of my time outdoors, it was the call of my country, ironically, to go to war, that was to some extent set me free and allow me my first exotic tastes of the "real thing".

Border bush patrols were my favourite as these allowed me not only the opportunity to take note of and experience the natural surroundings, but, of course, my eyes were on the constant alert for snakes and other interesting reptiles. My first encounter was with a harmless mole snake which innocently slithered across a game track not five metres ahead of the first men of the patrol section. This sighting was greeted with the resounding screams from half a dozen mouths; "SLANG! DAARS n SLANG! SKIET DIE DONDER!" (Snake! There's a snake! Shoot the bugger!) and an entire patrol section of ten men unmercifully opened up with all the considerable firepower at their disposal! The sound of it was deafening and any terrorists that may have been within kilometres of our position now knew exactly where we were!

Rushing blindly ahead and almost getting my butt shot up, I screamed in retaliation; "STAAK VUUR! STAAK VUUR!" (Hold your fire). But through the dust and smoke, there was no sign of the snake which I decided must either have been blasted to smithereens or escaped totally unscathed. Furious now, I turned on my comrades.

"Idiots!" I screamed in fury. "What the bloody hell are you firing at a bloody harmless snake for?" a statement that was greeted with open-mouthed astonishment, for not only was my scolding inclusive of our sergeant and corporal, (my superiors as I was only a lowly rifleman), but I was speaking in defence of the serpent – the harbinger of all the evils of the world, as it is written in "The Book".

Defiantly I glared at the men. Smoke was still exiting in wisps from the barrels of their rifles. In silence they stared back at me, mouths still open. Then Petser detached himself from the team to approach me. He and I had become close friends over the months of training together and were now accepted as a team. In other words wherever it was necessary for one of us to be, the other would be included. All operations in the bush war required that a man never be alone, not even to relieve himself when on patrol. So it was that everybody had their partners and Petser and I, unknown to us at the time, shared a bond that would see us together again in later years, when called up for Operation Protea, one of the major incursions into Angola.

Jan Petser was of average height, but with a thick set torso and arms, legs and neck to match; he gave the impression of being as wide as he was tall. With coarse, black hair, well-beaten nose (from boxing) and permanent beard stubble surrounding a heavy set jaw, he was a singularly perfect example of the Afrikaner nation; solid, steady, strong, fearless, while at the same time polite, hospitable and ever ready to crack a joke. His somewhat surly physical appearance in fact was in total violation of his true design and I grew to honour his reliability and friendship. With a curious, questioning tilt to his head, he now voiced what probably every man there was thinking.

*Previous picture: a back fanged sand snake uses its slender, agile body to move effortlessly through the branches of a tree*

"Haai Engelsman, is jy dan van jou kop af? Jy het nou amper jou gat gesien!" (Are you crazy Englishman. You almost saw your ass!).

"Well you can't go around shooting up the wildlife", I retaliated sharply, but a smile was forming on my lips as I, for the first time, fully comprehended just how ingrained their fear of snakes was. Here was a test for me if ever there was one. I decided there and then that I would introduce wildlife education, especially reptile education, into the war-making training programme of the South African Defence Force.

And so, after a number of further incidents with snakes, where I was more fortunate in catching the specimens, I soon had most of the men (not everybody) quite interested, and Petser very interested. It was natural thereafter that I be known along the lengths of the border as "DIE SLANGMAN" (The snakeman).

Little did I know at the time that this title would follow me all the days of my life up to the present day and that I would become known as the "Snake Man" of South Africa!

*A harmless but angry African egg-eating snake displays the black interior of its mouth as a defensive strategy*

# CHAPTER TWO

# Battle Wounds

To live Africa is to love Africa, with its primitive ways and pot-holed roads, its beauty, its wilderness, its poverty, and even its wars. For those of us born to Africa, it becomes a natural thing to follow its ways and for those that visit, their lives are often changed for ever. From the harsh desert regions to the north, through the vast tropical jungles of the central regions, and southwards to the rolling savannahs and wild bushveld country – there is no place like Africa.

And there is the wild game. Teeming herds of game of every description, from the largest elephant, the noblest of antelope, to the multitude of smaller creatures, found nowhere else in the world – only in Africa.

All this was displayed now, vividly, to us of the 4th Infantry Regiment of the South African Defence Force as we once more found ourselves being transported still further eastward along the most northerly rim of the Caprivi Strip, the eastern pan-handle region, where three front-line black African states shared a common border with Namibia, two at least of which, were known to support and aid the terrorist movement to the south.

We had just crossed the Kwando River which signalled the eastern extremity of Angola. North of us now lay Zambia, while to the east, as we were moving, lay Zimbabwe (at that time still Rhodesia). To the south lay Botswana, which also shared a border with Namibia to the west, and South Africa, some thousands of kilometres still further south.

In those early days of the bush war, the modern day landmine resistant vehicles had not yet been designed and troops were transported precariously along the sandy bush tracks in nothing more than standard Bedford five ton trucks and open Landrovers. The leading vehicles, however, had their floors, and where possible, sides, stacked with sandbags, in a rather pathetic attempt to deflect an explosion from below. This modification rendered the vehicles very heavy and uncomfortable for the troops now spread out on the sandbags, and thus only a few were so fitted and placed at the head of the convoy, where naturally, the landmines would be first encountered. Naturally near pandemonium reigned amongst the troops whenever the order was given to "climb aboard", as the entire company stampeded for the rear vehicles, desiring as much distance between themselves and the landmine "Detonator Trucks" as they sarcastically became known, as possible.

There were fights, screams, pushing, shoving and waves of abuse hurled in all directions as one hundred panic-stricken soldiers (actually still just boys) scrambled and fought to fit themselves on the already heavily overlaiden rear trucks, while out ahead stretched a convoy of empty vehicles, carrying nothing but their drivers and mounds of sandbags!

Finally it was the captain who set things right in no uncertain terms, with his own long and loud string of verbal abuse, directed strongly towards us "Cowards!" We found ourselves faced with a choice of the "Detonators" or endless months assigned to the "Shit Hole" (long drop bush-toilet trench digging). Thus it came about that, cowards that we might be, Petser and myself found ourselves unceremoniously "volunteered" by the captain, amongst others, to mount the "Detonator Trucks" for what was to be only our first of many convoys through enemy landmine country. Together, we clutched our rifles and stared out at the slowly passing

*An Australian sand goanna easily scales up into a tree to avoid predators*

foliage, feeling vulnerable and frightened.

However, other than the fact that the lead trucks were most vulnerable to landmine explosion, there were some positive aspects. The sandbags rendered us higher than was normal in the back of the Bedfords and lying flat, with rifles at the ready, four men to a side and two looking forward over the driver's canopy (usually Petser and myself), we experienced a reasonably unobstructed view over and through the surrounding Mopane trees, much of which was inhabited by various species of antelope, buffalo, zebra, hyaenas and even elephant. In fact, the first time we spotted the great, grey shapes melting away into the thicket, the radio cackled with alarm signals reporting possible troop deployment ahead. However, these fears were quickly dispelled when a small group of young elephants, urgently being escorted across the track by their mothers, broke cover not a hundred yards ahead of our path.

*Beating the heat in Angola whilst also keeping a watchful eye out for crocodiles*

This was to be but the first of many such sightings, as great herds of elephants migrated freely from Botswana in the south, across the Caprivi Strip, and on into Zambia's Sioma Ngwezi National Park in the north. On another occasion, coming across a shallow river crossing, the convoy was brought to a total standstill for the best part of an hour as a great herd of buffalo refused us right of way as they drank their fill in the setting sun. We estimated later that this herd must have been close to four hundred strong and only moved off reluctantly when nudged cautiously by the leading vehicles.

Many species of buck were evident, especially Impala which sometimes congregated in herds of thousands, saturating the surrounding bush with their brown colourisation for kilometres on end. Lion tracks, too, were identified every now and again, and the creatures' lingering, coughing grunts and powerful roars some nights rent the air close to where we camped. Hyaenas laughed their excited calls and jackals howled their songs to the starlit sky and, were it not for the rifles held fast in our hands as an ever present reminder that we were at war, we might have been in paradise, the wild paradise that is only Africa.

Based now in a continuous training camp some distance west of Katima Mulilo, a major Caprivi/Zambia border defence force installation, we underwent further training in the art of gorilla bush war tactics. The base was constructed almost entirely from sandbags which were packed some three or four deep and six high around the perimeter and in single dividing walls where interior division was necessary. At a number of strategic points along the outer wall were machine gun posts, where heavy-barreled Bren guns and the belt-loading LMG's kept a constant vigil. The soldiers on duty at these posts lived in trenches, dug within the posts and never left. They operated a twenty four hour continuous three hours on/three hours off relief cycle. Petser and I avoided this duty like the plague, preferring, in spite of the obvious dangers, to volunteer for border foot patrol. In this way at least we escaped the confines of the base and were, to some extent, free to enjoy the bush with all its interesting wildlife and nearby waterways.

Quickly the days and weeks drifted into months and we learned much and experienced even more. Although the northern regions generally remained warm throughout the year, October had passed, and the sun still burned down upon the bush and sandy soil. The November thunderstorms soon followed with their sudden downpours which flooded the base and turned foot patrols into muddy slogs. The rivers flooded and had to be negotiated with care, and where cable-hauled ferry barges

*Above left: a snarling lion vents his anger*

*Above right: the exposed fangs of a black mamba are both deadly and impressive*

were constructed to carry over vehicles, there remained now only twisted cables and shattered logs, such was the force of the storms.

One advantage gained from all this was the abundance of replenished waterholes, allowing our patrols much relaxed drinking habits. In fact, in the dry season, patrol routes were strongly delineated by the availability of water points, as men on the march over rough bush terrain, heavily weighed down by weapons, ammunition and supplies, under a burning sun, by necessity consumed large volumes of water.

But for everything there comes a price and though we now drank freely while on patrol, the nights were alive with insects, especially mosquitoes, including the dangerous, malaria-carrying species, we relied heavily on the anti-malarial tablets supplied by the defence force medical teams. Of course, snakes too were encountered, more often as much to the horror of some as to my delight. Many, having witnessed me catch and identify several species over the months, venomous and non-venomous, my reputation as the Snakeman was firmly established. In fact, though my superior officers did not fully approve of my keeping snakes at the base, they did realise the value of my ability and knowledge and on a number of occasions I was asked to lecture on the subject, with permission to display any live specimens that might be at my disposal at the time to enhance the talk.

Snakes remained my greatest passion and, when on patrol, my eyes were as much in search of sign of any, as they were for the enemy. On numerous occasions I repeatedly shocked my comrades by dropping everything, rifle included, to charge off into the foliage after a rapidly disappearing tail. Most often the reptile escaped my clutches, its sleek body being far better adapted to sliding through the thick bush than mine. However, on a number of occasions I was successful and returned from the foliage with a specimen dangling from my hand. Boomslang, (tree snakes) a sub-species of the Egyptian cobra, and puff adders were the most common venomous species spotted, while mole snakes and rock pythons were amongst the most common, non-venomous species.

The notorious black mamba, longest, fastest moving and most deadly of African snakes, was also in evidence. Once I even had chance to chase one, which speedily negotiated an over-hanging tree along the Okavango

River before plunging headlong into the water. Knowing what I do today about these reptiles, I am most thankful that I did not catch it, for though I had over the years acquired some technical knowledge of reptiles, and even a fair amount of practical knowledge, I was far from being a fully practised herpetologist. Venomous snakes, especially the likes of mambas, should be handled by experienced experts only, as their large size (up to four metres), quick strike and fast acting neurotoxic (nerve destroying) venom make it a formidable enemy should it feel threatened. As is the case with all snakes, however, even the black mamba will not attack anything but its prey, unless otherwise attacked itself.

December came and with it a transfer for our company. As we were due to complete our tour of duty in January the following year (1970), we were now to be relieved from the "red" zone, (highly active zone), by another long-term company, while we were moved some distance westward to be based at Rundu. At this time Rundu was no more than a collection of tin shacks and sandbagged trenches, guarded all around by machine-gun installations. Over the years it was to grow to be a major town in the area.

Rundu was the first base camp to be reached by new troops as they were transported from the airbase at Grootfontein, some two hundred and sixty kilometres to the south, (as we had been some five months earlier). It is situated close to the Okavango River and was used as a training base for these troops, not yet familiar with bush war tactics. So basically we were winding down our operation, performing no more duties than to man the machine-gun posts and demonstrate some of our gained experience to the new arrivals.

The region was lush with vegetation, the Okavango River running deep and wide here for a stretch of some three hundred kilometres, dividing Angola in the north from South West Africa. To the immediate east of Rundu, a tributary of the Okavango, the Omuramba Omatako River, cut sharply southwards. Thus the region was from two sides surrounded by water, attracting game and birds of every description, often in great herds and flocks, not only from the SWA side, but from Angola as well.

Here, each troop section was allocated a day off each week, at which time we were able to requisition a Bedford truck and, with sandwiches and beers packed, the day was ours to enjoy. Usually, this involved a slow cruise along the banks of the Okavango, where all about us herds of antelope ranged free, feeding greedily on the lush abundance of summer grass-shoots and the leaves of blossoming trees. Often, herds of elephants would be gathered along the water, especially in the late afternoons, when they drank their fill before playfully lowering themselves into the depths of the river. From the uppermost extremities of towering, long dead trees, the African fish eagle sounded its soulful call of the wild, before swooping down, talons outstretched, to grasp at a momentarily surfacing fish. Wildebeest, roan antelope, impala, giraffe and even kudu were plentiful, as were egrets, herons, storks and a horde of other water birds. Except for the rifles which were always close at hand, we might have been in Eden. On such days the war seemed so far, far away. It was here, without a doubt, that I first truly fell in love with Africa, where I truly felt its call, the call of the wild, and the feeling was to last a lifetime. Little did I suspect at the time what devastating effects the soon escalating war would have on this paradise of wildlife.

Back at Rundu base, time passed slowly with the inactivity and every man was counting down the days, first to Christmas, and then to home. I suspect that my interest in nature placed me to some extent at an advantage, for though I too longed for home and loved ones, my mind was kept active with the everyday possibilities of further wildlife experiences. Little did I imagine what a near disastrous situation this enthusiasm was about to bring into my life.

There remained but one week to Christmas and though we were stationed far from home, our enthusiasm for the occasion was no less. Certainly we would be celebrating in a somewhat different manner from what most of us were accustomed, but celebrate we would, and if there was one thing I learned to respect most about the Afrikaaners in my time spent in their company, it was their irrepressible spirit.

*Most noted for their magnificent spiral horns, these kudu bulls are amongst the largest of African antelope.*

It had been confirmed by headquarters that, though turkey was out of the question, each man in the operational area would receive at least a portion of grilled chicken, smothered in "home cooked" vegetables. Though I never got to see the day, I was later informed that this promise had indeed been kept (though there was a strong suspicion that the "home cooked" vegetables came straight from the tins). Apparently there had been no shortage of champagne, rum and beer either, and by all accounts the border war had been somewhat "ignored" for a number of hours that particular year.

It was well passed midnight when the rude awakening came. It was Sarge, and he was shaking me vigorously, calling my "name" – "Engelsman! Engelsman! Word wakker jong. Daars 'n slang tussen die manne!" ("Wake up Englishman, there's a snake amongst the men!"). Good grief I thought to myself as I came round and attempted to focus on the dark face in the gloom. "What do you mean there's a snake amongst the men?" But Sarge was rattled and obviously not in the mood to chat or elaborate. Following my change to English now, he screamed into my face! "Don't bleddy speak to your Sergeant from your bed! Get up and get out!" And with a solid yank, he had my bedding spread across the floor and me, starkers in the cool morning air. "Now get your blerry boots on and come catch this blerry snake before it eats someone!" He stormed out of the tent, leaving me still somewhat dizzy in the ears.

So now with boots and shorts hastily donned, I rushed out after our rattled leader, who quickly led me to one of the perimeter LMG posts, where a group of men had gathered together, seemingly as agitated as the Sarge.

"Daar's a blerry slang in die bunker!" they all exclaimed together. "Die blerry ding het ons amper gepik!" ("There's a bloody snake in the bunker and the bloody thing nearly bit us!"). My rather British use of the word "bloody" had quickly been adopted by my comrades from the start, as a novelty I guess. However, their Afrikaans accent delivered the word as "bleddy" and when voiced at speed, it evolved to "blerry".

A Namib Desert tortoise with time-weathered shell, emerges from tall grass to eat on succulent desert flowers after good rains

Quickly asking a few questions now, it seems that there had been some rustling noises coming from within the bunker not far away from where the machine gun was mounted. However, nothing was visible in the dark and, as there were often mice scavaging for food, little more was thought of the matter. That is, until indeed a mouse was spotted scampering across the floor, right towards where the men were stationed behind the LMG, and hot on its heels was an enormously fat, slithering snake. Needless to say, the bunker was evacuated at some speed. Having informed Sarge of the situation, and the fact that this particular area of the base was now unprotected, it was decided to call in my services in spite of the late hour. Here was a situation, the men insisted, that could not wait for morning!

The description "fat" immediately suggested a puff adder, as these rather sluggish reptiles were renowned more for their girth than for their length, usually averaging less than a metre. At the same time, however, these adders are fast strikers, with long fangs and a powerful venom. If this was the snake in question, there was no question about it, no man could, or would, return to the bunker until the reptile was removed. I, of course, was glad to have the chance to rescue the snake, to release it into the wild, rather than see it killed.

"Bring me a torch, please, and a short stick, and a pillowcase", I said, preparing to go into the dark of the bunker. The bunker, built entirely from sandbags piled high and canvas sheets, I soon discovered, was a snake's paradise. With numerous holes, gaps, tunnels and scattering of unfilled sacks, a snake could remain hidden for as long as it pleased. This report did not impress the men waiting outside and so, focusing the torch ahead of me, I systematically began to probe and investigate every visible opening. It was not long before my probing stick brought results in the form of a short, aggressive hiss. I had nudged the snake!

Disturbed by the sudden activity when the men had first evacuated the bunker, the puff adder, as indeed its powerful hiss told me it was, had most probably forgotten its attack on the mouse and itself scampered for safety into the closest available opening. The spot, under normal circumstances, would have been ideal – but not tonight. Borrowing a bayonet, it was a simple matter to cut the closest sandbag to release some of the contents and, within seconds, the narrow "snake tunnel" had been enlarged enough to see the reptile in its entirety. A few sharp nudges with the probe-stick and the, by now, quite distressed snake came slithering out in a last desperate lunge for freedom. I was ready, however, with pillowcase strategically positioned to allow the reptile to bag itself

*A Parabuthus desert scorpion - a highly venomous species found in the Southern African region and which can be identified by their slender pinchers and thick-set tails*

*The deep water spider crab may have a legspan of over two metres across*

entirely under its own steam.

Suddenly all the men, including Sarge, who had up until then kept his distance, crowded forward, eager to see the snake in the bag. Tired and wanting to return to bed, I allowed only a quick peek by torch-light, promising a full demonstration of snake, fangs and even venom extraction later in the day. The time was 2am.

The day broke like most others there in the beautiful north of South West Africa, with crimson sky and crisp summer air, but for me, that was where the similarity would end. It was to be a day that would forever be etched in my brain. It would be the day of my first experience of real pain – and shock!

The news of the captured snake had spread like wild-fire around the base, with those personally involved delivering (as only the Afrikaaner can), detailed, dramatic and totally exaggerated accounts of the night's "death defying" encounter with the most dangerous of reptiles, the dreaded "vrek adder", as the poor snake was labelled (adder of death). This, of course, came from misinterpretations of an earlier lecture, where I had explained how the puff adder, because of its reluctance to move out the way of approaching feet, was most often stepped on, and therefore, was responsible for some eighty percent of all snake-bite cases in Africa. This fact was absorbed with much drama and, to people otherwise not familiar with the ways of nature, such an "astounding" declaration conjured up bloody images of millions of people being attacked and killed by the said serpent, so it was natural that the title "adder of death" should arise. The fact that more people were killed by lightning alone in Africa than were ever bitten by snakes (of all species) did not feature. The fact that thousands were dying in road accidents every day, also did not register as nobody felt any apprehension when climbing into a car. But a snake; now that represented pure, unadulterated fear! Here death was a certainty!

Naturally, I did everything within my limited power to correct this thinking and indeed some did come to see the light. However, the day's events about to unfold were to strain the support of even my strongest converts.

The snake demonstration was scheduled for midday, allowing me an hour to lecture after which lunch would be served as was usual on the base. All the men not on duty were to attend as the captain felt the lecture would not only benefit the troops, but would, to some extent, relieve the boredom of those with time to pass between guard duties.

Collecting the puff adder from under my bed, where it had spent the intervening hours safely tucked away in the pillowcase, I tipped it out onto the table supplied for the occasion. Before me a hundred interested faces gazed up from where they sat cross-legged in the open arena and, as one, they craned their necks forward for the best possible view.

The snake, now quite stunned by the sudden exposure to bright daylight, lay motionless where it landed, with only its tongue flickering rapidly, in quick successive bursts. The reptile was in good condition, of average length and, by the short stubby tail, I deduced, was a female. With the thick-bodied snakes, as the puff adder is, it is usually possible to tell the sexes simply by the length of the tail. However, this method is far less reliably accurate with the more slender-bodied species, as they invariably all have long tails. Volunteering this "interesting" bit of information to the men before me, the fact was greeted with stunned disbelief. Not, I suddenly realised, because of the interest value, but rather because of the ridiculous assumption I had just voiced, that anyone in his right mind would want to sex a snake!

Hereafter, I decided to keep the lecture visual. The men were not really interested in any "fascinating" facts or figures; they were gathered to see me handle and extract venom from the dreaded "vrek-adder" and anything less was of little importance. Certainly not one of them was about to go out and practise their newly acquired knowledge of how to sex a snake, and the message in their faces as they stared up at me was quite clear; "Die bleddy Engelsman is skoon mal!" (This bloody Englishman is crazy!).

Having earlier prepared for the demonstration, I now displayed, for all to see, a slender drinking glass borrowed from the kitchen, over the top of which I had secured with the aid of an elastic band, a fine rubber membrane, borrowed from Petser's secret box of "emergency sex" apparatus. "You never know where or when" he had explained sheepishly to me when I first discovered the supply. It had taken some argument to acquire one sample for the particular need I had in mind. However, all things are possible in the army and, as I now raised this specially designed apparatus in my left hand for all to see, deftly, I grabbed the waiting adder behind the head with my right. This is a dangerous manoeuvre, as the puff adder is capable of a lightning fast strike, and should never be taken behind the head without the head first being secured by some method.

However, youth, ignorance and daring were in charge here and with one hundred men focusing their full attention on me, I was not about to be anything but the hero! Amazingly, the snake displayed little retaliation at my rude handling, and when its mouth was forced over the lip of the membrane covered glass, it showed great reluctance to bring the long, hinged fangs into play. Although I repeatedly forced the mouth over the membrane, the snake simply refused to bite.

Beginning to flush slightly now, embarrassed in front of the crowd by my inability to deliver the promised venom extraction process, I proceeded to do the most stupid thing possible. Releasing my index finger from around the adder's neck, leaving only my middle finger and thumb in place, I slid the finger along the snake's head towards the nose, the idea being that I might pull back on the upper lip and force the snake to bring its fangs forward into the striking position. And here now, the snake decided it had had enough. Taking advantage of my weaker grip around its neck, the animal twisted suddenly in my fingers, unsheathing one fang as it did so, to bring it down once sharply with a jab to my extended index finger.

Adders have the most advanced venom injection system of all venomous snakes. The fangs are large, too large in fact to be kept erect in the mouth, so they are hinged and folded back up against the roof of the mouth when not in use. From this position, however, the snake can quickly open the mouth and shoot the fangs forward in a lightning-fast strike, some having being recorded to reach speeds of five metres per second. Should the snake find itself gripped behind the head, as my puff adder now did, restricted from striking out, it can still quite easily drop the fangs forward and down beyond the bottom lip to stab out at the restricting fingers.

The pain was immediate as in my head the world seemed to move into slow motion and, with the knowledge that I had stepped beyond the point of no return, I watched helplessly as the gleaming, silver-white fang

*Austin catching a Spitting cobra in Borneo*

unsheathed and thrust down at the finger, now easily within its range. The pain was immediate, a frightening, burning pain, that told me venom was entering my system, venom with the capability to inflict terrible damage to the human body, even death!

Shocked, I relinquished my grip on both glass and snake, sending them crashing to the table, from where the snake came alive with energy and made a break for freedom, off the table and slithering as fast as it could, directly towards the one hundred somewhat stunned members of the audience. They had come to see the action and certainly they were getting it, but the fast approaching snake was just a bit more than they had bargained for, and one hundred strong, healthy, battle-trained men leapt into the air with a unanimous cry of "Oh Shit!" and ran for their lives. I had achieved in one simple manoeuvre, what the entire terrorist onslaught from the north had as yet never been able to do!

*An aerial view of the Okovango Delta region in the dry season, when flowing waters have been reduced to a minimum*

The pain in my finger increased by the second. It was obvious that I had received a serious dose of venom, and panic flared up inside of me. But I knew before anything, I had to retrieve the snake, or its life would be lost to a burst of rifle fire. Suddenly, Petser was beside me, as though reading my desperate thoughts. "Vang gou die blerry ding Engelsman! Hier's die kussen-sloop." ("Catch the bloody thing Englishman! Here's the pillowcase."). And he waved the bag in front of me. "Ek sal dit laat los." Jy moet na die medics toe jong!" ("I will release it. You must get to the medics").

So, forgetting for a moment my bitten finger, I rushed across to the snake where it was attempting to make all haste across the sandy floor. Grabbing for the tail, I literally threw the poor reptile into the bag in one smooth reckless movement and Petser took charge of it. "Kry nou jou ry Engelsman, ek sal sorg vir die slang." ("You get a move on Englishman, I will see to the snake."). And he was off. Thinking about it later, it suddenly dawned on me just how close Petser and I had become over the months. Another friend might have put more concentration into the fact that I was snake-bitten, but knowing me that well, Petser realised my concern for the safety of the snake would leave me agitated and worried, emotions that I did need to contend with at this time, considering what I was about to be faced with. I could now concentrate fully on the problem at hand. Petser would release the snake back into the wild at the first opportunity.

The snake safely removed, men now suddenly appeared from all over, to gather around me, craning their necks for a better look at my fast-swelling finger. Sarge was amongst them and, with a rapid burst of authority, sent everybody scurrying for safer, distant places. Quickly he ushered me towards the medics' tent, where a frantic staff-sergeant was emptying the contents from a cabinet, scattering them across the floor as he did so. He had been informed of my "accident" and he was now living his worst nightmare; stuck out in the wilds of Africa with a human snakebite casualty in his lap. Finally, locating what he was looking for, he turned and looked at me. His face was wet with sweat and the look on his face told me he was scared as hell and had never been faced with a snakebite case before. At this point I realised that my life was not going quite as I had foreseen it; and Christmas was just six days away.

One must consider that in those early years still relatively little was known about snake venoms, their clinical effects on the human body and even less about the treatment thereof. Though the staff-sergeant was a trained medic and naturally quite informed on various treatment procedures for various injuries, snakebite, a rare and unlikely eventuality, was a ball game all on its own! Though the staff-sergeant now dearly wished he was somewhere else, with another problem, any problem, he was stuck with me – and, unhappily, we both realised my life was in his hands!

Staff-sergeant Johan Swart was a likeable, jolly man, carrying more weight around his middle than was healthy for him, and it showed now as his face flushed pink and his palms sweated. In his hands he held a standard issue snakebite kit containing a tourniquet, a disposable syringe and needles, plus two ampules of polyvalent serum, (serum designed to combat the venoms of some adders, cobras and mambas). Gazing down first at my swelling finger, oozing a bloody discharge from the fang puncture wound, and then into my, by now, somewhat frightened, pain-filled eyes, he suddenly, as if having made a decision, sprang to life and proceeded heroically to administer all the wrong treatment that was at the time available to men of his profession.

Grabbing for a nearby length of nylon cord, he wound it tightly around my bitten finger a few centimetres above the puncture, effectively cutting off all blood flow to and from the area. This, he had been taught, would prevent the venom from spreading further up the limb. Next, he snapped open an ampule of serum, drew up the contents into a syringe and proceeded to plunge the needle repeatedly into my now enormously, and extremely painfully, swelling finger.

A half dozen times or more he did this, without removing the terrible nylon tourniquet and the injected serum collected and swelled my finger to the point of bursting like an over-inflated balloon until, finally, I screamed out loud with the agony of it!

Suddenly realising the reason for my distress, staff-sergeant Swart dropped the syringe and tugged hurriedly at the terrible, constricting nylon cord and, as it came undone, the rush of blood and serum up into my hand almost brought me to my knees in a further wave of agony. However, this was the relief needed though, unknown to staff-sergeant Swart, the damage was already done! I myself would at that time probably have treated a snakebite with similar ignorance, as snakebite treatment then was a subject still undergoing much speculative research.

Staff-sergeant Swart had administered my treatment roughly as he had been taught, the theory behind the teaching being that to apply a tourniquet would restrict the flow of the venom and then, by injecting serum around the site of the bite, the isolated venom would be neutralised before having chance to be further distributed throughout the body. However, today we know that snake venoms consist of a complex combination of enzymes and protein fractions, so complex that scientists still have not been able to duplicate them artificially.

In the case of neurotoxic venoms (nerve effecting) most often present

*A demonstration of venom extraction using a puff adder - the same species which nearly claimed Austin's life*

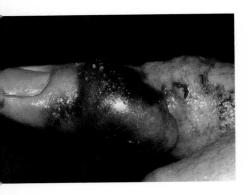

*Austin's finger showing tremendous discolouration and oedema from the cytoxic effects of the venom, two days after the puff adder bite*

in African cobras and mambas, a tourniquet can be of some considerable help in retarding the spread of venom. However, such a tourniquet should be in the form of a wide crepe, or stretch bandage, wrapped firmly around and along the entire length of the bitten limb. In this way the blood flow is not restricted, but slowed, as is the possible flow of venom even along the lymphatics. A narrow cord tourniquet, tightly bound around a limb, greatly promotes the chances of resultant gangrenous effects. This is especially the case with a puff adder bite as the venom is largely cytotoxic (tissue destroying) and should not be isolated by a sharp, tightly bound tourniquet, as the isolated and concentrated cytotoxins will destroy tissue in the area, beyond repair, thus promoting gangrene.

Serum should not be injected close to the site of the bite, especially when such a bite is located on a small appendage such as a finger, and especially not in the case of adder bite, as the further punctures made by the needle allow easy access for the destructive venom fractions.

At the same time, the restriction placed on the blood flow by the swelling of the limb caused by the venom is compounded by the swelling incurred by introduction of serum so close to the bite site. This, in itself, will promote the chances of gangrenous effects. Serum should be introduced only by an intravenous route, as snake venoms, for the greater part, are designed to spread quickly, making it impossible to isolate and neutralise them at the point of entry.

Standing back now, both Sarge and staff-sergeant Swart watched with big frightened eyes as I writhed in agony, clutching at my hand as I did so. The pain was terrible and my finger was already turning purple as the venom was making full use of all the advantages it had been afforded by the incorrect treatment procedures. Quickly, another ampule of serum was snapped open and the contents injected intramuscularly at the shoulder. There remained nothing else to do now but to lay me down as comfortably as possible and radio for a doctor.

No qualified doctor was present at the base at that time, but one was located some kilometres away in Rundu town itself and he requested that I be immediately transported to him. Meanwhile, my arm was swelling visibly by the minute and by the time I was being stretchered to a vehicle it had increased to twice its normal size and I was all but screaming with the pain of it. Never had I dreamed that there existed in the world such pain! I was, after all, just a boy, far away from home and at the very beginning of the exploration of life – free for the first time of parental guidance or distraction. Life, as I should know it, would forever more be of my own making, for good or for bad. I alone was in control, holding the power over my own destiny and at that moment I was making a real hash out of it! God-dammit! I cursed myself inside my head as I was loaded into the truck. How could I be so god-damned stupid! The pain in my swollen, purple-coloured arm was terrible.

Most of the camp seemed to be panic-stricken by my accident and the driver of my vehicle was no exception. With full theatrical exaggeration, he called to the gathered men around the vehicle in mixed English/Afrikaans slang: "Moenie worry nie! Ek sal die Englesman blerry fast transport!" And we took off like a dragster at the speedway, crashing right through the base entrance gate as we did so. In the back with me was Sarge and staff-sergeant Swart, clutching for their lives as the truck took to the sandy tracks at impossible speed. I think for the endurance of that ride, my life was in far more danger of being terminated by motor accident than it ever was from the snakebite! But thinking back on the situation some time later, I was honoured by the realisation that any of those men would have done anything within their power to help save my life. I am forever indebted to them. I was not to see Petser again for some eight years, when we were all once more to be called upon to serve our country.

The doctor at Rundu, whose name I never knew, immediately set up an intravenous drip into which he added more serum. Examining my hand carefully, his face expressed concern. Already a large blood blister was forming at the fang puncture site and, almost delirious now from the pain, I begged for morphine. When it finally came, after some further examination, I was muttering senseless words, half sobbing, almost crying, with my head lolling aimlessly from side to side in indisguisable torment. Above me, bright lights burned into my eyes, interrupted only by the blurred face of the doctor as he worked over and around me where I lay stretched out on a hard hospital type bed. Occasional, whispered words registered in my brain; antiseptic; antibiotic; hospitalisation; and some others. My brain was losing contact with my body as I slowly succumbed to a state of pain-induced shock. The morphine-carrying needle slipped painlessly into a vein in my arm and thankful oblivion overcame me.

I awoke some twelve hours later, just as the six-seater Cessna aeroplane I was being transported in banked sharply on approach to land at Windhoek airport, and I vomited the contents of my stomach all over the interior. Within an hour I would be in Windhoek hospital, the first snakebite case to be treated at this relatively new institution. My life was now in their hands.

For the eight days that it took for the cytotoxic properties of the puff adder venom to fully distribute its devastating effects along the length of my arm, I surfaced consciously only between morphine doses when the terrible pain forced me from the delirious blackness to the living hell of reality. Cytotoxins destroy tissue and blood cell walls, promoting haemorrhaging and necrosis, which will eventually lead to gangrene poisoning. In simple terms, to place one's arm into a fire and hold it there would roughly describe the painful effects of this tissue destroying venom, while the resultant swelling, blistering and exuding of plasma-like fluid from the bitten limb is frightening to witness. When, for the first time another day later, I saw my hand and arm unbandaged, the shock of it took my breath away. Swollen to twice its normal size, the upper regions were tinged purple, while below the elbow the flesh was black and hard, with a number of thick, raised, blood-filled blisters scattered across the top of my hand.

The entire arm was painful to touch, as were other areas of my body, especially in the armpits and the groin, where the lymph glands had swollen considerably. However, except for the actual bitten finger, the doctors seemed reasonably confident that the arm would eventually slough the dead tissue and regenerate new with the help of certain antibiotic drugs. The finger was another matter, however, having been exposed to the worst of the cytotoxic effects of the venom. Solemnly I was warned not to get my hopes too high as full recovery here was not possible and amputation was highly probable. When, several days later, I was told the finger was indeed saved, the sense of *relief* was palpable.

*Austin shows the still considerable effects of the same bite healing some six weeks after*

CHAPTER
THREE

# At the Park

Life at Hartebeespoort Dam Snake and Animal Park was, to say the least, life with never a dull moment. My years of interest in wildlife, especially reptiles qualified me as a natural, and I took to the work like the proverbial "fish to water". The fact that the park was home to a collection of mammals from around the globe as well as reptiles made it all the more interesting and I soon found myself deeply involved in the study of all natural creatures, their habits, localities and general behaviour patterns. However, though my interest in these natural things now broadened considerably, I was, and would forever (as things turned out), remain first and foremost a "snake man". And though I had at that time not the slightest precognition of things to come, I was on the first rung of my climb to claim the not so enviable title of "Snake man of South Africa"!

The construction of the park on the edge of the Hartebeespoort Dam had begun in the early 1960's, but the original entrepeneur somewhat lacked the true dedication essential for such a project to succeed, and a quick sale of standing buildings so far constructed, inclusive of all animals and reptiles so far housed within their walls, was made to Jack Seale, himself an eager and ambitious naturalist who had long had his eye on the site. Together with his wife Heather, the pair made a formidable team, she handling the financial development and re-construction of the monetary business, and he the physical further creation, construction and directing of what finally today, some thirty years later, has become the biggest privately owned snake and animal park in Southern Africa.

*Opposite page left: Austin performing a venomous snake show at the snake park*
*Opposite page right: making friends with a cheetah*

My title as "Curator of Herpetology" in fact did little to describe the true nature of my work. Herpetology (the study of snakes, lizards and frogs) certainly played a major role as there were even in those early days, some hundreds of reptiles housed in glass displays and open pits which demanded much cleaning, feeding and general all round husbandry. However, there were, the many mammal species to consider and though there was in the employ of the park a large African staff, whose sole job description was to be the consideration of these, there remained always the task of general supervision and decision making, not to mention the daily handling and liaising with the general public who flocked through the gates, more especially on weekends and public holidays.

Living on the premises as I was, automatically (as it sometimes seemed), rendered me on twenty-four hour duty, as Jack had no qualms about calling me up in the middle of the night to "suggest" that I quickly run down and check if all was well with some particular animal that might at the time be either ill or pregnant or whatever. Another favourite was "to pass the buck" when called in late at night to go catch a snake in somebody's house or garden or wherever.

Jack was a fair man, though often stubborn and most definitely set in his ways. He was from "the old school" and saw no reason to change or modify any adopted system or style, but rather living by the theory that, "if it has worked for twenty years…why change now!" Thus much of the design of the park is "rustic", as are some of the methods employed in its day to day workings. However, generally speaking, the Hartebeespoort Dam Snake and Animal Park was, in its development then, and is still today, a uniquely interesting and even exciting place for tourists, the general public and staff alike to attend. I was to spend many memorable years in its service.

The snake handling shows naturally were a favourite amongst the visitors and a strong draw-card at the gate. Although the lions, tigers, gorillas and general assortment of other mammals and birds were popular displays, the most popular question by far posed by the public was; "When will the next snake-handling show take place?" On weekends, in fact, many people would spend the day either gazing into the display cages or sometimes just lounging along the water's edge, but at the same time attending every

snake-handling show of the day, sometimes as many as half a dozen or more. Such is man's fascination with the serpent; excited to view it under safe conditions − terrified of a chance encounter in the wild! A similar settled mode of thinking is attributed to sharks, those similarly secretive and potentially dangerous creatures of the deep, and it is certain that it is man's lack of knowledge on these particular subjects, above all else, that lends to his loathing and fear of these specifically designed creatures of nature.

But, while it is difficult to teach people to respect rather than fear the shark, as close quarter encounters with the animal are generally out of the question for all but those few involved in undersea exploration, the snake is a much more readily available creature which can (at any reptile park) not only be viewed, but handled as well. This more fortunate situation offers the herpetologist an opportunity to educate the general public, not only by way of lecture, but more importantly, by way of actual physical contact with the subject. It has long been my experience that live demonstration leaves a far deeper and more permanent impression than the written or lectured word.

Naturally this does not mean that all visitors to a snake park automatically leave again later with an instantly developed love and desire to regularly fondle a snake. However, for those who are more willing to be educated, close contact with a snake, under the watchful eye of its handler, is a thrilling and usually educational experience. First to note always, (in amazement and contrary to that expected), the reptile's skin is dry to the touch, often shiny smooth, but never wet. Next, is the feeling of the gently working muscles below the skin as the creature slides easily and gracefully from hand to hand without any apparent effort. Not "revolting" as expected, but rather interestingly relaxing. Most noteworthy of all to the still trembling (either with excitement or fear) student, the snake does not blatantly go out of its way to bite, but moves rather continuously as though to escape, or settles down comfortably stretched out along the length of a supporting arm. Amazing! Having experienced this much at first hand, the person in question is now much more likely to accept the fact that snakes do not eat people and, indeed, have no interest even in biting people, unless attacked first. This, be the snake venomous or otherwise.

However, there are many factors to consider when attempting to educate the public in this specialised field and the public witnessing an experienced herpetologist handle highly venomous snakes with apparent ease, should not be led to believe this can be achieved safely by the novice. Venomous snakebite should be avoided at all costs! Also, it is important to consider that though a species can be generalised on, temperaments will invariably differ and, whereas one snake of a particular species may prove to be docile, another of the same species may prove more reluctant to being handled. There is no definite pattern; thus, though it is in the interest of all to be familiar with snakes to various levels or degrees, the actual handling of venomous species should be left to those more studied and with professional interest in the subject.

Most people, of course, consider those working with venomous snakes to be a "couple of tins short of the six pack", while herpetologists, on the other hand, will argue that the job is no more dangerous than many others, only more poorly renumerated, (Racing drivers are a popular example). However, it is a fact that those people who most often get hit by a motor vehicle are those who most often cross the street and likewise, those who most get eaten by sharks are likely to be those who swim most in the sea. So it stands to reason that those who get bitten

*Bottom left: Austin with a young springbuck in distress*

*Bottom centre: Austin displays a venomous tree snake to the public visiting the snake park*

the most by snakes are those working with, or at least living in close proximity to, them.

One would imagine that should anybody be in danger of being bitten by a venomous snake at a snake park, it should most certainly be one of the herpetologists, especially one involved in the performing of public demonstrations. Indeed, it is probable that a large proportion of the visiting public are there chiefly on the off chance of some greater excitement, much in the way one attends a bull fight, subconsciously hoping the matador will heroically go down under the horns. (I know what it's like – I've been there! Man craves excitement, as long as it does not endanger him personally. Thus, television is the most popular "adventure" in every home).

However, matters do not always proceed exactly as planned and over the years there have naturally occurred at the park, a number of unplanned accidents, some serious, some quite frightening, other humorous, (though not always at the time). For those people attending my show one day not long after my appointment, it was a frightening turnabout when they were suddenly faced with the potential prospect of snakebite while I, the "heroic" handler, was safe on the other side of the arena wall.

It was mid-summer Sunday, the last in the month of November and a popular time for tourists and general public alike. Christmas was around the corner, month-end salaries had been collected and generally it was a good day to drive out to Hartebeespoort Dam to picnic along the water's edge and, of course, go visit the snake and animal park, where one could be thrilled and entertained by handlers displaying live venomous snakes – from a safe distance of course.

On Sundays and public holidays the snake shows took place every hour, from ten in the morning until four in the afternoon, with sometimes a visitors harmless snake-handling session somewhere in between, when the situation called for it. Usually the midday to 3pm shows were the most packed with visitors and there would be hundreds of spectators crowded around the snake arena, all eagerly craning their necks for a better view. At this time grandstand seats were limited to about two hundred, while the rest of the crowd would simply gather along the arena wall, often four or five deep. The snake shows were ever popular,

*Bottom right: a very youthful Austin!*

*Bottom centre: Austin examines a docile and beautifully coloured puff adder from the Cape region*

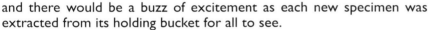

and there would be a buzz of excitement as each new specimen was extracted from its holding bucket for all to see.

The venom extraction process naturally attracted the greatest interest, and was actually what everyone had come to see. On this particular day an enormous puff adder, well over a metre in length, was delivered to the park by a passing farmer who had caught it along the road side and dropped it off at the park in exchange for the value in cash. I was amazed at the size of the reptile, not so much its length as its girth, which in conjunction with the short, stubby tail, strongly indicated the gender to be female.

Carefully removing the specimen from the grubby cardboard container into which it had been unceremoniously dumped, I was further astonished by the animal's reasonable nature. Expecting furious retaliation, I was handling the snake with a stout snake stick, all the while careful not to get any part of my anatomy anywhere within possible striking distance of those huge fangs. (The agony of a puff adder bite remained still freshly imprinted in my mind!). However, my fears were unfounded, as rather than display signs of anger as was her right, the heavy-bodied serpent seemed content to just simply dangle between my hand, which gripped her lightly by the tail, and the snake stick which supported her mid-body. There and then I decided this marvellous specimen of a serpent should be displayed for all to see, a fitting climax I reasoned for the midday venom extraction show. (Venom extracted from snakes, or "milked" during public shows was dried and sent to a medical research institute where it was used in the process of manufacturing anti-snakebite serum).

When the moment finally arrived, the grandstand was packed full and the entire arena was surrounded by eager, expectant visitors, who clapped and roared their appreciation at every move I made. The ringhals (spitting) cobra stood high and proud, as with venomous intent it determinedly lunged forward, again and again, to saturate my face and protected eyes with venom. And the crowd clapped and "oohed" and "aahed". The boomslang chosen for the show that day was bright green in colouration and furious at being disturbed from its midday siesta, inflating its throat to three times its usual size and lunging out at me from where I displayed it to the crowd at the end of a metre long snake stick.

Even the venom-less mole snake I offered to the spectators to touch was on form that day, hissing and striking out in a mock display of aggression, until eventually it turned and nipped me on the thumb, and the crowd were shocked into silence as blood trickled from the ineffectual wound, but clapped and cheered again as I dismissed the incident as little more than an irritation. Everybody was having a wonderful time, and I was the undisputed "hero" of the day!

*Austin examines damage sustained to the eye of an alligator after a territorial conflict*

Then it was time for the grand finale! The moment everybody had been waiting for, and, as I ceremoniously lifted the enormous puff adder from the holding bucket, there came a unanimous gasp from the crowd. The snake was enormous, fat and heavy, with a characteristically broad, flat, triangular shaped head, as wide as a small man's hand. There was no question about it; this was the biggest puff adder anybody out there had ever seen, not to mention actually being handled by human hands!

I, too, was still in awe of the snake, for indeed I don't think I had, up until then, ever seen such a specimen. I was further astonished, as cautiously I pinned the broad head firmly to the stone floor before grasping it securely between my bare fingers which just slightly trembled with expectation of vicious retaliation – but none came! Together, with the audience, I breathed a sigh of relief.

The puff adder was heavy and therefore difficult to hold so it became necessary to balance the bulk of her body along the length of my left arm, in the hand of which I now held the "milking" flask, over the top of which the tightly stretched plastic gleamed in the midday sun, ready to receive the penetrating fangs and gushing venom. Gripping the broad, flat head of the snake firmly but gently between the fingers of my right hand, I (thankfully) registered no sign of distress in the creature which was seemingly at ease with the situation.

I stepped forward now to the very edge of the arena wall, closest to the packed grandstand, all eyes focusing intensely on me as, all the while through the miniature radio microphone attached to my shirt collar, I lectured on the proceedings, explaining the process. Naturally too, partly for dramatic, but also as fact, I described the potential danger of the snake I held, how the huge head was capable of striking out at speeds exceeding six metres per second, to unleash hinged fangs of up to two centimetres in length, capable of delivering multiple death-dealing doses of a virulent blood and tissue destroying venom! The audience loved it, "oohing" and "aahing" as they revelled in the danger so close, yet so safely out of their reach. With five hundred expectant necks stretched to their limit, craning forward now in hushed silence, determined to witness this final scene, I slowly, and with dramatic deliberation, eased the great, venomous head towards the flask.

*The African black widow spider is well known for its potent neurotoxic venom*

This may have been the moment everybody had been waiting for; so too, it seems, was the snake! As the flask ever so gently brushed the edge of her mouth, the huge reptile suddenly, and with tremendous thrust, lunged forward, open-mouthed, and with huge fangs instantly erect, crushed down upon the plastic covered surface determined to vent her apparent long pent up frustration!

As the plastic covering, complete with attaching rubber bands, crumpled and snapped under the onslaught, and yellow venom gushed down into the base of the glass, the unexpected force of the thrust ripped the flask from my fingers, sending it crashing downward upon the arena wall, where it shattered and spewed venom coated glass in all directions. In the shock of the moment, my remaining grip around the neck of the puff adder slackened and, with one further thrust, the great, deadly serpent was free and tumbling after the shattered flask, over the arena wall, to land unceremoniously at the feet of the closest, gawking spectators!

For a single split second, in the wake of the tinkering sound of breaking glass, there came a deafening silence, as all about, frozen, disbelieving minds battled with the implications of what they had just witnessed. Now suddenly everything was turn about and not so exciting anymore! In fact, the only people really in any danger were those half dozen crammed in against the arena wall, closest to where the bewildered puff adder had landed. However, the entire grandstand and surrounding arena of some five hundred now not so enthusiastic spectators, threw their arms up into the air, turned and fled screaming for any available exit! Pandemonium reigned supreme!

*Double page picture overleaf: the deadly black mamba*

Directly in front of where I stood, the front rows of human bodies scrambled up into the grandstand, over those still there, while those in turn scrambled over those behind them. Those at the top were faced with the open-top crocodile enclosure and froze in indecision – puff

adder or crocodiles! On the ground some had stumbled and fallen and were immediately trampled by those from behind. At the far edge of the arena a huge woman screamed once before fainting and the advancing crowd was forced to split two ways around her plentiful bulk as they continued their frenzied stampede for the exits.

Adrenalin surging through my body, I leapt over the arena wall in a single stride, my eyes frantically searching for the giant snake, but almost instantly found myself trampled to the ground by a further wave of hastily departing visitors. However, from my floor-ridden position I was fortunate enough to spot a thick tail disappearing beneath the grandstand seats and, pulling on my elbows, I dragged myself in pursuit. I had no snake stick with me and I saw the snake was flattened in an awkward position in a dimly lit area below the seats. But no matter, and despite the chaos about me, I knew my priority was to recapture that snake before it disappeared forever into the bowels of the park. Jack would have my head, which surely after this episode was already on the block!

However, the puff adder now seemingly satisfied that it had clearly stated its case, neatly curled itself up in a dark corner, where I found it some minutes later, well settled in and preparing to sleep. Satisfied that she was not any longer on the move, I quickly scrambled back to the now deserted arena, collected a snake stick and within a further few minutes had returned the once more docile serpent to her holding bucket.

At the far side of the arena a small group of people gathered around the fainted lady, who began to recover slightly as she was being dampened down with a wet cloth. Quickly I ran to join them, that I might assist, but on first sight of me, the woman's eyes popped wide and she vented a muffled scream before slipping back once more from her sitting position, out cold! Twice more this happened, as with great difficulty I and the two assisting visitors attempted in vain to relocate the enormous woman to more comfortable quarters. Finally, after introducing a stiff whiff of smelling salts, she recovered enough to hurl abuse at me and threaten endless lawsuits against the park, before storming unaided out of the gate.

Good grief I thought to myself, my life is over as all about me the earlier looks of "our hero" were now replaced by scowls of distaste wherever I went. One would imagine I had purposefully and maliciously planned the whole affair as a bad joke, risking everybody's life in the process! And I dreaded the reprimand that was sure to come from Jack, once a report of the incident reached his ears.

However, all was not lost, as some time later Jack approached me, a big grin on his face and asked if I could possibly enlarge on a recent statement received that I had attempted to kill some five hundred or so of the visitors by hurling venomous snakes at them. Relieved that he obviously had dismissed this ludicrous report as the fantasies of somebody's overactive imagination, I hastily explained the events of the show, adding that I had recaptured the snake and marked it for display only, not public demonstration! It was a lesson learned that rather than allocate freshly arrived specimens for public demonstration, others of acknowledged temperament should be employed first

CHAPTER
FOUR

# Record Breaker

*Previous pages: a rare blue-tinted, green tree viper coils around a branch in wait of prey*

It is a fact that snakes, like most other creatures of the wilds, do not consider man to be natural prey and will not attack him unless in self defence. Where a creature is large enough to literally eat a human being, one can expect such a statement to be somewhat frowned upon, even discarded with contempt. But whatever one's particular opinion might be (educated or otherwise) it should not be difficult for even the most sceptical to reason that snakes, with the exception only of one or two of the largest species, cannot possibly consider humans to be potential food. All snakes swallow their prey whole. They are not able to chew their prey, but by utilisation of the rows of tiny teeth that line the mouth, simply draw the food animal into the throat from where it is forced down to the stomach by muscle contraction.

Thus, it can be reasonably ascertained that human snakebite casualties occur only under induced circumstances of misunderstanding on the part of the snake – or otherwise calculated self defence. Stepping accidentally on a venomous snake whilst walking through tall grass for example, would quite naturally evoke a retaliatory attack from the serpent. Although the victim in all likelihood will look upon this as an unprovoked attack, as there was no malice intended, the snake is not familiar with human reasoning and must quite naturally assume the worst and defend itself!

On the other hand, should a snake be cornered deliberately by a human, with intent to do bodily harm, the snake will, indeed must, defend itself with any means at its disposal. This is the natural way of all living creatures. And in the case of the snake, having no claws, arms or legs, but only a mouth full of teeth, be it venomous or not – it will bite!

*Opposite page: the North African spitting cobra is capable of squirting venom into the eyes of an attacker from a distance of three metres*

Some eighty percent of reported snakebite cases in the world occur below the knee, strongly suggesting that most such eventualities are caused by the reptile's retaliation when being stepped on. A few snakes are capable of a higher strike. The king cobra of Asia for example, grows to six metres and could quite easily raise itself up high enough to strike a man in the chest or neck. In Africa the same is possible with the black mamba which averages around three metres plus, and is well known for its ability to move along the ground with it's head held high up in the air.

Non-venomous species constrict their prey, throwing a number of coils around the victim to suffocate it by application of continuous pressure. Of these possibly only the green anaconda of South America and the reticulated python of Asia, are capable of attaining size enough to accidentally consider a human as prey. It is possible that one such species, hunting from the river, may have in the past grabbed a young child as they frolicked or bathed at the water's edge. Though there is no factual record of such an occurrence, the possibility exists that a giant snake might easily confuse the playful splashing of a small child for that of a prey animal. Certainly, where the disappearance of a riverside-living rural child is reported, the chances of crocodile attack or simple drowning are by far the more likely cause.

Working with snakes, venomous or non venomous, on a daily basis, obviously presents one with greater odds in favour of snakebite encounter than your average citizen who rarely, if ever in their life so much as gets a fleeting glimpse of a snake in the wild. However, this does not necessarily advocate that herpetologists are bitten on a regular basis. Herpetologists after all, are the experts and that very expertise should be their protection. In theory this is so, but as with all subjects or any business, there remains always the unexpected, the unexplained or, worst of all, that momentary slip!

It is not unusual to receive (sometimes even in one day), more than one harmless snakebite when, for example, cleaning out small laboratory cages or examining large numbers of the smaller specimens housed at the park. Such bites rarely cause more discomfort than would a pin prick, with minute specks of blood marking the spot. Consider this much in the way your hand might be scratched when encouraging a playful pet cat. These bites are not to be confused with those of larger species, or venomous species. Large non-venomous snakes are capable of inflicting a painful, slashing bite and are handled with far greater respect, while venomous species are handled only when absolutely necessary.

Herpetologists who have suffered serious snakebites have usually received them on the right hand, especially the index finger, the "working" finger. (As was the case with my first snakebite). But the situations that present themselves when working with dangerous reptiles, especially when demonstrating them, are many and the opportunities for the "exception" abound. This I was to discover, somewhat to my detriment, over the years.

Jack Seale himself had been bitten by a black mamba which rendered him in a coma and at death's door for some weeks, where after, under strict instructions from his wife, Heather, he avoided physical contact with highly venomous species where not absolutely necessary. Indeed, this was, after all, what I had been employed to do, handle the reptile section of the park's operation, leaving Jack free to perform his many other less harrowing duties. Thus, with the many hundreds of public performances I performed each year, combined with the many thousands of times I had handled venomous snakes in my daily routine over a collective period of some twenty years, a total of three serious bites (where serum was administered), two lesser bites (where no serum was administered) and one venomous lizard bite, is, by proportion I feel, quite reasonable!

The most unusual of these incidents was certainly the time I was delivered two doses of venom during the half hour period of one single public demonstration! Needless to say, Jack did his nut, accusing me (after my recovery) of dire negligence and unrelenting egotistical pursuit! Looking back now I can understand his distress and anxiety for my safety. But I was young and busy being the "hero" in front of the crowds and there was no way I was going to let a little thing like multiple snake venom poisoning topple me from my pedestal!

I had awoken that morning, after a late night out, to find myself suffering from a slightly painful, raw throat. It was winter and I accepted that somewhere through the evening I had possibly rendered myself vulnerable to a cold draft. The ailment persisted throughout the day, but presented me with little more discomfort than a slightly hoarse voice.

Came the mid-afternoon show with its usual huge crowd of spectators and I was cruising high on the crest of the wave that had, so far, been a particularly good day, with me performing at my dramatic best. Moving around the demonstration arena with practised confidence, I ignored the huge puff adder close to my feet where I was about to demonstrate the venom throwing abilities of a ringhals cobra I had just placed on the stone floor before me. I was familiar with the puff adder, a female that lived permanently in the show arena, along with a number of other

species. I knew the snake to be docile and quite accustomed to human movement and, even purposely, I nonchalantly stepped close to her on occasion, a strategic move that often brought cries of warning from the more nervous spectators, adding just that little extra spice to the overall effect of the show.

However, on this day, for reasons I am not able to supply, the puff adder suddenly and without any prior indication of discontent, lunged upward with some surprising agility, to imbed both fangs through the cloth of my trousers, just below my right knee! There the huge serpent hung, suspended by the huge, curved fangs. This, of course, brought more than just a gasp from the audience and stunned faces stared incredulously while those more disciplined grabbed for their cameras to record this moment of disaster at the snake park.

The situation from my position and point of view was, keep a straight face and casually make as though nothing unusual has happened, even though I was conscious of a slight burning sensation spreading from exactly where the snake's fangs had penetrated my trousers. However, glory before death and all that, not to mention keeping face before my "adoring fans", I casually plucked the puff adder from my leg with a tug from the tail end and, almost without missing a word, continued my introduction of the patiently waiting ringhals standing with raised head before me.

Astonished now by this performance, the audience's mouths dropped open in disbelief. The man in the snake pit had, after all, just been bitten in the leg by a huge, deadly puff adder! Why was he not toppling over in agony, or, at least, scrambling for medical attention? Bewildered, confused looks emanated from the crowd, goading me to offer an explanation. "Nothing to worry about", I lied, as the burning sensation increased and spread up my leg. "The fangs just penetrated my trousers. Often happens." Nonchalantly I lowered my face for the ringhals to throw venom onto my protective glasses.

Naturally, my heart was pounding somewhat from the shock of the bite, but I knew that I was in no immediate danger. Firstly I suspected that just one fang had penetrated my leg and, secondly, I knew from what I had seen of the exposed fangs, that, at most, only the tip had penetrated my flesh. Thus I concluded that very little venom had been injected and that I could therefore continue to play the hero, and complete the show, in spite of the spreading pain.

And now, while a still astounded audience looked on, I still further risked my life in the face of a venomous spray of ringhals' venom, which, of course, I knew to be harmless on my skin – unless in the unlikely eventuality of it penetrating an open wound. The crowd gasped as the sticky fluid sprayed onto my protective glasses and surrounding facial area – and a drop or two into my mouth! The latter I spat out ceremoniously, before explaining that snake venom could even be tolerated in the mouth without any ill effect, as long as there were no open cuts, or ulcerations – or raw areas, like when one has a sore throat! As I said it, the realisation of it hit me like a ton of bricks, and a second later I experienced the first spasm of tightening in my throat. I had been envenomated for the second time in just ten minutes and my body now faced the onslaught of both cytotoxic and neurotoxic symptoms. This was really it. In front of all those people. My life was over!

The burning sensation creeping up my leg from the puff adder bite was tolerable and would not force me to leave the arena prematurely; the

ringhals' venom, penetrating directly through the wall of my throat was an entirely different matter altogether! There was no time to waste. But, determined still to keep up a front, I continued with the show as I would per usual, but at a somewhat increased rate of pace, until finally it was over. Ignoring attempts by the audience to ask questions, I wished all an enjoyable further stay at the park, before staggering hastily away to find Jack. As matters worked out, however, he found me, as I sat in the laboratory with radio in my hand, gasping drunkenly for breath.

From here on it was a flurry of activity, with the local doctor hastily summoned and Jack preparing a hyperdermic syringe full of anti snakebite serum. The slow acting puff adder venom, especially in the small quantity that I had received, was of no threat to my life and would cause no more than a painfully swollen leg. Even the powerful neurotoxic ringhals' venom would not normally have had such an immediate effect, were it not for the fact that the location of the absorption was so strategically placed. Death by suffocation, caused by paralysis of the pharynx due to snake venom poisoning, would have been the sum total of the coroner's report. However, with medical attention close at hand, this was avoided and, as the first ten mil ampule of serum entered my veins, instant relief flowed through my body! A second ampule assured complete recovery. I was saved!

Jack however, was unimpressed with my behaviour and seriously reprimanded me, and, of course, he was right. I should have left the show arena immediately after the puff adder bite, no matter how inconsequential I may have judged the envenomation to be. Though the neurotoxic effects of the ringhals' venom were immediately relieved (as is usual in the case of neurotoxic envenomation), the cytotoxic effects of the puff adder bite, which are not relieved by the serum, remained with me for a further eight days in the form of a painful and swollen limb.

Having again experienced the terrible trauma of snakebite poisoning, I resolved to be more careful and swore that it would never happen again. But, of course, there were to be more bites over the years that followed, and after each time I promised myself "never again" before confidently once more pursuing my chosen career.

Of course herpetology involves not only snakes but lizards as well. But unlike venomous snakes which constitute some ten percent of the total number of species recorded, just two lizard species are venomous. They occur in the desert regions of the South Western United States of America and Mexico, and are closely related. The smaller species, and more colourful, is the Gila Monster (named after the Gila River along which it may be found), and is considered potentially dangerous to man as it possesses half a dozen grooved teeth fixed in the lower jaw by way of which it can convey a quantity of myotoxic venom (muscle effecting venom). The body covering consists of a pattern of mottled black and pink bead-like scales, and the head, trunk, tail and legs of the reptile are stout and strongly designed, with powerful digging claws protruding from the tips of each toe. These lizards thrive in captivity and are much sought after by collectors.

The Mexican beaded lizard is of much the same design as the Gila monster, but usually black and yellow in colour, and growing to twice the size of the Gila Monster, with some species recorded at over a metre in length. As with the Gila Monster, the beaded lizard has powerful jaws, containing a similar venom apparatus, and it was by one of these that I unceremoniously managed to get myself bitten!

*Opposite page top: Austin in New Mexico with a Gila Monster, one of only two species of venomous lizards found in the world*

*Opposite page bottom: the wings of a dragonfly reflect the last light of the day*

*The Australian thorny devil is one of the world's strangest desert lizards and feeds entirely on ants*

The park had imported a number of these lizards from a breeder in the United States and, as yet unfamiliar with the reptile's behaviour patterns, I was not completely at ease with the handling of them. When the day came that it was decided that each beaded lizard (there were four), should be dosed for worms, there was great consternation as Jack and I quickly discovered the lizards' determined reluctance to co-operate!

The usually simple task of gently pushing a short length of soft tubing down an animal's throat through which medication can be administered, now suddenly took on the proportions of the impossible as the beaded lizards clamped their powerful jaws rigidly shut in indignant refusal! Even just attempting to hold the lizard fast proved hazardous as their long claws relentlessly clutched and scratched our arms.

Finally, after many futile attempts to prize the first lizard's mouth open by pressure of the feeding tube, Jack decided that four-handed force was the only answer. Considerately, he volunteered me as the one to prize the mouth open with thumbs and forefingers from both hands, while he stood ready to quickly insert the tube between the gaping jaws. Heroically I agreed, and with renewed determination grabbed for the struggling lizard's jaws that I might wrench them apart with one hefty pull! However, the beaded lizard in question, seemingly was ready for just such a move and, as my fingers clamped down securely along the edge of its top and bottom jaws, the reptile suddenly jerked its mouth open, lunging its massive head to the side as it did so. Without further ado, my right hand thumb slid neatly between the waiting rows of needle-sharp, venomous teeth and the powerful jaws clamped down like a vice!

Jack, who stood stooped in front of me with the rubber pipe held at the ready between his fingers, focused his eyes momentarily on my thumb clamped between the lizard's jaws, then snapped his head to look up at my face. For one split second we stared at each other, somewhat in disbelief, as though seeking confirmation from each other that it had really happened. But it had, of that there was no doubt in my mind! As the first blood squirted out from between the lizard's jaws, accompanied by an intense burning pain, I howled my distress to the roof! "Aaaaarrgghhh!" I screamed, jumping up and down as I did so, the beaded lizard still determinedly clamped to my thumb! The pain was terrible and I screamed to Jack to get the bloody thing off me. Jack's eyes were now as big as

*Crowds flock to see a new Guinness Record being set by Austin*

saucers, but instantly he jumped to my assistance. However, the lizard would have none of it and, despite our combined efforts, the reptile's jaw remained clamped. Every lizard has his day and this one was making the best of it.

Pain seared through my thumb, across my hand and up my arm as the venom spread like wildfire. So terrible was it that tears forced their way along the rims of my eyes. The more I jumped about, the greater the pressure the beaded lizard exerted! "Jack! Dammit. Get the bloody thing off me".

By now I had hopped clear across the laboratory where, suddenly, through streaming eyes, I spotted the water system and, with the giant lizard still grimly hanging on to my thumb as though its life depended on it, I jammed my hand into the sink and opened the cold water tap to full throttle! Streaming blood, now mingled with water, splashed all over me and Jack, the floor and the walls. But still the bloody lizard hung on, seemingly more determined than ever!

Jack now suddenly disappeared out the door, I assumed to get some device which might encourage the lizard to open its jaws, something like the cattle-prod we kept for wild animal emergencies! A second later he was back, but not with some weapon for my salvation but a camera. A bloody camera! "Jack, what the bloody hell are you doing?" I roared at him, my legs quivering beneath me as I battled with the monster creature attached to my throbbing hand. "Get this thing off me and get me to a bloody hospital, dammit!"

Moving in close now, his eye pressed tightly into the viewfinder, Jack released the shutter. "No reason for hospital", he remarked casually, as he re-positioned the camera for another exposure. "There's no serum for

*The spotted bush snake of Southern Africa in defensive pose*

beaded lizards, and, as far as I know, this is the first bite recorded. So I'm recording it". A series of clicks and flashes greeted my open-mouthed stare of disbelief! Was this then definitely it? Was my life over at last? The pain seemed to surge through my fast swelling hand with renewed vigour!

Bursting now with frustrated anger and in a last desperate attempt to free my thumb from the lizard's jaws, I dug the thumb and forefinger of my left hand hard into the base of the jaw bone, where the upper and lower connected. Jack moved in for a close up shot, just as, at last,

the powerful jaws relaxed slightly their vice-like grip and I tore my thumb free in a splattering of blood and shredded flesh. The lizard dropped with a plop into the half-filled basin, where it stood itself high on its forelegs to glare defiance at me, its jaws crimson with my blood. I was free, but the pain continued to be terrible and I now turned to glare my discontent at Jack!

Forty minutes later saw me in the Pretoria General Hospital, where a collection of worried faces gathered around my bed. Jack was not amongst them. I was in good hands he had said and he was off to have the film developed. He was going to be famous, he said and would write a paper, on the first recorded beaded lizard bite, with pictures no less! As I lay in the hospital bed with a drip stuck in my arm and that collection of "uncertain what to do next" medical attention around me, I fumed!

As things eventually turned out, the pain and swelling of my bitten thumb and hand subsided after just a day and, though the still concerned hospital staff insisted I stay for further observation, I signed an RHT and walked out the front door, still fuming! As for Jack, his camera had had no film in it at the time of the photographing of the incident and he spent the next four days in self imposed isolation in his office, presumably banging his head against the wall! But after a time, when all wounds had healed and tempers calmed, we once again got together to continue the business of running a zoo. Light-heartedly we discussed the happening and agreed, that had he managed to capture the bite on film, we would indeed both have been famous (amongst herpetologists anyway).

However, unknown to us at the time, a similar photographic situation was to materialise some years later, and would dramatically display to the world the startling picture and behind the scenes story of the 107 Day World Record Venomous Snake Sit-In! It was to be a most traumatic and dramatic time of my life!

*Austin with some cobras for company in the world record cage*

Over a period of some years there had every now and then been one or another attempts made by various individuals around the world to set some sort of record for the time spent living in a cage with snakes. Some did it for glory; some claimed scientific research; others to attract higher attendance at the gate of the park sponsoring the sit-in. One of the earliest such record attempts in Southern Africa was set with African rock pythons, and the person in question claimed a world record of fourteen days spent in a cage with these huge, but generally harmless snakes.

Soon other record sit-in attempts followed, some with crocodiles, one with lions, but most with venomous snakes. Here Jack Seale himself had taken the lead in the middle sixties, when he spent sixteen days in a cage with twenty-four highly venomous African species, including black mambas. This he did to attract interest to his budding park, while claiming at the same time, proof for the first time ever, that the infamous and greatly feared black mamba, if not provoked, will not attack man, even when confined in close quarters with him.

Of the many later venomous snake sit-in records set, none included the black mamba, as it was generally accepted that, no matter the facts, this species with its quick temper, lightning strike and virulent neurotoxic venom, was not one to be fooled with, and beyond the status of casual risk! By the middle eighties, some twenty years after Jack's original sit in, the world record claim for spending time in a cage with venomous snakes was reported to be somewhere in the region of a staggering sixty days.

At this time the Hartebeespoort Dam Snake and Animal Park was once again in the news with a new breeding section for highly endangered species under construction. One of the main topics of discussion was our attempt to purchase a female gorilla mate for Kaiser, our only resident male gorilla. Jack had decided that the gorilla situation in Africa being what it was, it would be in the interests of conservation of the species to set up a breeding program for these magnificent creatures. Locating a captive-bred female gorilla, however, was no easy task, not to mention a price tag of close to half a million US dollars when, and if, successful. It was this seemingly insurmountable problem that first fired Jack's imagination with the idea of an all encompassing, totally undisputable world record, venomous snake sit in, (including black mambas), by which to bring to the public's attention our need for support in our quest for a mate for Kaiser, the lonely gorilla! Thoughtfully, Jack volunteered me for the task!

"A hundred days." I voiced my dismay as Jack in his usual, casual manner dropped the bombshell. "A hundred days and nights", he corrected, nonchalantly stroking his walrus moustache. "We want this to be the biggest, best and most daring sit in ever attempted, with you never leaving the cage. Imagine the news value! And instead of twenty four snakes we'll put in thirty six. Puff adders, Egyptian cobras, boomslang… and black mambas! What a sensation we will make; and all for a worthy cause, a mate for Kaiser!"

And the more Jack said "we", the more it sounded like "me". The more he elaborated on his idea, the more nervous I became. But nevertheless, just a few days later found me sitting nervously on the edge of my bed, inside a three by four metre glass cage, surrounded by what seemed to be hundreds of scurrying, slithering snakes of highly venomous composition. Outside, looking in, was a horde of eager pressmen and their photographers, a crowd of curious visitors and Jack, his face beaming with delight. He had talked me into it and it was day one of what eventually would turn into the longest venomous snake sit in ever completed. One hundred and seven days and nights! A record that still stands today (as described in my first book, Snakes in my Bed, Penguin 1992).

*A highly venomous boomslang settles on Austin's arm whilst drinking tea in the cage*

As I was soon to discover, living locked in a cage with venomous snakes was very different from working with them from the outside. Even with all my years of experience and knowledge of the species, I now suddenly found myself as though a novice, starting from scratch. But there was more involved than just the snakes. There was the day to day eating, sleeping, ablutions and other general twenty-four hour a day living, all from the inside of a glass cage into which thousands of people stared everyday! Then too, there were the daily visits from press, television stations and assorted magazines, local and international.

There were the daily telephone interviews, some from as far afield as the United States and Australia. Many of these, because of the time difference, took place late at night or in the early hours of the morning. To authenticate the whole business, visitors were allowed to enter the park at any time of the night, under police escort, to verify that the man sitting in the cage of venomous snakes, was indeed sleeping in the cage as well. Having described this much, one can now consider all the further consternation brought about by the presence of the snakes themselves!

The black mambas, most feared and reviled of all African snakes, in fact gave me little trouble, with the exception of the one time I stood on one by mistake and experienced a rather tense few minutes frozen on the spot while the enraged snake, with jaws open in the ready to

strike position, stared me in the face, daring me to move a muscle! Mostly, however, these three metre serpents slept under the bed, out of my way and I was only aware of their movements at night when one or more would slide gracefully across my neck as I lay dozing in the bed.

The boomslang, though considered to possess one of the most powerful haematoxic venoms known to man, were well behaved and spent most of their time stretched out in the little tree provided for them. These snakes generally are docile and shy, avoiding confrontation when possible, though quick to inflate their throats and strike out when angered.

The puff adders, with their long, hinging fangs, terrible cytotoxic venom and six metre per second strike, were a constant threat, as they spread themselves out lazily about the floor, just looking to be stepped on. Although I experienced a number of close calls with these, I fortunately was never bitten by one. Such a bite, with its traumatic tissue-destroying effects, would certainly have ended any further attempt at the proposed one hundred days and nights!

*Austin on the phone to his wife Barbara during the 107 day record sit-in*

But of all these species, it was ultimately the Egyptian cobras that presented me with the most arduous of times, partly because of their numbers, (there were eighteen of these cobras in the cage), but mainly because of their insistence to dominate the bed! Virtually from day one, these cobras, each averaging close to two metres in length, proclaimed the bed to be theirs, despite my obvious presence. The battle for the bed became a regular daily routine, from which I seldom emerged the winner, and which frequently presented me with uncomfortable, sleepless nights spent in the chair. Later, I managed to modify and adapt to the sharing of the bed with my deadly companions, but it is not surprising that at a later time I was to be bitten by one of these snakes.

It was, in fact, exactly on the morning of day ninety six. By this time I was close to exhaustion, having endured three months of living in the cage of venomous snakes, with little sleep to speak of and the constant daily pressures of gawking visitors and the media. Naturally this was all to be expected as part of the operation and I accepted it, but this did little to ease the strain. Eating, sleeping, reading, writing, scratching, bathing – all were done in full view of the daily gathered crowds, with my only privacy being the few minutes I might spend each day hidden behind the tiny canvas enclosure that was my toilet! Even here, everybody watching from the outside knew exactly what I was doing and, undaunted, waited expectantly for the "snake man" to return! But the public support I received in the form of letters, prayers, radio messages and personal visits more than compensated for the discomfort of being constantly on view and it was this unstinting support that ultimately aided me through the more desperate of periods.

Naturally too, the media played a vital role as their reports spread the message of the one hundred day sit-in around the globe and, for a short period of my life, my name became a household word (though headlines always referred to me as the "Snake Man"). But the constant pressure asserted by members of the media to acquire exclusive material from me eventually pushed me over the edge somewhat!

I understood the necessity for dramatic pictures portraying me in dangerous proximity with my companions in the cage. But what each additional photographer did not seem to understand, when pushing me for that "different" picture, was that the request was unanimous amongst all media photographers! On some days I would be faced with as many as half a dozen assorted magazine and newspaper teams, all eager to get that "different" picture. Inevitably, each photographic interview entailed me draping handfuls of usually un-cooperative venomous snakes all over my person, while posing either eating, sleeping, reading or whatever else the particular photographer in question could dream up!

One prestigious French magazine sent their "top" photographer with the usual demand – "different". But when indeed that particular interview, taking place right in the cage, did offer a unique picture opportunity, in the form of an angry cobra striking me hard on the forehead with its nose, the bloody idiot was so busy watching the action as I risked my life for him, he didn't get the picture! And, when incredibly a second later the snake repeated the strike, the fool French photographer was too late with the shot! By now I was in a state of shattered nerves, having suffered three earlier such photo sessions that day already. With a frustrated howl, I grabbed the idiot Frenchman's arm and bit him hard on the wrist! Then, dangling the enraged cobra in his face I screamed: "Idiot! Here, you hold the snake and I'll take the photograph!" With a startled, wide-eyed gawk, the Frenchman dropped his camera like a hot potato, and screamed out the door, holding his wrist high, as though it were snake-bitten!

*A guy's got to have a wash, even when sharing your bath tub with several deadly snakes*

One can imagine that by day ninety six, with just a few days left to complete what would be the undisputed world record venomous snake sit in, I had had my fill of risking my life for magazine and newspaper pictures, and was filled rather with anticipation of the "coming out" ! But early that fateful morning when Jack introduced me to two American gentlemen from National Enquirer Magazine, one of America's biggest selling weekly magazines at the time, I knew that we were making the BIG news and I would have to pull out all the stops!

*Austin receiving anti-snakebite serum after being bitten by a cobra during his world record sit-in*

So it came about, that while providing the team with a selection of unique picture poses, worthy of the coverage they would get around the world, one of the Egyptian cobras I was working with, for no distinguishable reason, suddenly lunged out and bit me hard on the wrist, pumping volumes of deadly neurotoxic venom into my system as it did so! If ever my life was prematurely to be over, this was surely it!

At the time all I could think was, "Oh dear God! Now I will never complete my world record goal!" But at the same time, while a standby medical team was rushed to my side, I begged Jack not to let me be removed from the cage unless there was no hope of recovery otherwise. Through a delirium of pain and nightmarish semi-consciousness that lasted four days, my body, with the aid of anti snakebite serum and an assortment of other treatments, battled against the terrible venom. When I regained my composure and the terrible neuro-effecting symptoms abated, I found myself on my back looking up into Jack's smiling face.

Even before I could bring myself to speak he said: "You're still in the cage and the record is yours!" From outside the cage a roar of applause rang from a waiting, expectant crowd, gathered to wish the "Snake Man" well, and congratulations on his new world venomous snake sit-in record! Somehow, I had made it again!

As things turned out, however, and partly because of the interest aroused by the cobra bite, I opted to spend another week in the cage, that my record, irrespective of any other, be considered the undisputed record. This record of one hundred and seven days and nights remains unchallenged still today, with the picture of the actual bite dramatically recorded on film by the very capable National Enquirer photographer, to remain forever a first in photographic journalism!

*A nervous moment as a deadly four metre long black mamba rests its head on Austin's arm. The mamba is widely feared for its nervous temperament, toxic venom and speed of movement*

*This is what one might call a close shave!*

# CHAPTER FIVE

# Stardom Awaits

*Previous pictures: a mixed herd of springbuck and wildebeest graze on the grassy plains of Etosha*

One day, after completing a show, a pretty blonde woman named Debbi Allan, whom I recognised immediately from her "Adventure" television series, approached me and without hesitation, asked if I would be interested in bringing my reptile show into the SABC studios to record a show for broadcast on national television. Without a second thought to the matter, or to the problems such a show would present, I accepted! This was the "big one" and I knew it! For though the park, myself and other members of the team had made numerous appearances on television, never before had there been an offer to perform our own episode on a highly acclaimed series as was "High Adventure". Little did I suspect at the time that so successful the show would be, that public demand would bring me back for two further appearances.

Jack was pleased, in spite of the fact that I had not consulted with him before accepting the proposal. The value in publicity such an episode would generate for the park, I suspect he realised, heavily out-weighed any administrative irregularity performed by me (this once anyway!). Just two days later, at the crack of dawn so as to avoid the terrible onslaught of Johannesburg city traffic, I found myself negotiating my way towards the SABC studios, the Nissan Cruiser packed with reptiles of all species, shapes and sizes! I was determined this was going to be a show the country would never forget! And for those at least present in the studio that day, it certainly was!

It all began with security as I brought the Nissan to a halt outside the big rear entrance gates. These diligent young African gentlemen insisted that no matter the fact they had been notified of my expected arrival, my vehicle should be thoroughly searched, as was customary security procedure for all vehicles authorised to enter. However, on the ceremonial opening of the rear door, the first thing that greeted their eyes, were the gaping jaws of Brutus – Hartebeespoort's own friendly alligator, who, adamantly, and with persuasive showing of razor sharp teeth, had point-blankly refused to be transported in any confining sack or other container for that matter and was therefore eventually allowed to settle comfortably in his own space amongst the stack of reptile-containing boxes and bags.

Needless to say, this little episode was broadcast to all within a two kilometre radius of the studios, as the now not so diligent security team voiced their horror loudly and clearly before fleeing the immediate area. In fact, Brutus was basically harmless and vented anger only when forced to travel in the confinement of a container. However, his open-mouthed, toothy grin was certainly not what one expected to encounter in the back of a van in the middle of metropolitan down-town Johannesburg, so the security guards' reaction was not without justification. With Brutus still "smiling" toothily from his comfortable position amongst the crates of other reptiles, I shut the door, opened the gates and let myself in.

*The very effective camouflage of a gaboon viper displayed here*

Because of my unusual load, arrangements were made for me to manoeuvre the Nissan Cruiser almost to the very entrance of the massive soundproofed studio. Five other studios operated in the same complex and, though most were occupied with some recording or another, word had gotten around as to the nature of today's "Adventure" recording and everybody was there to greet my arrival. Debbie was there with her assistant Gordon Pickford, a tall good looking man who spoke with a British accent, and together they quickly introduced me to the video and sound controllers, the director of operations and the camera crew.

The formalities taken care of, willing hands now offered themselves as I started to remove the boxed reptiles from the Cruiser, but there came a startled hush of uncertainty as Brutus appeared at the door, apparently fed up with the confinement and eager to escape. Lunging forward with a bellow, he toppled headlong out the back, over the tailgate and onto the smooth concrete floor and for the second time within twenty minutes of my arrival at the SABC studios, the air was rent with the sounds of screaming, fleeing people! Only Debbie and Gordon managed, with some effort, to keep their composure, the nature of their "High Adventure" show over the years having somewhat conditioned them to such "minor incidents!"

However, matters soon returned to "normal" as, without effort, I guided Brutus across the studio to a dark corner where he quickly settled down again, happy to be out of the truck and content to relax quietly and watch the proceedings. Brutus had never seen the inside of a television studio before and his usually vacant, staring eyes now seemed to shine with the new experience of it all!  Knowing the alligator's distaste for confinement, I decided, and explained to the crew, that where Brutus lay was where he should be left until called to appear on screen. Everybody nodded in somewhat dumbfounded agreement!

This much achieved, I now proceeded to unload the entire contents of the Cruiser. Boxes and bags of varying sizes, shapes and weights, each containing a specific species, some local, many exotic, from around the globe. I intended this to be a show as never before witnessed on television!

Finally, after much preparation, planning and explaining on my part, the performance was about to begin, and the studio was cleared of all except those involved. Overhead, behind the great walls of soundproofed glass, the control room was packed with eager spectators and crew from other studios, their own projects seemingly forgotten in the wake of the show about to take place here in studio 2. It was all systems go: Lights! Cameras rolling! – Action!

"Good evening and welcome to tonight's episode of "High Adventure", Debbie began, looking directly into camera one, and paused as Gordon came in: "Yes, good evening. Tonight we have a very special show for you. Something to make your blood run cold!" he punned, while looking to Debbie to react. Debbie shivered with some exaggeration as she appeared back on screen, then continued: "With us tonight, live in the studio with some of his cold blooded "pets" is Austin Stevens, curator of reptiles at the Hartebeespoort Dam Snake and Animal Park". And turning to me now: "Austin, reptiles are a greatly misunderstood group of creatures, most often shunned and feared by man. Can you tonight help to dispel some of these fears and give us the facts about these cold blooded animals?" The floor was mine!

Having decided to conduct the early part of my show much as I would at the park, I immediately produced the first snake, a huge gaboon viper, largest of all the vipers, with its amazingly complicated colour pattern shimmering under the studio lights, I knew it would be a definite crowd pleasing opener!  Incorporating Gordon's assistance with the handling of the hefty one and a half metre body (much to his horror), I proceeded to inform the later viewing audience about the snake, and those belonging to the same family. The gaboon viper in question was a docile reptile, as

*A gaboon viper exposes its fangs which are the longest of any snake in the world, reaching up to 5cm in length*

indeed gaboon vipers generally are, but with fangs reaching a record five centimetres in length and housing a powerful nerve and tissue effecting venom, it was not a snake to fool with unnecessarily.

*Opposite page: a green iguana from South America*

With the camera zooming in close, I explained the need for venom extraction for the manufacture of anti-snakebite serum and prepared the audience for the scene to come. When it did, the huge head, with giant fangs fully exposed, filled the screen with yellow venom gushing noisily to the bottom of the plastic covered flask. I knew it looked sensational!

Gordon breathed a sigh of relief as the giant snake was returned to its holding box, as I think did the rest of the crew within close proximity. However, this was just an opener; I had far greater things planned as they all were soon to discover. It is a good thing that the entire programme was being pre-recorded for later broadcast, as from this point on, drama ensued, necessitating a series of compulsory retakes!

Next, I ceremoniously pulled from a box, the biggest ringhals cobra ever seen anywhere, I think, in the entire country! This specimen was three times the average thickness usually associated with the species and well past the average metre plus length, leaning closer rather to the two metre mark, a magnificent specimen, delivered to the park by a farmer just the day before. Though I well knew the risks of utilising an unfamiliar snake for public demonstration, it was as though the reptile had been delivered especially for my big television debut and I just simply had to show off the animal in all its spectacular glory!

*A gaboon viper, sometimes known as the "butterfly adder"*

But the snake seemed not to share my sentiments, as with great deliberation it raised the first two thirds if its thick, black body straight up into the air, focused its dark, beady little eyes on the unfamiliar surroundings, and with a seemingly inexhaustible series of dramatic forward lunges, proceeded to spray venom on everything within its quite considerable range!

"Slap. Slap. Slap!" The echoing sound of the forward-crashing body connecting with the studio floor reverberated around the studio, while Gordon, Debbie and two of the three cameramen dived for cover! "Slap. Slap. Slap!" Angry, and totally dedicated to venting its anger, the snake streamed a shower of venom with each forward motion. A dramatic scene indeed, and thankfully one cameraman still filming, though his head was tightly tucked in under his arms.

I had, of course, briefed everyone beforehand as to what to expect, explaining that as long as the snake's full concentration was focused on my close, "threatening" proximity, the venomous spray would be concentrated solely in my direction! However, it seems I had neglected to inform the snake, who now still continued to hurl metres of lethal fluid at anything and everything, be it moving or otherwise!

Suddenly, it dawned on me that most likely the furious reptile was being blinded by the powerful surrounding lights, and in its confused rage, simply took to defending itself any which way, left, right and centre. This concluded, I quickly recaptured the ringhals with the aid of a grab-stick and, with some difficulty, forced the disagreeable animal back into the holding box from which it had been taken.

Again there came the audible sighs of relief, though they were short lived as I explained the problem and prescribed the remedy. Quite simply, we would have to re-enact the entire scene, this time however, incorporating less floor lighting, relying more heavily on overhead illumination. My entire face, protective goggles, chest and arms were covered in venomous spray, as were camera lenses, their operator's arms and most of the surrounding props. Fortunately, I had insisted beforehand that all wear protective goggles or glasses, though not for one moment expecting venom to reach anybody but me! Again I was living the nightmare of using an unfamiliar snake for public performance!

However, all was not lost and, with everybody washed down, the lenses cleaned and the light adjusted accordingly, we attempted a second take. My theory proved correct, with the ringhals once again rising to its full height, to aggressively hurl a still seemingly inexhaustible quantity of venom, not at anything and everything about, but strongly and directly at me, its closest antagoniser !

The scene was dramatic and powerful, and afterwards I held up my venom saturated goggles for the camera to screen in close up. I knew the audience would love it! Then, for final effect, I captured the still enraged serpent carefully behind the head and introduced it to a previously prepared plastic covered conical flask. This being the final outrage, and desperate to kill something now, the ringhals bit at the flask with great force, to render yet another tremendous dose of the clear, neurotoxic venom splashing to the bottom. Enough potentially I suspected, to kill a dozen men! I made a mental note: this snake for display only, not for public demonstration!

So the day progressed, with periods of easy, co-operative reptile display, interspersed with periods of quiet panic, bordering on near hysteria! The latter especially when Tina, a five metre Asian reticulated python, (the biggest, most powerful snake I had ever worked with), happily curled herself around Debbie as though in a lover's embrace, and point blank refused to let go! The more we tugged, pulled and unwound the massive coils, the more determinedly Tina held on, seemingly satisfied that she had found her place in life. All this, and Debbie's purple face while attempting to keep up a smile for the cameras and audience to be!

Later, when determinedly I attempted for the first time in my life to extract venom from a deadly scorpion, it was my turn to panic when the venomous tail, gripped somewhat overtightly between my thumb and forefinger, stuck fast to the skin when supposed to be released! Sensing its chance for retaliation, the little creature twisted and groped with open pinchers at my splayed fingers, in an attempt to gain leverage by which to bring the deadly sting into effective operation. Reflex action getting the better of me, I jerked my hand skyward, sending the angry scorpion flying in an arc through the air, to land squarely on Gordon, who in turn now jumped up and down hysterically, frantically slapping at his hair with both hands like some demented lunatic! I thought; "Oh good grief! Here we go again. My life is over!" But it wasn't and there was still more to come! And it is just a miracle that by the end of the day, still nobody had been killed!

Poncho, the two metre long, green iguana from South America, a normally docile, lazy reptile, who generally exercised a little more than his jaws when stuffing himself with vegetables and leaves provided at the park, today, in front of three rolling video cameras, methodically set about shredding my unprotected arms with his razor sharp claws, otherwise designed for climbing trees! As if this were not enough, at that very moment, Brutus, who up until then had been content to doze in his darkened corner, now suddenly decided to make his move, bellowing as he did so and toppling over half a dozen loosely latched snake containers as he boldly strode into camera!

For the next few, but seemingly endless, minutes, my career and future once again teetered on the edge, as frantically I tore Poncho from my arms, dumped him hurriedly in a box and charged about the studio recapturing the fast disappearing snakes which had so unceremoniously been hurled from their containers. One puff adder, one night adder, a harmless mole snake and - oh Lord – one three metre long black mamba, most potentially dangerous of all snakes!

Fortunately, everybody had made themselves scarce, rendering me free to concentrate fully on the task in hand. Although the highly irritated black mamba with its long reach and lightning fast strike, desperately tried to kill me as many times as possible, I otherwise managed, at a feverish pace, to entice the entire lot safely back from whence they came! For the umpteenth time that day, everybody unanimously released a great sigh of relief! Only Brutus now remained on the floor, his jaws open in a toothy grin, his dark eyes gleaming in the lights. Obviously it was time for his performance.

And what a performance he gave! Standing, raised at full stretch on his short, stocky little legs, he ballooned his throat and bellowed gutturally as he would when calling for a mate. Thereafter, he easily allowed me to turn him over that I might display for the cameras his soft underbelly, the region so desired by the leather trade for the production of useless items for people. Finally, there was an examination of the teeth and inner mouth, which Brutus brilliantly displayed by stretching his jaws to maximum, directly in close up view of camera one. This achieved, the show was concluded with the alligator rather comically waddling off the stage, roughly in time with a piece of music entitled "The Butterfly's Ball". For this, Brutus received resounding applause from all the studio team, and was thereafter everybody's favourite, friendly alligator!

So it came about that some days later the show was broadcast across the country on prime time television. Expecting the worst, I sat before the set at my parents' house, dreading to watch, but unable not to. Then suddenly the show was on with its usual introductory theme music and dramatic briefs taken from previous episodes. Soon I appeared, moving through my paces, smoothly and with no hint of the behind-the-scenes drama that had plagued the making of the programme. The editing was superb, with each event dramatically highlighted with exciting close up visuals. One exciting demonstration led to the next, until finally, there was Brutus, in all his alligator finery, waddling across the floor in time to the closing music!

For the following three days the phones at the park never stopped ringing with public congratulations, press interviews and a host of new adoring fans for me! I was now the undisputed "Snake Man" of South Africa and two more shows were scheduled for the not too distant future! Even Jack strutted around the park brandishing a huge smile on his usually sullen face and, judging by little hints dropped by Heather, quite possibly the time was right for a little salary increase! I was everybody's hero again and life was great, with the future promising wonderful things.

At the weekends visitors came from far and wide to experience the shows at the park, to see the "snake man" from TV! Letters poured in from around the country with congratulations and invitations. Mostly women wrote, some simply in a friendly gesture, others with blatant suggestions of closer intimacy. The more aggressive sent me nude photographs of themselves, signed with a phone number! One of these persisted to the point of finally confronting me at the park. She was tall and beautiful, with jet black hair, deep, dark eyes and an all over tan (I knew this from the photograph) – I thought she looked Italian.

So, one night we went out to dinner. Later we returned to my flat, well inebriated and lingering in the anticipation of further developments. However, her husband was waiting outside the door with two henchmen. He was Italian and well connected! I just managed to escape in my fast accelerating, Mazda Rotary Coupe as I was chased through the streets of Hartebeespoort town by his Jaguar XJS! And I cursed the woman for omitting these "minor" details from her otherwise so descriptive resume! I cursed myself for falling headlong into this. When some hours later I returned cautiously to my flat, the door hung by its hinges and the interior was a shambles. Now I cursed the "Mob" for their efficiency and for the following weeks I suffered numerous near heart attacks as suddenly the roads in my rear view mirror seemed alive with Jaguar XJS's!

Later, the two further scheduled television programmes were completed at the SABC studios, and were again received with rave reviews by the press and public alike. No question about it, I was the best thing on local television that didn't sing and dance! Life was wonderful and I was everybody's hero! Every dog has its day and I was wallowing in mine!

Then, in the same week that my final television show was broadcast, a letter arrived for me - one of those dreaded brown envelopes marked "Private and Confidential" and bearing the seal of the South African Defence Force ! Suddenly, as I read the call-up notice with shocked disbelief, all the wind was sucked from my sails and my brilliant future rendered listing somewhat miserably on the rocks. In drastic contrast to the friendly atmosphere of the park where I would heroically be displaying some deadly serpent for the crowds, two weeks later found me instead kitted out and once again slogging my way through the insufferable heat and bush of Southern Angola, a rifle clasped firmly in my hands!

It was November - suicide month as it is known by those familiar with the soaring temperatures, billowing dust and (dry) desert, so typical of that time of year just before the rainy season.

Below me, the sandy grey-white floor glared up at me as, with exhausted deliberation, I forced one booted foot before the other. Scared, thirsty and fed up to hell with the goddam' stupid war, I cursed softly to myself. What the hell was I doing there anyway? I was a lover not a fighter! This wasn't even my goddam country! Besides, I was needed back home at the park where my fans no doubt were in deep mourning at my untimely departure. One would think that the "Snake Man" of South Africa would be exempt from such demeaning an obligation as war! I thought to myself: "My life sucks!"

*Opposite page: a juvenile African mole snake emerges from a dried calabash in the Kalahari Desert*

*A Tokay gecko from Asia, so named for the sound it makes, is one of the largest geckoes in the world*

*Opposite page bottom: the dazzling scarlet ibis of South Amercia*

CHAPTER

SIX

# Germany

Leaving the Hartebeespoort Dam Snake and Animal Park was a decision not easily taken. I had put much thought into the matter over a long period of time. But deep inside of me there was a growing restlessness and uneasiness with my position in life. It was a frightening decision! I knew nothing else; the park was my life, my very way of life. Yet who can explain those inner feelings that grow within one's being, to inevitably steer you in a particular direction, however unsuitable a course it may seem at the time.

At the park I was in want of nothing. My salary was enough to keep me comfortable in my simple needs and my future was secure in a world where unemployment runs rampant with the advent of global overpopulation. Though Jack confronted me with many such realistic arguments in favour of my continued employment, the inexplicable feeling inside me prescribed not so much to leave as to move on.

I had learned much about reptiles and other wild animals and, working closely with them in captivity had gradually fed me with a longing to experience them further in their natural state. Naturally the many field trips that I had undertaken over the years for the park and in my own time had further whetted my appetite, until, finally, the urge to travel distant places and experience new things overwhelmed me. I knew only too well how easy it was to slide into a comfortable rut, surrounded by man-made false securities. One need only to look around to see that ninety nine percent of the human work force on the planet exists in this fashion. Without question, my chosen career had supplied me with much adventure and excitement, far beyond anything most people could ever imagine, but still I felt that there should be more to life than just "The Park".

But though my fondest interests lay in Africa and all African things, I felt too the need to experience other cultures and lands, far removed from those I knew so well, that I might broaden my thinking and absorb what knowledge was to be offered. However, one would suppose that Germany, of all places, with its cold climate and lack of natural wildlife, would be one of the last countries considered for my new beginning: it was indeed to be my first!

My reasons, however, were not without some logic as a German friend of mine, Jurgen Hergert, a keen herpetologist who had spent some time in training under me at the Hartebeespoort Dam Snake and Animal Park, had on many occasions asked that I join him in his endeavour to create an open air reptile park in the Harz Mountain region of Northern West Germany. After reading news reports in Europe of my world record attempt, he had once again expressed to me, in the form of a dozen or more urgent letters, his desire that I join him at his now newly established reptile park, just opened to the public and in dire need of my expert attention! Considering my restless temperament at the time and my insecurities created by my desire to leave Hartebeespoort, the move was a natural first choice and a release from my dilemma!

Arriving in Germany in May with my then wife, Barbara, in tow, we were somewhat taken aback by the cold, rainy weather that greeted us, after Jurgen had in some detail in his most recent letter described how wonderful Germany looked now that "summer" had arrived. This however, was but the first of many such obstacles we were to be faced

*An Australian green tree python,*

with in our new home. For me especially, freshly departed from Hartebeespoort Snake and Animal Park, where the most modern conditions and up-to-date methods are incorporated, I found myself now suddenly hurled headlong into the raw beginnings of Jurgen's small, badly designed and very disorganised reptile house.

Jurgen's English was as bad as my German, so admittedly there existed the probability of some misinterpretation between us, but it did not take me long to realise too that Jurgen had very much exaggerated, and in some cases excluded, the truths! Even though Jurgen had spent some time with me at Hartebeespoort, it was blatantly obvious that he had returned to Germany with only the barest knowledge of animal and reptile management.

Jurgen's park is situated two kilometres outside the sleepy, little touristy town of Schladen, in the Harz Mountain area of North West Germany. Schladen is one of a cluster of small, Gothic village-styled mountain towns to which tourists flock every winter to ski the slopes and skate the lakes. The region is lush green with forests of pine and fur, while the red and orange, steeply sloped and pointed roofs of the towns sparkle gaily at the foot of the mountain slopes. Here, far from the maddening crowds and bustling city world that is so much a part of Germany today, true German hospitality rose up to me, Barbara and to welcome us with open arms. The year we spent there was to be one of the most memorable of our lives.

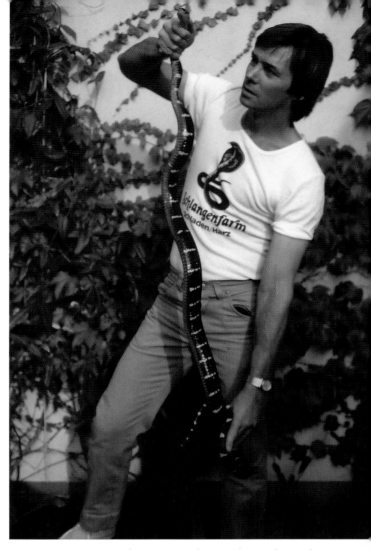

*Austin wrangling at the snake park in Germany*

However, the first months of that year were fraught with problems and difficulties, as urgently I threw myself into the task of redesigning the interiors of each cage to better suit the occupants. Everywhere I turned new problems presented themselves. The structure of the park was designed much in the way the early open air parks had been in South Africa, with rows of glass fronted cages strung out along the lengths of the mainframe walls of the building. In the centre was constructed an open pit for local species, a glass hothouse for tropical species and an open arena where reptile shows could be performed for the visiting public. All this, in a South African styled, open-air type design, right there in the Harz Mountains of West Germany, where snow fell for some months of the year and temperatures dropped to –20 degrees centigrade!

"Oh Austin!" Jurgen exclaimed in delight, when returning to his park after a two week business trip to Holland where he had contact with reptile importers and dealers: "You make my park all different – like new!" He threw his arms around me in firm embrace, almost crushing the life out of me as he did so. "I knew you to be a good manager here for my park. We make a good team, ja!" Happily he strolled along the rows of cages admiring my work. Certainly there was a change to be seen already, but I knew I was a long way from what was needed. However, the basics were completed, with all the cage interiors redecorated to better suit the particular species housed, the hot water heater system improved and repaired, the dilapidated and mouse-eaten electrical wiring for the overhead lights repaired or replaced, and the reptiles correctly classified and divided into their appropriate sections. Now, at least, visitors could see the reptiles in their tidy displays and read about them on the legends I had mounted on the wall outside each enclosure.

Of average height and build, with sandy hair and pale eyes set close together and a smile ever present on his lips, Jurgen was in many ways a typical German – hard working and energetic, always on the go, having already made arrangements to perform snake shows around the rest of the country. Figuring that I was now "managing" the park, he decided this now left him free to take his show on the road, thereby promoting the park and gaining potential tourist interest. Indeed this was a brilliant strategy, as there were no other private parks of this nature in all of Europe, where people could come into close contact with reptiles from around the globe and experience the thrill of venomous snake handling and venom extraction demonstrations.

I had been in the country less than a month and was somewhat astounded when Jurgen happily announced these future plans to me. "But..but..but.." I stammered stupidly as he gestured wildly and excitedly with his hands, while explaining how famous we would become in all of Europe, even the world, and how we would "milk" millions of snakes and perform thousands of shows and be on national TV and be rich beyond our wildest dreams! This was all very nice, but my immediate concerns lay in the fact that Jurgen was scheduled to leave immediately to launch the first of many tours planned for the year!

"What about me here at the park?" I attempted to cut in on his fanciful imaginings. "What about the work here at the park, the tourists, the shows..?" But Jurgen cut me short with a careless wave of his hand. "This is why I bring you here, Austeen (he always pronounced my name this way). You are professional! I know you can handle all." With a casual air that indicated that all was taken care of down to the last detail, he rose to leave. Jumping up quickly I followed after him.

"But what about the public shows, Jurgen?" I pursued the matter. "I can't speak the language and you've got bus tours booked by the dozen and…." But Jurgen cut me short, obviously annoyed that I brought such "trivial" matters in an attempt to spoil this glorious beginning to his soon-to-be revitalised career. "You find a way Austeen. You professional, I know you do a goot job, ja." And he was gone!

*Austin with Gunther and python during his days at the German snake park*

So it came about that on that very next weekend, with Jurgen off somewhere in Germany with a van-load of reptiles to gloriously promote his park to the public at large, I stood nervously in the centre of the demonstration arena and faced the huge crowd of German tourists that had just arrived in six bus loads! Thunderously they had disembarked, determinedly trudged through the park to the show arena and set themselves down in expectation of the dramatic, "death defying" venomous snake handling show the tour guide had assured them they would witness! With rubber knees and pounding heart, I stared back at the hundreds of eager, expectant faces, craning forward to catch my every move! Meekly and softly, in an uncertain voice, I uttered my first word of German to begin the first public show of my career in that country.

"Gutten tag." The barely audible words sounded from my downturned face. With a resounding chorus of enthusiastic voices there came a return greeting from all present! "Guten tag! Guten tag!" This was followed immediately by an exaggerated round of energetic applause – and the ice was broken!

To my delight I was soon to discover that my lack of expertise concerning the German language was of little concern to the tourists, their concentration being entirely drawn rather to my actions with the snakes. Indeed they seemed to take delight in my struggling attempts to convey my knowledge to them and helpfully aided me in my search for elusive words. After every show, without fail, the crowds applauded my performance with the snakes, and enthusiastically shook my hand or thanked me whenever they met me personally. Soon, in spite of being in a country so far away and very different from my own, I was made to feel completely at home, and welcome.

Jurgen's roadshow was proving to be a success with the park becoming well advertised plus an ever increasing number of bus tours being booked for a visit, locally as well as from other parts of Europe. Thus, of Jurgen himself, I saw little as he would return from one tour only long enough to exchange his reptiles before departing for the next tour. Generally these tours lasted a few weeks at a time, with Jurgen moving his displays from town to town at regular intervals, all the while making further bookings for the show and the park as he travelled. All in all it was a great success and when finally German National TV enquired as to the possibility of doing a feature on the park, it semed indeed as though Jurgen's predictions of grandeur were to be substantiated.

*The Australian blue-tongued skink flashes its brightly coloured tongue in an attenpt to scare away predators*

However, back at the ranch so to speak, I was still alone and struggling to keep up the pace as tourism to the park increased and my time to attend to the reptiles diminished. There were cages to clean, snakes, frogs, crocodiles, lizards and a host of other smaller creatures to feed and attend, not to mention the general everyday chores that keeping of such a park demanded.

There were rats and mice to be fed and bred for the purpose of feeding to the snakes; there were reptile breeding programmes to be attended to, with incubation facilities to be designed; there was medication and treatment to be provided for injured or sick animals; there was a laboratory full of import quarantined reptiles to attend to. The list was endless and through it all I was faced with sometimes as many as six venomous reptile handling and venom extraction shows each day, depending on the number of buses booked by Jurgen, who, it seemed, continued to believe unwaveringly that because I was "professional" I could handle it all!

Finally, out of desperation, I managed to corner Jurgen briefly one day between tours and begged permission to hire an assistant. Reluctantly he agreed, after much "umming" and "aahing" as he let me know in no uncertain terms that the whole idea of his hiring a "professional" like me in the first place was to deter any further "unnecessary" expenses. The fact that I needed an assistant obviously blemished my record, showing I was not as "professional" as Jurgen's "standards" demanded! I was furious with the man's newly-acquired, pompous disposition which had materialised since the advent of television interest in the park. To

*A dramatic picture of a pelican in full flight*

prevent any unpleasantness, and satisfied that I had won an assistant, I held my tongue. I knew that Jurgen was new in the business, and now excited by the positive prospects looming on the horizon. There would be time enough to mellow into the working facts of the matter later.

Unfortunately, Jurgen took it upon himself to choose a "suitable" assistant for me, without any consultation. Thus it was with some dismay two days later, that my eyes registered the presence of Gunther Stark in my office, who, somewhat uncertainly, introduced himself to me as the new assistant!

I know as well as anybody that looks might be deceptive and that any employee must be granted time to prove his worth. But, two hundred pounds of solid fat, well decorated in green, blue and red tattoos along the arms, with shoulder-length, dull, black hair and facial stubble to match, dressed loosely in faded black, leather boots, faded, black denim jeans and similarly faded, cut-off, brass-studded t-shirt, did not to my way of thinking, epitomise the usual herpetologically minded park assistant! Without any qualms or evasive excuses, Gunther assured me that though he was interested in the business, he had not the slightest knowledge concerning the business! And, though indeed he was very interested in snakes, he further informed me that he had never actually touched one before! Proudly he stated that he was a true German, having never set a foot out of the country in all his twenty two years and spoke therefore not a word of anything but pure, unadulterated German! I thought to myself: "Oh good grief! These bloody Germans drive me crazy!"

Still, despite his somewhat dubious resume and unorthodox appearance, Gunther proved to be as interested in the business as he claimed and a more gentle, compassionate person I am yet to meet. What he lacked in knowledge, (which was everything), he made up in pure enthusiasm, though he deftly avoided physical exertion like the plague! Thus for the first month at least, in the hiring of Gunther as an assistant to alleviate some of the work load, Jurgen successfully doubled my task, as much of my time was compulsorily expended in the aftermath of Gunther's enthusiastic blunders!

*The highly endangered black rhino of Namibia*

The language barrier naturally added to the confusion; nevertheless forced to communicate only in German, my vocabulary increased in leaps and bounds as Gunther took some pride in correcting my speech and identifying new words. At the same time Gunther saw the opportunity in my poor construction of the language to conveniently misinterpret certain instructions, especially those where physical labour was called for.

A good example of this technique manifested itself one day when sadly one of the larger Asian pythons died of a virus infection of the intestine. Fearing the spread of the virus to other serpents housed at the park, I instructed Gunther that the carcass be incinerated immediately after autopsy. Nodding his head vigorously, Gunther acknowledged the order and disappeared in search of a bag and wheelbarrow.

The snake was large, over four metres and weighing around 100 kilograms. Especially in its dissected state it would prove to be an ungainly and difficult carcass to handle. Jurgen's incinerator being what it was, an old wood log stove with a tall smoke pipe reaching some metres into the air, it would call for many loads of wood and a number of hours of attention before so large a reptile could be completely transformed to ash. Indeed, just transporting the huge plastic bag of dissected reptile remains to the site by wheelbarrow was strain enough to produce some serious perspiration to the brow of the now not-so-enthusiastic Gunther. To thereafter spend hours chopping up logs with which to fire and feed the flaming incinerator was more than could be even considered by the man, and quickly he "misinterpreted" my instruction and dumped the carcass in the shadow of the spectator grandstand, where surely nobody would ever notice!

At this time Germany was experiencing a rare week of extremely high temperatures which rendered the reptile show arena a furnace, packed with hundreds of spectators. It was with some consternation on that day following the python autopsy, that I found myself performing my usual "death defying" feats for the public, while they, in turn, shuffled restlessly amongst themselves, their noses squeezed firmly between thumb and forefinger as their eyes scanned the hall for the source of their distress!

By midday the stench had become intolerable even to me where I stood in the centre of the arena. But search as I might for that dead monitor lizard or turtle or snake or any other of the many species that frequented the arena, I could not locate the source! By late afternoon the complaints were coming thick and fast with tourists, however eager to see the snake show, refusing to enter the hall. Already those before had left in a hurry, cursing me as they did so, as if I alone were the cause of their discomfort. Indeed I could not blame them. They had been promised a "death defying" show with live reptiles, not a nauseating, aromatic display of dead ones! And everywhere I was confronted not with the usual barrage of interested herpetological type questions, but with one single unanimous: "Was ist der Starke gestank?" (What is the big stink?)

Finally, desperately, I decided to search beyond the arena itself, suspecting that a stray cat may have died somewhere under the grandstand. It did not take me long to realise that this area indeed housed the source of the smell, but the eventual discovery of the greatly inflated, putrid, decomposition-filled plastic bag, was more than I had bargained for! With bile surging up into my throat and my head reeling with the terrible stench of the nauseating mess, I rushed out of the hall screaming for the immediate attention of Gunther!

"Gunntthhaar! You bloody, ignorant German misfit! Where the bloody hell are you?" In terrible rage I rushed around the park in search of the source of my distress, much to the dismay of those tourists still remaining, who gave me a wide berth as I passed through their midst.

Finding Gunther, strategically hidden from my attentions behind the workshop area, peacefully munching on a sandwich and sipping a coke, I came down on him like a ton of bricks. With every nasty word I could muster I cursed his hide, his very existence on the planet. Catching my drift in no uncertain terms, Gunther lunged to his feet, his eyes wide at my rage and the sudden realisation of his mistake, and he streaked off towards the grandstand in the hall, a spade and a wheelbarrow hurriedly collected as he went. For the twenty minutes that followed, standing at a safe distance from the stinking hall, I took gleeful pleasure in the vile wretching sounds that emanated from the interior as the man battled with his nausea while scraping up the putrid remains of his "misinterpretation"!

For Gunther, assistant "herpetologist" at the Nord Harzer Schlangenfarm, life would never be quite the same again; I would make certain of it!

*Live snake shows in Germany, unlike in Southern Africa, were confined to an enclosed hall, heated against the cold*

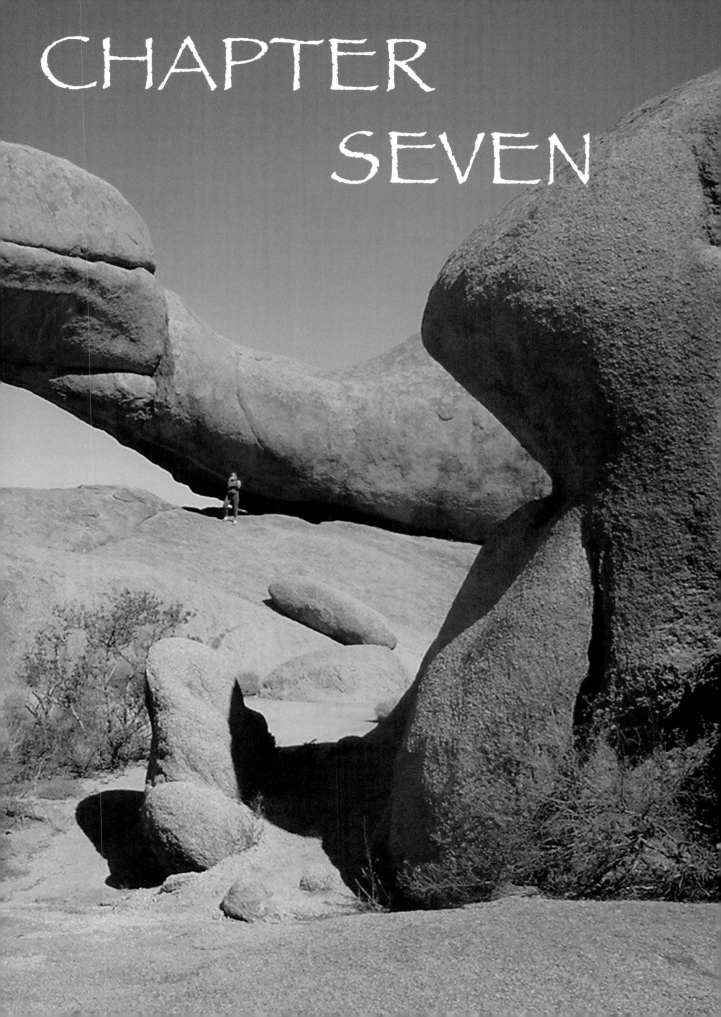

# CHAPTER SEVEN

# Celebration

The months that followed saw me ever confined between the four walls of the park while Jurgen ever increasingly expanded his snake tours of the country. Although I appreciated and took full advantage of my personal overall position as park manager, there naturally arose at times matters which I felt should be discussed with the owner, Jurgen, that he might approve some critical alteration or modification that I had planned. So brief were Jurgen's appearances at the park, that I was eventually forced to leave notes on his desk, in that perchance he might at least read my proposals and scribble down his views, before once more disappearing for yet another unspecified period of time. But even this last desperate attempt to confer with the man was usuccessful as all notes left for my attention were similarly adamant in their message; "You are professional! You know what to do best. Signed Jurgen."

Generally, I had everything running smoothly. My improved perception of the German language now allowed me to convey a more interesting reptile demonstration for local tourists, while Afrikaans sufficed for the Dutch, and English for the Swiss, (this always by their own request). In the ticket office, Jurgen's close friends, Ziggy and Renata, a semi-retired couple, handled the gate while Barbara helped out with general office work and the selling of ice cream, a most profitable secondary income for the park.

Gunther meanwhile relentlessly (if unwittingly) pursued his chosen path of constant mishap, bringing ever greater consternation to my already excessive quota of daily problems. His enthusiasm was boundless, with only his inability to pursue it successfully hindering his own progress. He had learned much over the months and basically knew his daily routine well, though somehow, he still managed to incur a string of minor disasters.

Feeding Suzy, the five metre pride and joy of the park, was a relatively simple task. The snake, in spite of her enormous size and formidable array of teeth, was gentle in human company, displaying her lightning strike and powerful coils only when offered dead rabbits, her staple diet at the park. Raised in captivity over a period of some fourteen years, before being donated to the park, Suzy had become accustomed to having her meals offered to her at the end of a metre long snake tongs, from which she snatched the dead animals with startling vigor!

Gunther, after many initial nervous attempts, had finally mastered the technique and was proud of his ability to feed the giant Asian reticulated python, often demonstrating the procedure to interested groups of visitors. Unfortunately, one day, Gunther was performing for a crowd of young, mostly lovely, female zoology and biology students on tour of the parks and zoos of the country, and found himself somewhat distracted from the task. Suzy, on the other hand, suffered no such distraction! On the contrary, when presented with the smell of freshly killed rabbit, Suzy's single mindedness of purpose is clearly displayed by her speedy approach to the open, cage door and her lightning grab at anything that moves within the radius of that "aromatic" smell!

Proudly boasting his ability to deal with the giant reptile's feeding requirements and with all eyes rigidly, excitedly focused on him, Gunther boldly flung open the door to Suzy's cage and, with inflated chest, nonchalantly waved a recently defrosted rabbit before the reptile's attentive nose. His eyes and attention still firmly fixed on the girls around him instead of on the speedily approaching reptilian head, Gunther's casual discourse was suddenly terminated as Suzy inexplicably bypassed the offered rabbit and attached her abundance of needle-like teeth into the hairy scalp of our "hero", Gunther, instead!

All hell broke loose as Gunther let out a blood curdling scream, and pulled back frantically from the cage, with five metres of python tumbling out after him. His original shriek was easily surpassed by the resounding chorus emanating from the mouths of the panicking, trampling, dispersing females around him! Five metres of python were firmly attached to the back of Gunner's scalp by six rows of needle sharp, half-inch long reptilian teeth! As I approached at urgent speed to investigate the high pitched uproar, I thought I had seen it all!

There was screaming, shouting, trampling and stumbling throughout the park as other visitors, without even knowing the cause of the panic, joined the frantic surge for the exit! In thirty seconds flat the park was deserted, all except for the terrified, whimpering Gunther, who clutched ineffectually at the huge mouth affixed to the rear of his head.

The fact that Suzy had made no attempt to loop coils around Gunther was proof enough that her strike at Gunther's head was an accidental misjudgement, brought about by the overpowering smell of food to her senses, connected to the movement of Gunther's, shaggy head in her eye. Immediately realising her mistake as her teeth embedded in Gunther's scalp, the reptile refrained from further attack, but too late found herself unable to retract the long, curved teeth from the accidental victim. It took but a minute for me to unhook the giant snake's teeth from Gunther's scalp which liberally exuded blood from every one of the fifty or more razor-like cuts which had been inflicted. It looked worse than it actually was, nothing that an antiseptic wash would not cure within a matter of days.

Suzy was thereafter quickly and easily returned to her cage, where she greedily consumed the originally intended prey, and a further dozen that followed. No amount of discussion, however, could convince Gunther that the giant reptile had done anything but premeditatedly attempt to eat him alive. He swore never to go near Suzy's cage again! He also refused to show his face outside the park laboratory, where I treated his wounds, until the now pacified and returned group of student girls had left the premises. For Gunther it had not been a good day – but then it was little worse than most others spent as assistant "herpetologist" at the Nordharzer Schlangenfarm in Northern West Germany. As for me, I thought to myself: "these bloody Germans drive me crazy!"

As the European tourist season reached its zenith and passed, Jurgen's countrywide reptile shows finally reached their end and triumphantly he returned to the park, free at last to once more assume personal command of his now booming business. This was good news for the poor reptiles that had been shunted from town to town in their semi-permanent display cages, and I noted immediately that, in spite of regular exchange, many were in dire need of some serious nutritional replenishment. Reptiles, especially snakes, do not take well to constant upheaval and travel, sometimes refusing to eat until once more introduced to ideally suited conditions. Thus for the following weeks my priority concern was the fattening up of these returned specimens, as well as all others housed at the park, in preparation for the long, cold winter months that loomed on the horizon.

To celebrate the success of the park and the return of the "prodigal", Jurgen, a huge barbecue and German-style fest' was catered for by Barbara, Renata, Jurgen's girlfriend, Frauke, and "Mutter Hergert", Jurgen's mother, who, at eighty plus years, wide as she is tall and strong as she is wise, immediately took charge over all concerned. By late afternoon that very next Saturday, the park courtyard was alive with colourful decorations and streamers. Lines of tables were liberally stacked with cakes, salads and an assortment of other delicious foods, while a hastily erected bar sported countless barrels of "echte deutches bier". Soon a horde of no less than one hundred friends, relations and other acquaintances had passed through the entrance gate, each brandishing some further delicacy or special drink, and to round all this off, from the park public address system, roaring relentlessly, came the forceful, crashing overtones of German oompah music! No expense had been spared, no detail omitted. It was to be a celebration to remember!

Indeed it was out there in the North Harz mountain region, inside the walls of the Nordharzer Schlangenfarm, just outside the sleepy little town of Schladen, that I was for the first time to be fully introduced to the true meaning of the term – "Let's party!" as on into the early hours of the following morning those crazy Germans, with their irrepressible fever for having a good time, uproariously drank, sang, danced and ate their way into a semi-comatose state, as though there was no tomorrow!

As the first light of the dawn tinted the distant horizon, and the last morsels of food had been consumed or otherwise strewn across the scattered tables, and the last drops of beer wrung from the round wooden caskets, Jurgen was, by aid of many hands, ceremoniously hoisted up upon a rickety table, from where he was unanimously called upon to demonstrate the traditional "northern down-down" and make a speech.

With bloodshot eyes and legs of rubber, his hair in disarray and a tankard of beer in each hand, Jurgen drew on his last reserves of stamina, that he might carry forth the tradition, undauntingly, heroically, before all those cheering around him. For two minutes he stood there, swaying gently from toe to heel, till finally, with tremendous concentration, he lifted his left leg straight out before him as though in mid goosestep on a German military parade ground. Miraculously, he held this pose, for ten seconds or more, while all around him the crescendo of cheering voices boomed with ever increasing volume.

This much achieved, Jurgen now lifted and poured the contents of the first tankard down his throat, all in one long, gurgling gulp! A miraculous achievement by any standards, considering what the man had already consumed that night, not to mention the still rigidly outstretched leg! The roar of approval from the cheering, swaying, singing crowd was unanimous.

For a further thirty seconds Jurgen remained this way, rigid as a rod, his eyes seemingly focused on the distant wall, though his toe to heel sway now dangerously increased, close to the point of over balance. With big brass "oompah" music relentlessly, thunderously echoing across the courtyard, and one hundred voices cheering him on, finally, Jurgen raised the second tankard of the cherished liquid and placed it on his head!

Further critical seconds elapsed as Jurgen attempted to release the tankard, that it might balance upon his swaying head. From where Barbara and I stood, with bloodshot eyes and aching legs from a night of endless celebrating and dancing, I saw clearly the concentration in Jurgen's eyes, as, with a final tremendous effort, he removed his hands from the balancing tankard full of beer! For one split second he remained so, poised precariously on one swaying leg, with the other still rigidly outstretched before him, with balancing tankard of beer impossibly attached upon his head, while all about him the crowd, now worked up into a total frenzy, called for the anticipated speech!

Opening his mouth wide, his eyes still rigidly focused upon the distant wall, Jurgen declared clearly and gutterally in his best German, to all those present before him: "Liebe Freunde..!" and no more, as suddenly his eyes glazed over and slowly, without bending at the knee, he toppled forward, to land with a resounding crash, face down on the table, never to rise again! (At least not for the duration of that particular celebration!)

This dramatic conclusion to what would be termed for months to come in the Northern Harz region of Germany as "The Great Celebration", was received with loud applause by all present, and jubilantly many hands reached out to remove Jurgen to safer quarters, while, for another hour ,those still able to stand or walk, relentlessly pursued what time was left to "Party!" All in all, the celebration had been a resounding success, with Jurgen the undisputed "hero" of the day.

Steadily, the days grew shorter and colder, while the sky became grey and lifeless. As the winter approached, so the tourists dwindled in their numbers, until finally in the last days of November, the park closed its gates. The previous year had been harsh, with snow storms buffeting the region and temperatures dropping to almost −20 degrees centigrade. There was no reason to expect anything less from the season to come, so no effort was spared in preparing the reptiles for the months ahead.

The restlessness I had felt in my bones more than a year earlier when I decided to leave Hartebeespoort was back, and it was with some regret that I informed Jurgen that I would not return for the re-opening of the park that following year. I explained to him my urge to travel, to further experience new things and places. Reluctantly he accepted my wishes, assuring me at the same time that should I change my mind, there would always be a position waiting for me. As matters turned out, I was to return twice more in the years to follow.

*Opposite picture: the vivid colours of an Amazon tree boa*

*A yellow tree boa from the Amazon rain forest*

# CHAPTER EIGHT

# Call of the Wild

**A**frica is a troubled continent with ever changing moods, with its wars and dictators, its droughts and its plagues, its crimson dawns and remaining wild herds, its overpopulation, starvation and unstable future. Even though many regions of the world might recite a similar description, those who have been touched by the wild, restless abundance that is Africa, leave their hearts with her, forever.

Africa is a land of numerous races and religions, of vast deserts and forests; the land of the big five, and the multitude of wild animals that further serve to balance this eco system of immense proportions. It is a land of cities and shanty towns, of poverty and of wealth, of industry and conservation. Africa is all of these and more, but above all, Africa is the wilderness, where dreams and adventures stride boldly side by side.

I had brought back with me from Germany some eight thousand Deutchemarks, which at the time converted into roughly fifteen thousand South African Rands. But the price pasted up on the big ex-army, forward-control Landrover, where it stood in the parking lot of a little out-of-the-way four-by-four service garage in Honeydew, South Africa was sixteen thousand Rands! However, after some bargaining with the owner, (not to mention much pleading), I finally drove the vehicle home, where I immediately began the task of converting it into a reliable and comfortable four wheel drive mobile home. And just ten months later, after much cursing, struggling and slaving long hours into the night, the vehicle was ready.

Big and clumsy looking, like a tortoise with too big a shell on its back, but fitted with everything I could devise for comfortable off-road travel, we christened it 'Little Monster'. Over the next three years, this was to be a home away from home for long periods of time, as my wife Barbara, and I, travelled and photographed the wild places and wild things of Southern Africa.

Barbara and I had 'met' many years earlier, while I was still working at the snake park, but she was the only girl that I did not meet *at* the snake park. It was by invitation of a friend that I turned up one night at the Kyalami Ranch Hotel, famous not only for being the regular haunt of international racing drivers performing at the nearby Kyalami Race Track, but also for John Rothman and his fabulous Kyalami Lovelies. This was a nightly show of international standard, much like something one might expect to see in Las Vegas, but on a much smaller scale. It was the baby of John Rothman himself, lead singer, dancer and creator of the Kyalami Lovelies, a group of stunning young dancers all dressed in the flamboyant style that is expected of a high class cabaret show. Totally liberated, and completely unabashed, John Rothman was years ahead of his time by South African standards, where the somewhat conservative government of the time frowned upon such displays of showmanship and near nudity as was being witnessed at the Kyalami Ranch. None the less, each week rated the show way ahead of any competition, and John Rothman, with the Kyalami Lovelies, performed at the Ranch for some 16 years.

Barbara had danced most of her professional years at the Ranch and, next to John, was the longest participating dancer of the group. Having being trained in ballet from the age of six years, she would later train in many different styles, but finally, by special invitation from John Rothman himself, found here place in up-market cabaret.

*Barbara holding a sea snake*

It is without question a fact, that when I first laid eyes on Barbara that night, as she stepped out from behind the curtains to the musical rendition of 'Where do you go to my lovely', -- my world, as I knew it, stopped right there, and began anew. What I was witnessing was a conglomeration of everything I had ever imagined perfect and beautiful in a woman. I stared in awe, and knew this was to be my destiny.

Thus the rest of the night was spent making a total fool of myself as I drank too much wine and tried every trick in the book to get back-stage to meet this magical woman. My childish attempts were easily thwarted by security, who had obviously seen it all before, though possibly not with quiet the determination I was demonstrating. Finally, under threat of being evicted from the property, I was forced to remain at my table and behave myself.

I will never know if it was by some simple factor of luck, or some more powerful instinct, that a short while later something urged me to look back over my shoulder to catch a fleeting glimpse of a graceful figure hurriedly departing the lounge through a darkened foyer. Whatever the case, in a flash I was up and running, all the way along the foyer and

out the front entrance, my alcohol-soaked heart beating like a drum. There I caught another glimpse, just a movement, as she seemed to float away into the dark of the parking lot. I stumbled on quickly, straining through bloodshot eyes for another glimpse. Suddenly there was the roar of an engine and bright lights headed straight at me, blinding me, followed quickly by the screech of tyres as the little Mazda pulled up short just inches from me. "Are you OK?" a concerned voice called from the driver's window. "I didn't see you there for a minute".

*Barbara dancing in the Kyalami Ranch where she first met Austin*

Am I OK -- ? If she had hit me full on I would have been OK. This was 'her', the woman of my dreams and she was talking to ME. Suddenly I became very conscious of my personal state, staggering and bleary-eyed and foolishly stalking a woman I didn't know even existed till just a few hours ago. From her open window she looked quizzically at me, and I felt like I had died and gone to heaven. It was now confirmed, from close up, as it had been from a distance, that this was the *ultimate* woman in the world, and she had almost driven over me in the parking lot. I was thrilled. "I'm f-fine", I stammered, while trying desperately to get some control of myself. "It's my fault. I wanted to speak to you, but they wouldn't let me. Sorry". I wobbled uncertainly, knowing full well that this woman had full right to tell me to go to hell if she so chose. Instead she said. "Come to see the show again. I'll watch for you. But I have to get home now". With a curt wave of a delicate hand, she drove away into the night.

I don't know how long I just stood there, but I do remember a joy building up inside of me as I had never experienced before, and friends later told me that the silly grin plastered all over my face had persisted unabated for days. Little did I suspect that this was just the beginning of many years of perseverance on my part, throughout which time Barbara and I would meet and talk through a hundred evenings when I came to watch her dance, but throughout which time she refused to (officially)

go out with me.

It is true that women mature more quickly than men, and are generally more level-headed. Seeing the youthful wildness in me, I suspect she knew only too well the dangers. Barbara gave precedence to her dancing career, as she felt I should to my chosen career as a herpetologist. We were both just twenty six years of age; plenty of time still needed to mature and find our way, though I personally would have dropped everything right there and then, were it not for her clear thinking stubbornness.

Then, on a fateful night, after some six years of haphazard, unscheduled visits, I arrived late at the Ranch, and walked into Barbara just as she was leaving and for reasons probably forever known only to her, she stopped in front of me and said, in that slow calm voice that I had come to know so well; -- "Take me home to your place, please". Six weeks later we were married.

The house in which we now lived belonged to Barbara. She had purchased it from her mother who seemed to have lost all interest in its up-keep since the death of her husband some years earlier. The house thus sold to Barbara, the old lady moved into the small cottage constructed on a far corner of the four acre property, while Barbara and I took up residence in the main building, which was of English cottage design, complete with thatch roof and lead-rimmed windows.

Money was in short supply and each month we just barely managed to cover the house bond and other general expenses. Barbara drew on her many years of dance training and experience to form a small teaching school, while I unleashed my still-to-be-proven talents as a writer/photographer onto the market. Wildlife photography being my main interest, with reptiles my speciality, I constructed a number of short articles with pictures and to my delight they were published by a local magazine. The financial rewards for my efforts I was soon to discover were poor, though the encouragement great and gradually the idea of writing a book entered my mind.

So I began to write in earnest, drawing text from my years as a herpetologist at the parks and in my private capacity, including reptiles, animals, people and places, with the emphasis on humour. Were I at the time aware of the difficulties involved in the writing of a book, not to mention getting it published I may never have begun the work. However, as matters turned out, some three years later I was to see my first book published! "*Snakes In My Bed*" (Penguin, 1992) and it was the greatest feeling of personal achievement I had ever experienced!

*Picture left: Barbara strutting her stuff at the Kyalami Ranch*

Immediate plans for our first incursion into the wilds of Africa were cut short by the death of my mother, who after many years of suffering weakness due to one lung having been permanently damaged in a motor vehicle accident in her youth, finally succumbed to the effects of pneumonia. Though I have never been particularly close to any of my family, except my brother, the untimely death of my mother, though not entirely unexpected, left me somewhat in a state of ignorant confusion. I did not seem to know how to react to the situation, as I think neither did my father, who let me know that he would be grateful if all arrangements were handled by me.

That time remains a confusing blur in my memory, which only lately, many years after, I am beginning to question, finding myself saddled with a heap of uncertainties and feelings of guilt. I knew I hadn't given my mother the time and attention a son should give a mother, but I had always been younger in mind than I was in years, and possibly not as responsible and aware of certain obligations as I should have been. My mother had been a writer of short stories, published in various magazines with some of her work being dramatised for children's television and it was not until I too began to write my first articles that the realisation struck me how much my mother and I would have had in common.

*Extreme left picture: Barbara and Austin's wedding*

However, if I have learned anything about life, it is that one must carry on in a forward direction, allowing the past to be just that, though not necessarily forgotten. I believe firmly that mistakes are not entirely a bad thing in life, as long as something has been learned by their passing. There will always be those mistakes that never allow a second chance with which to exploit the knowledge gained. One only has one mother – once.

I think my first glimpse into the responsible adult world that lay ahead of me came the day I had to view and identify the body of my mother where she lay in her coffin, in a miserably bare little room filled with the quiet tones of miserably depressing organ music which served only to further strengthen my belief that there is no glory in death, only misery! As I stared uncomprehendingly at the pale, ghost-like face of my mother, tears welled up and filled my eyes to overflowing and ran down my cheeks and onto the polished surface of the coffin. It was like a lifetime of emotions, slowly released for a woman, my mother, whom, I suddenly realised, I had hardly taken the time to get to know.

*Elephants amongst the camp in Botswana*

Embraced by a sudden overwhelming feeling of aloneness

# THE LAST SNAKE MAN

*During times of drought, with surface water all but evaporated, elephants wallow in the last remaining mud.*

*The beautiful hoopoe of Southern Africa, so named after the sound of its call*

and despair, I cursed my father for not being at my side! I cursed my brother who was waiting outside and had opted not to come in with me! Finally, and more honestly, I cursed myself for neglecting the simple needs of the woman who had given me life! None of it made me feel any better and unable to bring my sobbing heart to stay in any longer, I rushed from the miserable room and back into the real world outside.

Here I was quickly set upon by the undertakers, waiting unashamedly outside the door, where they were quick to point out that, without an immediate cash advance, the funeral arrangements were unlikely to proceed beyond this point. With a sudden surge of anger curtailing my flow of tears, I ripped the already prepared cheque from my jacket pocket and stuffed it into the closest undertaker's hand, cursing him to hell and damnation as I did so, before storming off into the street. Somehow this did make me feel better and when I joined my brother again, where he sat waiting for me in his car, his red, swollen eyes told their own story, and I knew that in one way or another, he, my father and I were all living the same nightmare and I could no more begrudge them anything than "fly to

the moon", (as my mother would say).

Finally, with the cremation of my mother's body, this bewildering period reached an end (physically at least) and more than ever I felt the need to escape the confines of society, that I might feel free to explore my deeper emotions, far from the norms of everyday life. The "Little Monster" was ready, packed and prepared for just about any eventuality I could imagine, and it was with some relief for both me and Barbara, I think, that finally we were on the road and headed for a different world.

A wise man once said: "A journey of a thousand miles begins with just one step" and indeed this was where Barbara and I now found ourselves, on the first step of what was to develop into years of bush travel experience and learning. Suffice it to say, much of this learning came by way of mistakes, some dangerous, some accidental, many humorous. Combined with encounters with people in similar travel mode as we, our lives were enriched to extremes that were not imaginable back in the dreary monotony of everyday, so called, civilisation.

First encounters, of course, are likely to leave the most lasting impressions and may therefore to some extent influence one's approach, should similar episodes materialise. Learning from the experience is of course all important and can stand you in good stead in the future, just as our first encounter with wild elephants somewhere in the heart of the Okavango Delta in north Botswana forever educated us in the more precise art of

bush campsite selection.

It is one thing to have visited the Kruger National Park in South Africa, or any other tourist-orientated wildlife area where safe camps are provided and the animals are familiar with human activity and vehicles. However, in the more remote regions, for example the Okavango Delta, where the animals remain wild in the truest sense of the word and little provision has been introduced for the ways of man, these animals exist as they were designed to, and tolerate man only as long as he presents no obvious threat. This is especially true of elephants who are of the few animals capable of enforcing their law, should man in any way infringe on their right of way.

We made no major affair of selecting a campsite in those early days, simply stopping the truck where ground was level and shady under some leafy trees and if there was water, as close to that as possible. Tables, chairs, gas cookers, lamps and all other relevant camping paraphernalia would quickly follow and be spread out around the truck as suited the spot. Thereafter would follow much relaxing, a beer shandy or two to combat the heat and wash away the dust before getting down to the serious matter of cooking supper. By this time, boxes of supplies, water containers, tarpaulins, stretchers, sleeping bags and a host of other gear would be comfortably scattered about as the setting sun lit the sky with glowing colours of crimson and gold and Africa settled itself for the night.

On this particular evening, our first along the edge of the Okavango Delta, Barbara and I congratulated ourselves on the commandeering of so perfect a site, a tiny alcove, surrounded on three sides by fresh, clear Okavango water, shaded entirely by a number of huge, leafy Marula trees, their branches laden with ripe Marula fruit, a considered delicacy amongst man and beast alike. Indeed, it was the month of May and the Marula fruit had been obvious to us along our route, not only hanging from the branches, but dropped and scattered on the ground below, from where their fermentation filled the air with a somewhat bitter/sweet, not unpleasant aroma.

On a number of occasions we spotted baboons feeding on the fruit, high up amongst the Marula branches and this in itself should have provided some insight to the potential hazards of camping within close proximity to such fruity trees at that particular time of year. However, though not entirely ignorant of the patterns of the African bush, Barbara and I were more preoccupied at this time with the novelty and excitement of everything around us to take much note of the potential implications depicted to us by the fruit eating activity of the baboons. This little matter however, was soon to be rectified, as that first night, camped in our little alcove under the Marula trees dripping with fruit, Barbara and I crawled into our sleeping bags, contented after a bush cooked meal of sausages, potatoes and peas. Within minutes we were both sound asleep under a canopy of Marula trees through which the stars twinkled brightly in a clear, moonless African sky.

Elephants are well documented for their close family ties, gentle ways and patience. They are also famous for their ability to move through the bush with amazing stealth, despite their enormous bulk. Elephants are, of course, also partial to the Marula fruit, now so tantalisingly suspended from the Marula branches and scattered on the ground, from where their fermenting aroma clearly conveyed their presence on the wind. If the days are hot, some elephant groups may prefer to travel and feed by night, especially breeding herds which have young to protect.

It was with some disorientation that sometime after midnight I was drawn sluggishly from my slumber by soft shuffling sounds of movement. It took only another second for the sluggishness to dissipate and be replaced by stark terror as all about where Barbara and I lay, spread out amidst the rest of our camp, huge, moving, breathing shadows loomed ominously above us! While my brain clearly indicated this to be an excellent example of a good time to panic, scream and run, my muscles froze rigid where they were, all except those controlling my eyes, which were protruding dangerously from their sockets and rolling in circles in an attempt to confirm what I only dared imagine to be true.

Urgently, hoarsely, I whispered Barbara's name under my breath and in the dark, hushed shuffling quiet of the night, my voice seemed terrifyingly loud and I cowered deep into the pathetic "safety" of my sleeping bag. Suddenly she came awake, sluggishly, as I had surfaced earlier, as anyone who surfaces from a deep, contented sleep. I was about to whisper a warning as to our precarious situation before she startled, when automatically she groped for her torch and switched it on! In that split second, as suddenly, and for the first time clearly, the huge shuffling shapes about us were illuminated, grey against the enveloping blackness, I vaguely comprehended the likelihood that our lives now were surely over! After one further second of sudden and complete silence, wherein all shuffling abruptly ceased, and the world seemed to hold its breath, there followed the most terrifying and thunderous chaos humanly imaginable!

With an ear-piercing cacophony of startled and indignantly enraged trumpets and bellows, the herd of peaceful Marula-feeding elephants instantly transformed into a raging, hysterical disorientation of lumbering five ton bodies! Contained by the surrounding water, there was no escape

*Extreme left picture: an elephant enjoys the river*
*Left: an elephant in close up*

*A black mamba raises its deadly head well off the ground in a defensive pose*

*The African secretary bird is well known for the inclusion of snakes and other reptiles in its diet*

other than back the way they had come, past our truck and through our, widely-dispersed camp. And come they did, from all sides, like an avalanche of giant, tumbling, granite boulders, innocent of malice, unstoppable in momentum! The very earth beneath us shook from the force of it, as one might expect it to, with the coming of the end of the world! Without further ado, as one, Barbara and I launched ourselves from our stretchers and dived for the hopeful safety of the undercarriage of the truck, where we collided shoulder to shoulder, to land unceremoniously in an undignified heap on the sandy floor, our hearts charged with adrenalin and pounding in our chests.

Clinging to each other, our bodies pressed flat into the earth, we panted, wheezed and choked in the enveloping clouds of dust, as the trumpeting, thundering activity around us reached fever pitch. Suddenly the great beasts had passed, with continued evidence of their hasty departure conveyed only by the distant crashing of bush and trees as they went. Suddenly it was all over, the bush silent once more, as though nothing had ever happened, but still we remained flat under the truck, shaking with fearful anticipation, reluctant to venture back out into the night. When finally we did, the scene that greeted us was one of mild carnage!

Though the elephants had easily avoided collision with the truck, they had paid little heed to the surrounding camp gear, which was now strewn far and wide, twisted, buckled and flattened. Food boxes had erupted and spewed their contents for metres around, some of it retrievable, much of it lost to the sandy earth. The flimsy-framed camp chairs and tables now resembled something spat out of a trash compactor, buckled and bent, with the sharp edges firmly embedded in the ground. It was a mess and one, I recognised immediately that would seriously effect the rest of our bush trip. (At least until reaching a town where certain items could be replaced).

The incident was entirely to blame on us, the human factor. I had not anticipated the potential problems relating to the ripe Marula fruit, added to which, in this case, the sudden light of the torch had been the catalyst. The fact that the herd had so calmly and quietly gone about their business of feeding in spite of the close proximity of man is credit to their tolerance and further indication of their peaceful nature. It is certain that had Barbara and I simply remained quietly motionless in our sleeping bags, the great animals would have continued about their business with little concern, before once more disappearing into the surrounding bush.

It is a fact with elephants, as it is with most wild animals, that if you are quietly present at a place of their destination, for example at a waterhole, the animals will arrive and proceed with their drinking as per usual, though likely with a diligent eye focused in your direction. Barbara and I have on numerous occasions, (since that first harrowing experience), found ourselves completely surrounded by great herds of elephants, (especially along the banks of the Chobe River in Botswana), sometimes numbering in the hundreds, as they nonchalantly pursued their ritualistic drinking, bathing and dust bathing, unconcerned, although within only metres of our vehicle. One time a huge bull elephant took the liberty of utilising the back of the truck to relieve an itch, sending pots, pans and other loose utensils clattering about the interior as he did so – not to mention our nerves! Occasionally young bulls would eye out the vehicle, suspiciously, raising their tails and flapping their ears in irritation, even threatening a charge. But this is all bluff, young animals attempting to assert their authority, with no real malice intended. However, no elephant should be taken for granted, and no liberties should be attempted, for though

they are tolerant and gentle by nature, they remain the largest and most powerful of the land mammals on earth, with physical strength, agility and determination far beyond our comprehension.

In Botswana, where the elephant population is estimated to be in excess of sixty thousand, there are plentiful examples of their great strength in the thousands of trees pushed over for no reason other than to feed more conveniently on the fresh leaves at the top. In the Etosha Pan National Park of Namibia some years ago, a new design of "elephant proof" concrete and cable fencing was erected in an area where elephants were to be kept out. A single huge bull, however, passing through the area on his way to his favourite waterhole, was spotted sometime later, nonchalantly strolling through the bush and dragging behind him some hundreds of metres of cable and concrete pillars of "elephant proof" fencing. It is little wonder, and somewhat an understatement, where in high density elephant populations areas of Africa, signs along the side of the road read; BEWARE! ELEPHANTS HAVE RIGHT OF WAY!

*The Chobe National Park in Botswana is one of the few places where herds of elephants numbering in the hundreds can still be seen*

*Cape fur seals gather in large breeding colonies along the Skeleton Coast of Namibia*

# CHAPTER
## NINE

# Colossus of the desert

*Previous picture: a bull elephant crosses paths with a zebra*

Deserts are known to people as harsh, dry climate regions, wind-blown and relentlessly scorched by an ever present sun. Thus, it is often with some surprise that people learn of the small creatures living in these seemingly, inhospitable places, and they are amazed at the special adaptations that these animals have evolved to make this existence possible. Having established this much, it then does not seem unreasonable that small creatures needing little moisture, could cope well under desert conditions.

However, one is most often greeted with a startled look of disbelief at the mention of larger animals surviving, indeed thriving, in these waterless realms. The receiver of such news may eye the informer with some suspicion, as his mind battles with the logistics of the statement. At this point, to venture even further and claim the existence of elephants in certain desert regions is likely to get the speaker either ridiculed, or at the very least, considered a joker! After all, elephants in the desert, where barely a reptile manages to sustain life; where nothing is visible to the eye but endless expanse of sand and rock; ridiculous!

*Spectacular colours spring out of the arid desert*

Ridiculous indeed, and those not in the know would be easily forgiven for their doubt – but the statement is true, and in the Namib region at least, to some extent, a result of the hand of man.

Over the millennia, many creatures have adapted to live in the deserts, some small, others bigger. There are snakes, lizards, beetles, pangolins, porcupines, various antelope species and even ostrich. But admittedly, the suggestion that the largest land mammal on Earth, averaging around six tonnes, and needing to consume some two hundred kilograms of green food and one hundred and sixty litres of water per day, finding itself comfortable amongst the great sand dunes and rocky mountains of the desert, does somewhat boggle the mind.

The circumstances surrounding the arrival of elephants in the harsh desert regions of north west Namibia (Skeleton Coast, Damaraland and Kaokoland) are not entirely natural, but to some extent influenced by man. These elephants are, in fact, no different from others seen in the Etosha Pan Game Reserve, or the Kruger National Park, (Loxodonta Africana), but their harsh surroundings have rather forced these giants of the bush to adapt their survival methods to accommodate the situation, or die!

The regions where the "desert" elephants are most often encountered consist of vast plains, fringed by spectacular, rugged, mountain scenery and dry, river valleys. Once these great beasts migrated freely across the plains, from where the Etosha Pan Reserve now stands in central Northern Namibia, to the west coast and back, and north to the Kuene River bordering Namibia with Angola. In fact, the German Colonial Government in power in 1907 proclaimed the entire region from Etosha, west to the Skeleton Coast and south as far as the Ugab River as game reserve. Big game flourished, their numbers controlled only naturally by the dictates of the environment. The northern regions (Kaokoland) meanwhile was a combination of both game reserve and area reserved for Herero and Himba tribesmen, where man and animal lived in harmony with one another.

As late as 1970 there were hundreds upon hundreds of elephants roaming the north western regions, freely migrating across the country as food supply dictated. But this was to be the last such year, as the Odendal Commission (a commission created in 1962 by the then Prime Minister of South Africa, Dr. H.F. Verwoerd, to examine the welfare and future development of South West Africa and its peoples), recommended the de-proclamation of the western parts of the Etosha Pan Reserve, in order to create ethnic homelands of Kaokoland and Damaraland. This effectively resulted in the eastern and western elephant populations being separated.

*A nocturnal Namib Desert spade-footed gecko collects condensed fog-water by extending its tongue across its huge eyes*

Those elephants remaining within the borders of the now smaller Etosha reserve increased in number, but were unable to migrate west, as the Etosha Park became surrounded by farms and the newly described homelands. These animals then had to be culled.

Those elephants stranded in the western regions (mostly Damaraland and the lower reaches of the Skeleton Coast river beds) were afforded no protection, and fell prey to poaching and uncontrolled trophy hunting. This situation was further compounded by the drought conditions of the early eighties and, by 1982, there were just seventy of the bewildered animals left, somehow carving out a meagre existence in the most inhospitable regions of the desert, where few men ventured.

Though the action of the Odendal Commission was deplored by conservation groups at the time, the government made no effort to provide any protection for the stranded game. In fact, rumour had it that excessive hunting of big game by high ranking civil servants and cabinet ministers and South African Defence Force personnel was taking place. These rumours reached the ears of the Wildlife Trust and a group was dispatched to Kaokoland to correctly tabulate the numbers of elephant and other game animals remaining in the region. Only fifty elephants were counted.

*Desert succulents are often coated with a waxy layer to help preserve water content*

To make matters still worse, SWAPO then opened a western front in Kaokoland to further its struggle against the South Africa Defence Force. South Africa retaliated and the war in the region played havoc on what little game remained. Tribesmen of the region were issued with some three thousand, old 303 rifles and ammunition with which to "defend" themselves against the SWAPO insurgents. These guns were quickly turned against the wildlife. As if this was not enough, the demand for rhino horn

*A rough scaled gecko explores the colourful desert fauna*

and ivory increased dramatically on the black markets of the Far East and, by the early eighties, to all intents and purposes, all the big game of Kaokoland had been wiped out! Of the western elephant population there remained now only those few still battling to survive in the harsh desert regions of west Damaraland and the Skeleton Coast.

Due to constant persecution few calves survived, as great treks were undertaken across the desert and it was feared these few, now desert-adapted elephants, too would soon succumb. Finally they were categorised as "Endangered" and this population has now been designated as high priority for conservation by the International Union for the Conservation of Nature (IUCN).

In recent years the desert elephants of Namibia have received much press coverage and, to some extent, they have been endowed with an aura of mystique, even romanticism. There have been whispers that they have special adaptations such as large, spongy feet, with long legs for travel across the sandy dune regions, where they exist for long periods without water, and desert travellers have reported only sweeping shadows passing their camps at night, or shimmering shapes in the distant heat of the day. In fact, the desert elephants (more correctly termed the desert-adapted elephants), are taxonomically no different from those found in the Etosha Pan or other parts of Southern Africa. However, by special virtue of the area that they now inhabit, these elephants have adapted behaviourally. Because of the high day temperatures experienced in the desert, the elephants travel mostly by night.

Strung out in single file they follow regular paths, most often leading to secret water points and fresh vegetation. They have a wide range and must often travel for distances of sixty kilometres or more at a time, over rugged terrain to reach different springs. Often it is necessary to dig holes in dry river beds in an attempt to reach the water below and, if the hole is too deep for a young elephant to reach, water will be passed up to it by an adult. Often there is vegetation present in river courses such as mopane, tamarisk and even reeds. Also bark is taken from acacia trees. There have been reports of small welwitschia plants being eaten. (Welwitschia mirabilis, the oldest living plant occurring only in certain regions of the Namib Desert and southern parts of Angola).

The elephants of Africa have long been known for their destructive eating habits in regions where food is in abundance. Trees are stripped of bark and left to die, while others are pushed over for little more reason than to sample a few of the tender leaves sprouting in the upper branches. In some regions entire forests have been decimated by the presence of large elephant herds. However, a totally different attitude has been adopted by the desert elephants, as though they sense the need to preserve the vegetation for continuous supply. Only small portions are taken from each plant or tree, while great care is taken not to promote more damage than is absolutely unavoidable by their great size.

*A welwitschia plant thrives despite the hostile desert locale and is the oldest living plant on earth with some specimens being over two thousand years old*

During drought periods, when even the trees and shrubs that grow along river beds and drainage lines are exhausted, the elephants are able to grind up dry twigs in their jaws, which supplies some low protein content. At such difficult times calving will decrease and often the very young and very old will die, thus allowing a better chance for the remaining healthy majority to survive until conditions improve. Even when conditions do improve and rain falls and bushes grow, the elephant breeding rate remains low, ensuring that their numbers do not overwhelm the food supply. Rainfall in these desert regions never exceeds 150mm per annum.

The home range now of the desert elephant appears to be limited to the area between the Huab and Hoanib River catchments. Having been perpetually disturbed and harassed, the animals are today still apprehensive of humans, making contact with them most difficult and close photography all but impossible.

With all this history and other general bits of information concerning the desert elephants securely tucked away in the back of our heads ready for instant recall, Barbara and I found ourselves bouncing along the rutted dustbowl of a track that was once the floor of the Hoanib River. Dust billowed up, not only from behind the wheels of our 4x4 vehicle, but clouded around us from the front and sides as well. Fighting to keep control of the steering as the front wheels were continuously twisted and wrenched this way and that by the contours submerged below the thick layer of powdery dust, I chanced a glance to where Barbara sat, clutching the seat next to me. Incredulously, though no more than fifty centimetres separated us, she was invisible to me, lost in the permanent cloud of dust that caused turmoil in the cab!

For some kilometres this situation remained until, finally, the dust track gave way to a more heavily sanded floor and, though the wheels now dug deep for traction, the powder dust was left behind and we could breath clear air again. For another four kilometres the track wound through the desert, the Giraffen Mountains steadily closing in on us as we went. Stark cliffs loomed ahead and suddenly the track dipped left and down to bring us to the very centre bottom of the Hoanib floor, where sign of underground water was clearly evident by the unexpected appearance of greenery. There Mopane and Tamarisk and, as we proceeded further into the canyon, even some reeds.

The low sun quickly disappeared from sight behind the cliffs as they loomed ever closer and higher around us, and we decided this to be as good a place as any to set up camp. As yet there had been no sign of elephants, though we suspected that such an area of greenery might well attract them. However, considering that these elusive small groups had free range over many hundreds of square kilometres of desert, we were not surprised or disappointed. We knew the likelihood of coming across elephants was small and we had prepared ourselves for disappointment. We would concentrate our excitement to the search, rather than simply to the finding.

Locating a suitable spot, we settled in for the night, our bodies tired from the hard day's travel. We were astounded the next morning, as we explored back along our tracks, to find them covered in places by the obvious, enormous, almost round imprints of elephant feet! They had passed in the night, not a hundred metres from where we slept.

For the rest of that day we searched the surrounding area by foot and in the vehicle, but to no avail. Footprints were plentiful, supported by the occasional collection of droppings. But try as we might, all leads seemed simply to disappear into thin air, impossible as that may seem.

The afternoon was hot, the desert having warmed up steadily through the day, and by evening we were grateful for the long shadows provided by the cliffs. We had explored the river bed westward for some ten kilometres, up to the point where the Txusab bed joined the Hoanib and, though we discovered a number of game trails, some obviously elephant trails, we were unable to locate exactly where the fresh tracks originated. The terrain was harsh and mountainous, making for slow, sometimes

*Desert elephant footprints preserved in the clay bottom of a long dried up river bed*

*A Damaraland kudu bull surveys the desert landscape*

*Pictures above: an angry elephant from amongst the reeds in a dry riverbed, seconds before it charged Austin and, a herd of desert-adapted zebras blend in with their surroundings*

dangerous going, even for the 4x4 vehicle. There were steep slopes of loose mica-shale slabs that threatened to cut the tyres to ribbons as the wheels slid and skidded on their surface. Smaller, long-extinct river flows, now a jumble of wind-blown boulders, tilted the vehicle at alarming angles, while areas of deep sand necessitated the lowering of tyre pressure. In most of these regions signs of elephant were encountered, mostly old, some not so old. But of the great beasts in the flesh, there was no sign! It was most frustrating!

Once back at our camp, we treated ourselves to a cool wash down, taking care not to waste any of our meagre, fifty litre supply of water that had to last for the five days we would be in the desert. Already the heat of the day had forced us to drink more than we had planned and we realised we would have to use the water sparingly, or be forced to leave the valley prematurely, thus forfeiting some of our time needed to locate the elephants.

Up early again the next morning, Barbara scanned the distant valleys with our powerful 10 x 50 binoculars. Our campsite was on fairly high ground, making it possible to see out of the canyon entrance, across to the rocky ranges beyond. Suddenly she pushed the binoculars into my hand. "Take a look at that row of shrubs growing up the slopes of the furthest valley", she said, rubbing her eyes. "Are they moving, or is the early light playing jokes with my eyes?" Invariably Barbara would have the lenses out of focus and, as I fine-tuned them now on the area she had indicated, my heart almost skipped a beat! These bushes were indeed on the move and though they were a great distance away, too far even for the powerful lenses, there was no mistaking the fast moving gait of the elephant! We were back on the trail!

It was without doubt the fastest camp evacuation we had ever executed, and literally within minutes we were battling the track across to the distant valley, all too aware that the desert giants would be long out of sight when we arrived. This proved to be true, but we were at least rewarded with fresh tracks in the sand, and the absolute knowledge that the animals were not too far ahead of us.

Quickly I photographed and measured the tracks where they were most clearly displayed in the soft, dune sand. Next we consulted our detailed

geographic and contour map to familiarise ourselves with the terrain into which we would be heading. The map showed a rugged mountainous area. So what else was new! Bundling ourselves back into the vehicle, we set out after the meandering elephant tracks. There seemed to be about a dozen or so of them, but this was just a guess, remembering the view earlier through the binoculars. Before us on the ground was but one track, along which many feet had passed. We were heading roughly north-west and everything was in our favour, cool morning air, freshly-sighted elephants and their footprints to lead us. Soon we would catch up to the herd.

By late afternoon, as the burning sun, now unobstructed by the walls of canyons, persisted relentlessly to scorch the desert earth below, Barbara and I found ourselves somewhat bewildered, somewhat lost, very tired, dirty, thirsty, and extremely frustrated! We had by now driven and walked every slope, space, niche and cranny in the region, relentlessly pursuing tracks that, one after the other, inevitably disappeared into stony ground. Of the elephants "Just Ahead" there was no sign, and it took us up until dark to find our way, firstly back to our vehicle, and then back to a more suitable, new camping site. We decided to remain in this valley where the elephants had at least been spotted.

Two more days of waiting, scouting and exploring this valley proved futile, so finally we packed the camp and headed once more for the cooler, greener regions of the Hoanib River proper, where we had camped the first night. Driving now further along the river bed, we finally emerged into a fairly lush area, where rivulets of water flowed between holes in the ground presumably fed by an underground spring. Though not in over abundance, the water was enough to afford small areas of lush reeds and other foliage, the perfect place to wait for thirsty elephants!

Some thirty metres up the side of a slight cliff face, we spotted a shallow cave and decided to carry our camp up there, as the height would afford a bird's-eye view of the valley below. No elephant could pass without our knowing about it. This was our last chance as the following day was to see the beginning of the long trek out of the Hoanib valley, then southward some five hundred kilometres to Swakopmund, our home base town.

Matters took a sudden, drastic and unexpected turn, as we struggled

*Pictures above: A desert elephant prepares to charge and, a Damaraland desert giraffe*

up the steep slope to the cave, laden down with the bare-essential, camping paraphernalia. Throwing ourselves down in the cool shade of the overhang, Barbara and I gazed out across the blotched green and brown valley below, as we struggled to regulate our breathing. Sweat was pouring down our faces, stinging our eyes. Rubbing them clear, we both stiffened, rubbed our eyes again and gazed out again. It was true! Standing like statues, unmoving and grey, in stark contrast with the surrounding green, were four elephants. No, hang on, five elephants! Or is that another pushing through the distant foliage? Yes it is! No hang on. There's another, and look, a calf! In fact, by the time the sun was setting we had counted no less than seventeen adult elephants, with two calves! Not only that, but it suddenly dawned upon us that we may indeed have driven right past in the river bed and never have been the wiser! It all seemed so obvious now. "Desert" elephants, as we had learned, are after all just like other elephants and would therefore spend as much time as was afforded them in the greenest areas, where underground water was enough to support vegetation. The only difference here was that this area was situated somewhere far off in the Namib Desert, where few people ventured.

Long into the night the elephants remained, but on our awakening at dawn, they had all once more disappeared. Or so we thought. For, as I was exploring amongst the reeds for sign of direction the elephants had taken, I was suddenly confronted by one! Possibly a straggler, or possibly just a loner, I don't know. It was a young bull and his appearance was a frightening reminder of the size and power of the beasts.

Obviously long aware of my presence by smell, the animal had remained still and motionless, giving me the benefit of the doubt – until I approached, however innocently, too close! With a trumpeting charge the elephant bore down on me where I stood at the edge of a cluster of reeds. But I knew something about elephant behaviour and, trusting that the same rules might apply here, I held my position just long enough to release the shutter of my camera. Indeed the great animal did stop his charge, confused by my reluctance to move before his threat. But, a second later, he once more trumpeted his rage for all to hear and, lowering his head, came at me once more. The sound was shattering and the huge head filled my viewfinder beyond its capabilities at 70mm wide, and I saw nothing but forehead, eyes and tusks. I turned and ran for all I was worth, adrenaline pushing my heartbeat to its maximum, enabling me to cover rocks, deep sand and all other obstacles like an athlete at the Olympics!

Breathless and shaking now, I emerged close to where Barbara too found herself, high up on the cliff face, out of reach of the elephant. Panting, we looked back, but the elephant, content now that he had made his point, continued to browse, slowly moving away as he did so. The excitement was over. We had seen and photographed "desert" elephants in the wild!

Enquiring for more information about the Namib elephants back in Swakopmund, I was encouraged to hear that the elephants were indeed growing in number, however slowly. But it seems that poaching is still a problem and, considering the vast and rugged region in which they find themselves, it is a difficult task indeed to protect these adapted animals from the rifle. However, at present there is a public awareness of their plight and, as stated earlier, the International Union for the Conservation of Nature has designated these animals as a high priority for conservation. Also, a study of the elephants' home range is under way, in the hope of a better understanding of their way of life and their movements.

More recently, following the discovery of an anthrax-infected elephant carcass in the Hoanib River, a plea for financial assistance from the World Wildlife Fund was made by the Namibian Ministry of Wildlife, Conservation and Tourism, to conduct a vaccination operation on the elephants in the region.

Anthrax is not common to the area and it was feared that the elephants would be easily susceptible to the deadly effects of the disease. One hundred and fifty thousand Rands were received for the operation and, by incorporation of a two seater Super Cub, the Hoanib River area was combed for sign of the elephants. Once spotted, a message was relayed to a waiting helicopter from which the animals were approached and darted with the vaccine.

During the air search, some 29 desert elephants were spotted, though due to rough terrain that could possibly cause injury to the animals, eight were not vaccinated. However, the remaining 21 elephants and one black rhinoceros were successfully inoculated from the air by use of disposable, barbless darts, which released the anthrax spore vaccine on impact.

During the operation it was noted that all the elephants were in good condition and those sighted subsequent to the inoculation seemed none the worse for wear. Unfortunately the vaccine is effective for just 12 months. Follow up action will include ground work as well as regular aerial surveys and, with luck, it can only be hoped that the disease will be held in check.

CHAPTER

TEN

# Plagues and Elephants

*Previous pages: Lions attack a buffalo in the Chobe River in Botswana*

*Opposite page: An infamous Banded (or should that be "bandit") mongoose*

The dangers presented by wild animals for the overland traveller are negligible, with the onus once more placed squarely on the shoulders of the traveller to know what he or she is doing. Here, knowledge of the behaviour patterns of potentially dangerous animals is all important, especially if such animals are to be confronted for the purpose of photography or research or any other reason that brings one into close proximity with them. Even thus knowledgably armed, it must never be forgotten that wild animals are indeed just that, wild, and familiarity must never be allowed to breed negligence!

Most wild animals today are confined to protected areas or national parks and it is therefore only those inclined to visit these areas that are likely to make contact with said animals. Indeed, if one prescribes to the general rules, there is no reason to contemplate any personal danger. At the same time it must be pointed out that not only must respect be afforded the larger animals, but the smaller species too, and some knowledge can only be gained from experience alone, as Barbara and I were to discover on more than one occasion!

The northern border of the Chobe National Park in Botswana includes a thirty five kilometre stretch of the Chobe River itself, an area famous for its sunsets, where it is certain every photographer that has passed this way collected a unique picture of his own. With luck there will be hippos present in the shallows, sometimes stretching their gigantic jaws in a cavernous yawn, as across the water, over the bushveld of Caprivi, the sinking sun makes silhouettes of them in its orange glow. Or possibly, the clinging tendrils of papyrus reeds left behind from the last floods, still held fast in the arms of wild fig trees at the edge of the river, will create a natural frame for the distant, setting ball in the sky. Whatever the case, sunset time along the banks of the Chobe River is as wild and beautiful a time as any in Africa. This area is also the haunt of a number of large colonies of banded mongooses. ("Bandit", I feel, might be a better description).

Banded mongooses are small creatures, much the same size as a cane rat. They are gregarious animals, often living in colonies that exceed thirty in number. They are diurnal and spend their nights in holes dug in the ground or sometimes abandoned termite mounds. They feed on just about anything that moves, and most of what does not, from insects and rodents to reptiles and eggs. At the time of our arrival at the edge of the great river, after a long day of driving in the burning heat and choking dust, Barbara and I were only too glad to unload at the closest potential campsite. It was close to sunset hour and, keen to get a few pictures, we quickly unpacked the bulk of our supplies from the truck, bound them tight in a plastic tarpaulin, before driving further down river in search of a sunset photograph.

On returning about an hour and a half later as the last light was fading, we were greeted by a frightening sight. The tarpaulin lay torn and discarded to one side while all the supplies lay scattered for metres around - bottles, tins, packets and everything else our lives depended on for the weeks ahead. Six dozen eggs, were scattered and crushed, every last one of them. Stunned by the sight, we could at first not comprehend what had happened. However, as I pulled up to the would-be campsite, a dozen little heads suddenly looked up from the carnage. "Banded mongoose!" I yelled as I lunged from the vehicle. Another twenty or more heads

*The attractive leopard gecko, unlike the majority of other gecko species, has moveable eyelids*

popped up in alarm. "Scram you little buggers!" I screamed, picking up a stick to hurl at them, but, to my total astonishment, they all ganged together and stood their ground, facing me with teeth bared! This was their find and they were not going to give it up without a fight! I had not expected this and skidded to a halt. If a lot of toothy little fish in the Amazon can devour a man in minutes, there was no guessing what this lot might do!

Grabbing for a tent pole, I beat it against the ground, closer and closer to the little monsters, until finally, reluctantly, they scattered for the bushes, with one or two still trying to get a last bite at something tasty, as though I were not anyway considered a major threat. Our supplies lay scattered far and wide, with everything edible, either partly or totally, devoured. Only tins and bottles remained intact. The six dozen eggs which were to last a month, had been reduced to a gooey mess of crushed shells and it was these, I realised, that had attracted the mongoose to the supplies. Few animals can resist the smell of an egg. As for us, we collected together the remains of our stocks and headed wearily down river in search of safer grounds. The weeks that followed were the longest we were ever to experience without the little luxuries of biscuits, rusks, butter, bread and eggs!

In any African country each year there is a plague of something or another. Many regions of the continent experience perpetual drought conditions which generally are relieved every so many years by torrential downpours, which inevitably again lead to flooding. There exists no accurate balance of proportions in Africa. Certain species of wildlife have adapted to these extremes of nature and are therefore either absent or in abundance, depending on the prevailing conditions at the time. For example, some frog species burrow underground and remain there, dormant, sometimes for years, in wait of the water from the heavens. They hurriedly surface, seek out a mate, breed and then eat as much as they can before once more disappearing underground for whatever time nature decides.

In the most northerly regions of Namibia, one year, close to the Kunene River which divides Namibia from Angola, late rains somewhat dampened the earth enough to stimulate the movement of nests of Matabele ants. These ants are wanderers, sometimes seen moving in columns two to three metres long and half a metre wide, while occasionally huge formations of twenty metres or more are reported. Each individual ant may measure up to 20mm in length and, should they be disturbed or threatened in any way, the entire column will immediately break rank and mill around in search of the cause of the disturbance, while at the same time venting an excited, high-pitched squeaking noise made by vibrating certain body segments. Should the need arise to defend themselves, the Matabele ants will readily deliver an extremely painful sting. This I was to experience at first hand one dark, cloudy night in Kaokoland, as I searched in the headlights of the truck for a reasonably dry spot to settle for the night.

The sporadic downpours during the day had granted some respite from the extreme December temperatures experienced in this region, though almost immediately thereafter the humidity content increased dramatically. Unsuspected by me, these conditions had stimulated the movement of nests of Matabele ants, which wandered now across the area in search of food. For the most part the rocky, winding track I had been negotiating was closed in on both sides by thick Mopani bush, but which opened up briefly now and again to offer bare patches suitable for camping. Having passed up several of these spots for various reasons, finally, exhausted

from the long day's drive, I pulled off the track, positioned the truck on level ground, swung open my door and, with great relief, jumped out into the dark of the night to stretch my legs.

For one fleeting second my bare feet sent messages of delight to my brain as they spread out on the cool, damp earth. But as I stretched my arms to the heavens and yawned luxuriously in my delight of a hard day's drive ended, the air suddenly was alive with an eerie hissing, almost high-pitched buzzing sound, of the like I could not immediately recall ever having heard before. Another second and the messages of cool delight transformed to urgent warnings of pure fire and, with a tremendous yell of startled, painful fright, I leapt for the sky like an Olympic athlete training for the high jump! The only immediately, logical explanation my brain could conjure up at that moment was…Scorpion!

"Bloody hell!" I'd been nailed by a scorpion! I danced around frantically on one leg as desperately I attempted to pull up one foot for closer examination. Then the other foot caught fire too and, with further screams and much more jumping up and down, I called urgently to Barbara to bring a torch. But she couldn't find it and, as she searched, I tried vainly to pierce the darkness with my eyes for any sign of the scorpion that I was convinced must be there! As the pain in my feet increased, so did my frenzy as I realised the desperate need to identify the species that had stung me, that I might judge my predicament - life-threatening or not. If I was going to die I wanted to know from what! Meanwhile, the incessant, high-pitched buzzing sound roared in my ears, but registered nothing to me in my state of overwhelming panic!

Suddenly the surroundings were bathed in light as Barbara produced the missing torch and, to my astonishment, the entire area about where I was hopping and searching was alive – not with scorpions, but with ants! Thousands of them, as far as the dim light could penetrate the blackness. The angry little monsters were in a fury, charging around in tight circles, desperately looking for something to kill, while those already sampling my bare, hopping feet already were doing a pretty good job of it! To further the humiliation, Barbara now burst out laughing as with relief she registered my "life-threatening" predicament to be little more than a humorous miscalculation on my part. I was not impressed and, after moving the vehicle to a safer location, spent the night sulking while the stinging pains in my feet rendered me wide awake and unable to sleep. I would not easily again forget to don my shoes before leaving the safety of the truck by night!

On another occasion, in the wetlands of northern Malawi, we were plagued this time by moths. Not ordinary moths whose path of travel one might simply deflect with a careless wave of a hand, but "Kamikaze" moths that dived straight for your plate of food or cup of drink, regardless of, or seemingly oblivious to, the potential consequences. This more often than not resulted in long drawn out meals, interrupted by frantic bursts of defensive activity as Barbara and I swatted and swiped at the invading creatures, whose unerring accuracy inevitably rendered much of each meal somewhat moth-flavoured!

In Zambia, close to the Victoria Falls, a larger species of moth appeared each evening soon after sunset. Commonly known as "hawk" moths, their bodies are thick but streamlined, with powerful wings well adapted for rapid flight. Some are beautifully marked, a fact that at first incurred my attention, and I encouraged one or two to settle on my arm or leg for a better look. I paid little attention to the little wet spots left behind

by the insects, simply wiping it away without a second thought. That is until a few days later my legs and arms suddenly appeared riddled with painfully itchy, red welts. This condition persisted for some weeks at a time and I was later informed by a local doctor that this was indeed the result of the hawk moth's urine deposited on my skin. Should the urine be immediately washed off with water there would be no such reaction. I, on the other hand, by encouraging the moths to settle on my person, suffered an acute bout of the itches which plagued me for weeks and necessitated constant and liberal coatings of calamine lotion, which though to some extent eased the problem, otherwise rendered me looking much as though inflicted with some frightening skin disease.

This however, was not the end of the matter, as red, itchy welts continued to appear on my shins and around my ankles, though certainly I took all precautions to prevent hawk moths from settling anywhere on my bare skin at night. It was with some distress, after many days of further suffering, that finally the riddle solved itself, as while traversing a particularly heavily corrugated section of track that caused the truck to shake and rattle with bone jarring effect, hawk moths suddenly appeared out from under the front control panel. Suddenly the interior of the truck was alive with the bloody things and in some state of panic I brought the truck to a jarring halt and unceremoniously dived for open spaces. Barbara followed my example and, as we sat on the hard ground outside the truck, suddenly the ludicrous nature of the situation dawned upon us, and we rolled over howling with laughter. There we were, two grown adults sitting on the ground outside our truck, terrified of a dozen or so little moths that fluttered pathetically against the window glass. Bloody Hell! This "itchy moth" business was turning out to be more worrying than a herd of Marula-eating, stampeding elephants!

The moths it seems, after completing their nightly foraging, were delighted with the discovery of the dark, safe interior of the vehicle's front control panel, and claimed the area for their daylight roost, all the while merrily urinating on my bare ankles and shins as we all travelled merrily together to the next destination! A few sprays of insect repellent soon changed their minds and, once all were cleared out of the truck, I was at last on my way to complete recovery, with no further itchy welts appearing on my legs or any other place. Another experience survived; another lesson learned.

Not only are insects capable of plague proportions. Some species of small mammals, for example mice, may also suddenly appear in great numbers. Again this may largely be due to climatic conditions, where sudden rains after drought can promote a sudden acceleration of the birth rate. Though one might consider these cute, furry, little animals preferable to the hordes of buzzing, flying insects, they are easily capable of rendering your camp a shambles in a very short time. Naturally, insect repellent has no effect on them at all, and it is impossible in the bush to expect to eradicate the hordes with merely a mouse trap.

Camping for a time in such a mouse-plague, infested area at the southern tip of the Okavango Delta, Barbara and I had our work cut out for us as every item of food had to be meticulously used and replaced in sealed containers or at least as out of reach as possible. However, it soon became apparent that no amount of care would solve the problem, as the hordes of mice grew greater in number and bolder in nerve with every passing day and night! If you pulled out a drawer, there was a mouse inside. If you opened a cardboard box of supplies, mice would come scrambling out. Soon every soft container was riddled with holes and the contents

*Opposite page top: this giant moth was filmed in Costa Rica*
*Opposite page bottom: the Namib large-headed gecko is the largest gecko found in the region*

*A tree mouse in Botswana, ever watchful for a morsel to nibble on*

widely distributed amongst the local mice, who by now had obviously invited family from far and wide!

When we were busy inside the truck, everything edible outside was being dragged off into the bush. When we sat outside in the cool of the evening, the noises emitted from within clearly announced "mice at work"! Sleep became impossible as infuriating little chewing noises would keep one wondering what was now being destroyed, while the pitter-patter of hundreds of little feet all over the truck rained on our eardrums like a Chinese water torture!

We left the camp for a few days to travel the Delta by canoe, to attempt some wildlife photography from the water. Not unexpected to us on our return, the mice had well established themselves in the truck, despite my diligent effort to seal it up tight before we left. Nests were everywhere, some with little pink, squeaking shapes in them, all crying to be fed. It was like a bloody zoo! And I was the curator supplying comfortable housing and food! Worst of all, I didn't have the heart to destroy the little animals, but instead spent the entire day removing the little nests of squeakers to outside accommodation, hoping that the parents would follow suit. However, that very same night the mothers returned their brood to the lower levels of the truck, where they immediately set about the reconstruction of new nests, incorporating all available on the spot material that they found so plentiful inside the truck! So the battle raged on for days and days!

Finally the day came for us to move on to other parts and, with all camping equipment and supplies gathered and packed, I turned the key in the ignition. But instead of the comforting churn of the starter motor that would fire the truck's reliable engine into life, there came only silence! Deafening silence! The implications attached to being far off the beaten track in the wilds of Botswana, stranded in a vehicle that cannot fire into life, are daunting to say the least! Again, I turned the key, but with the same result. Quickly I checked the fuses. All in perfect working order. The starter motor must be shot! There was no way in hell the truck could be pushed; it weighed a couple of tonnes and was positioned on soft earth. We were stuck, possibly to die in the remote wilderness that is the Okavango Delta, hundreds of kilometres from the slightest civilisation with the mice the only witness to our demise! Demise! De-mise? De-mice?! Suddenly the thought occurred to me! The mice! Quickly I removed the engine cowling and peered inside.

It was as I suspected. Frustrated anger flared up inside of me and, if there had been a mouse in sight at that moment, I would surely have committed murder! I screamed the words out at the top of my voice – "The wires! The bloody mice have chewed all the wires! Aaarrghh!" For the rest of that day the quiet, peaceful silence that is the very essence of the Okavango, was rent with sporadic bursts of liberal profanity as awkwardly I lay in an upside down position, painstakingly stripping, joining and taping dozens of well chewed wires all about the engine compartment!

By nightfall the job was completed, but too late for us to depart, so camp was set up. As usual, the mice were there in force, scurrying about; apparently delighted by our extended stay and determined to get their value. This meant another sleepless night for me as relentlessly I kept vigil over the delicate auto-wiring so recently repaired! The following morning, as the truck fired into life and we pulled away from the campsite, I almost imagined the looks of sadness on the faces of the mice as their somewhat brief, but luxurious, livelihood pulled away from them. I almost felt sad

*A pair of African toads, emerged from beneath the earth, mate after the first rains of the year*

myself and imagined poor, starving little mice wandering aimlessly around in the bush. That is until that very same night, at another campsite, the infuriating chewing began again, and I realised that either we had some hitch-hikers or we were still within the plague area! In exasperation, I thought to myself: "Who the hell said wildlife travel would be fun?"

Of all the potentially dangerous creatures to be encountered in the wilds of Africa, the lion must surely head the list, not simply because of its ferocious power, but because of the animal's ability to avoid detection in its natural habitat. In other words, though the lion may not go out of its way to attack humans, should the opportunity be offered on a plate, no blame can rest with the animal as it reacts to its natural instincts. In our ignorance one day, both Barbara and I came frighteningly close to setting a terminal example.

The Savuti region of Botswana is known to have the highest density of lions in Africa. The area is wild and remote, the scattered thorn bush and tall grass vegetation an ideal location for a variety of herbivores, which in turn attract the attentions of great prides of lions, sometimes exceeding twenty in number. Negotiating the Savuti region is certain to bring the traveller into close contact with lions, or at the very least, their echoing roars at night as they advertise their presence.

*Young lions position themselves on a fallen tree to better view the surrounding area for potential prey*

On one such night, we had just settled down to a relaxing evening of preparing supper under the stars, when suddenly there came a tremendous chorus of deafening roars from the very edge of our camp. Another second, and a pride of six lions came boldly strolling out of the tall grass and into the clearing where all our supplies and equipment lay scattered awaiting attention. Needless to say this necessitated a compulsory dive for the safety of the vehicle, from where we watched with watering mouths as our meat on the low camp fire steadily burnt to charcoal as the lions lingered close by, seemingly curious about our camp. We made no complaint however. This was exciting and what wildlife travel through Africa was all about and whenever possible, I sneaked a flash photograph from a window.

However, after some hours, with the lions settled comfortably, carelessly under our trees, it became apparent that they were in no hurry to leave, possibly enjoying the dim warmth radiating from the embers of our fire and charcoaled meat. Eventually we fell asleep, but were suddenly awoken later by the violent rocking of the truck. Moving to the front of the vehicle, I was about to peer out into the gloom when suddenly a huge dark shape lunged onto the bonnet and up over the windscreen. This

weighty movement rendered the truck once more swaying and rocking, as I realised with some dismay that the lions were climbing up onto the roof! Indeed this is where they remained for the duration of the night, while Barbara and I cowered somewhat nervously inside. The experience was both exciting and nerve-wracking at the same time, but by sunrise the animals had disembarked and once more welted away into the bush.

This was not to be the end of the matter as two days later, while preparing to cross a particularly wide and deep looking area of marshy flood plain, Barbara and I both left the vehicle to explore the section ahead, a normal precaution before attempting a water crossing. Usually only I would walk ahead, with Barbara remaining behind with the vehicle to keep an eye out for predators. But seeing as the area in question on that day was wide and open, there seemed little reason for this and Barbara was keen to stretch her legs at my side. Bad mistake! I should have known better, for when, after traversing the marsh on foot, we judged it not too dangerous for the truck to cross, we swivelled to return to the waiting vehicle and were stopped dead in our tracks!

Gathered around the truck, their faces showing pure delight at the reuniting with their "favourite" play thing, were the same six lions of a few nights previous! As we stared in terrified disbelief, the first lion lightly jumped onto the bonnet of the vehicle and onto the roof! A few incongruous minutes later saw us still frozen on the spot where we stood thigh-deep in the marsh, while just sixty metres distant on dry ground, our truck and only hope of safety stood stark in the sunlight, its roof adorned by the lithesome shapes of six adult lions. It was as close an example to my worst nightmare as I was ever likely to experience!

Barbara was trembling at my side which, combined with my own shaking, all but turned the water around our knees to foam. We were not in a good position and, as I slowly swivelled my head about, the lack of any specimens of tall trees accentuated the fact. On the truck, the lions lazed comfortably, seemingly content with their vantage point. None seemed to be interested in us and I guessed that possibly they were not even aware of our presence in the marsh. Of one thing I was certain, our only hope was not to attract their curiosity by any sudden movement, for that would surely render our lives prematurely ended! I knew as well as the next man that lions have no fear of water, especially when pursuing prey, and therefore did not for one second imagine that the marsh in which we now stood would provide any protection. However, I did know that the lions were unlikely to take the water route if there was a dry alternative and thus I made the only feasible decision possible for our rescue. Tugging Barbara gently by the hand, I motioned her to

*These pages and previous pages: the spectacular Epupa Falls - home to the Kunene River between Namibia and Angola*

slowly lower her body with mine into the water, until all but our heads were submerged, to make ourselves as inconspicuous as possible. There we sat, motionless, barely daring to breathe, for two and a half hours, until our bodies shivered violently from the cold and our submerged skins shrivelled on our bodies, while a short distance away the small pride of lions lounged comfortably in the warm sunlight, backing down on the roof of our truck. It was a time we would not easily erase from our memories!

The worst moments came just as the end neared for, as the lions finally descended one at a time from the roof, each in turn gazed out across the marshy plain, as though contemplating the crossing. An eternity seemed to pass before thankfully the six animals turned and wandered off in the opposite direction, never to be seen again. When eventually we were returned to the safety of the truck, our bodies were racked with spasms of cold and nervous tension and tears welled up in Barbara's eyes, and I held her close while silently cursing myself for my careless mistake and endangering our lives. This was a lesson learned the hard way if ever I experienced it and for many, many sleepless nights thereafter, my thoughts tortured me with the potential alternative outcome of the incident. The ways of the wild are not to be taken for granted, but to be respected, and the laws abided by. There are no two ways.

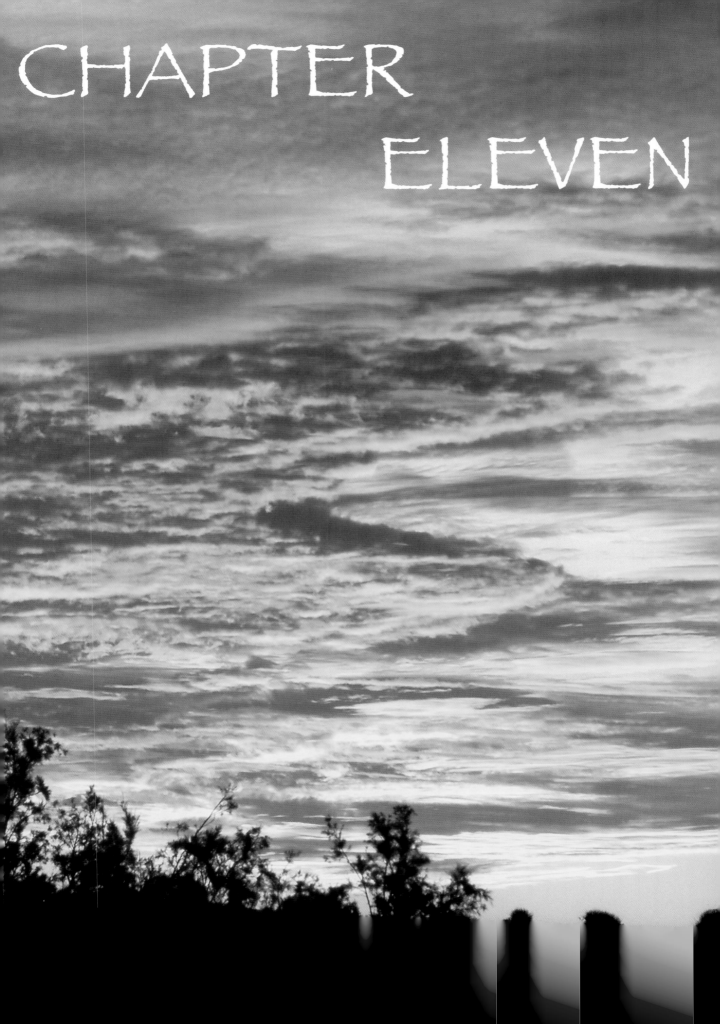

# CHAPTER

# ELEVEN

# Wild Dogs

*Previous pages: A breathtaking view of sunset over Damaraland in Namibia*

The mention of the last remaining wild dogs of Namibia being endangered by man's encroachment on their domain, was the initial spark that set myself and Barbara on the trail of further investigation. The history of the wild dog population in this country is not encouraging and further deterioration of the remaining wild dog population is, well, unthinkable!

Wild dogs require vast areas in which to roam, hunt and breed. They move continuously, relentlessly, in search of prey often covering as much as fifty to eighty kilometres in a day. This fact alone has made the tracking and recording of their habits extremely difficult. Even those once present in the vast Etosha Pan Game Reserve found it necessary to travel beyond the park's boundaries, where they were set upon and eventually wiped out by farmers.

A number of unsuccessful attempts to reintroduce the species unfortunately failed, as the hand-reared dogs found the abundant opposition of more powerful predators in the park overwhelming, and they either starved or were killed. It was in fact, at the Okaukuejo Camp in the Etosha Reserve, where the most recent group of young wild dogs were being prepared for reintroduction into the park, that I first made contact with the animals. However, as Ranger Lou Scheepers showed Barbara and myself around the specially erected private enclosure, he expressed his doubts as to the success of the venture and thought the animals would be more likely to be relocated to a more suitable environment in a private South African reserve. Later I was informed

*Pictures on this page: wild dog pups soaking up the sun and an adult wild dog surveys the lanscape*

that this was indeed the case and the Etosha Reserve remains today, still without a wild dog population.

Pursuing the matter further, I made contact and introduced myself to Mr Ben Beytell of the Ministry of Wildlife, Conservation and Tourism of Namibia, who informed me that the only remaining wild dogs in the country were to be located in the Bushmanland/Kavango regions of north eastern Namibia. Here they roam freely through the thick bush, sometimes crossing back and forth into Botswana. Ben informed me further that although the animals were afforded protection within the Kaudom Reserve located in that area, the animals' range was far greater than the reserve's borders, resulting in conflict with steadily encroaching human populations. Forseeing the inevitable outcome of this situation (as was experienced with the Etosha dogs) a biologist by the name of Flip Stander was assigned to the area in an attempt to collar and record the movements of not only the wild dogs, but also the other prominent carnivores.

This information further spurred my interest in the wild dogs of Namibia, and one glance at a map of the area, which clearly depicted a noticeable absence of the usual, familiar topography, promising rather an area of tantalisingly, undisturbed wilderness, made up my mind, and I applied to the ministry for permission to spend some months photographing in the region. My application was forwarded to Mr Polla Swart, the Director of Wildlife, Conservation and Research at that time, who graciously approved, suggesting that Flip Stander might well appreciate any assistance my presence in the area might afford, especially in terms of wild dog surveillance.

Travelling from Swakopmund on the west coast of Namibia, it is a six hundred kilometre, north-easterly drive to Grootfontein, the last outpost of civilisation before heading due east for the heart of Bushmanland. Some fifty kilometres short of the Botswana border we encountered the little "town" of Tsumkwe, which in fact consists of no more than a handful of old houses, one of which serves as a police station and another a hospital. The largest existing house is that of the conservation offices

*Pictures on this page: A lone wild dog and a pack indulging in a mud bath*

whose staff occupy the remaining few houses. The tiny shop/combination petrol station offered all the necessary "survival goods" for a lengthy safari, like tobacco, chewing gum, Vick's body rub and...no petrol! Our enquiry to the possibility of fresh meat eventually, (after much debate) produced the carcass of a partially plucked chicken that seemed to have turned green sometime before it turned to biltong. It began to dawn on Barbara and me that the supplies we had brought with us were to be "IT" for the duration of our adventure. At the conservation office, amid an exciting gathering of Bushmen and others displaying conservation insignia embroidered on the sleeves of their blue overalls, we met Duane Rudman, (then chief conservation officer of Bushmanland) as he was unloading a recently shot leopard from the back of his Land Rover.

Duane quickly responded to my questions, explaining that leopards were plentiful throughout Bushmanland, thriving in the thick bush with its abundance of small prey animals. However, as is always the case, and will always be the case where man and wild beast "share" common ground, there develops conflict should the beast, in a moment of weakness, prey upon man's livestock. Inevitably the end result is always the same. The beast is hunted down and destroyed. In this particular case, Duane had been the hunter, though reluctantly so, as he expressed his desire to rather trap or dart the problem animals for relocation to safer parts, like the Kaudom Reserve, just sixty kilometres to the north. This was easier said than done, however, as funds and manpower were in short supply. It was hoped that the presence of the biologist, Flip Stander in the area might soon offer some solutions.

Having received detailed maps showing all water points and possible campsite locations from Duane, we headed northwards along a bone-jarring, gut-wrenching track that offered relief only when falling away suddenly to deep sand that bogged us down to a snail's pace. Six hours later, finally saw us battered, dusty and exhausted across the border and close to Sikereti, the south camp of the Kaudom Reserve, where unceremoniously Barbara and I crashed for the night, oblivious to our surroundings.

*A rare close up sighting of the elusive, nocturnal brown hyaena*

Dawn came and we made contact with Katura, an Owambo Ranger in charge of the Sikereti tourist camp, which consisted of four, rustic, log bungalows with outside ablutions, and a further number of clearings cut in the thick bush for campers. Explaining to him our plans for an extended stay and the need to be close to water, Katura obligingly indicated a good spot not too far from the camp. However, water, he informed us, was not available at this time as the elephants had ripped up the borehole pipes a few days earlier. He seemed not perturbed, assuring us that this situation would soon be rectified by his team.

It was November, "suicide month" to those experienced in these northerly regions, and the midday temperatures were well into the forties. The drought had taken its toll and though we constructed our camp in an area surrounded by tall trees, there was not a single leaf to provide shade. Some serious rain across the region would be needed to rectify this condition.

The Kaudom Reserve itself falls within the Kalahari sandveld. Though we operated across a vast area, from Kaudom eastwards through Kavango and south throughout Bushmanland, we spent much time to make contact with game forced to these points by the persistence of the drought conditions.

All activities, had to correspond strictly with the supply of petrol available. Here, Katura offered some respite, promising (for some small renumeration) to collect for us a two hundred litre drum while replenishing Sikereti supplies at the northern Caprivi town of Bagani – soon. The Owambo definition of "soon", I was to discover, varies anywhere between tomorrow and next year! Although I remained grateful for Katura's effort, the sixteen day expectant wait for the promised petrol effectively reduced me to a nervous wreck, as steadily the last reserves in the truck's tanks dwindled below any visible reading on the gauge!

Meanwhile, the elephants persisted with their attacks on the borehole, ripping up the pipes, toppling the pump and all but totally levelling the framework that was the pump house. Not satisfied with these little midnight extravaganzas, the animals next proceeded to amble into Sikereti Camp, where they nonchalantly dislodged the overhead tank of stored water and had a shower! This at a time when Katura and his team were away to the north collecting supplies and fuel. Although I implemented crude repairs, every second night at least would see the elephants return to quickly and decisively undo my work. Even huge log fires stacked to burn the entire night did not deter the animals.

It must be noted that though the drought was at its extreme in November/December, with no surface water present, the boreholes in operation throughout Kaudom and Bushmanland continued to ensure water points for the game. The Sikereti elephants' nevertheless, chose to ignore these muddy waterholes in favour of the fresh, cool water pumped through the pipes. With the intelligence and physical ability to secure this source, these animals simply did what came naturally.

*African wild dogs, also known as Cape hunting dogs, are extremely social animals, with tremendous reserves of stamina which they utilise when running their prey to ground*

We had heard spotted hyaenas calling close to our base camp at night, but we had seen no sign of their physical presence other than tracks left in the soft sand. Suddenly, on the third night of our surveillance at our closest waterhole, Tsotsana, we witnessed a battle of some ferocity as three large spotted hyaenas attacked and drove away a lone lioness from the waterhole. Catching just a fleeting glimpse of this activity at the very limit of our spotlight as we approached the spot, we watched as the animals pursued a running battle into the bush and were lost from our limited sight, though we tried unsuccessfully to follow.

Encouraged by this activity, we remained in the close proximity of the waterhole for another two nights, and were finally rewarded by the reappearance of the three hyaenas who, with much indifference to our vehicle and light, led us a merry chase through the thick bush to gather around the remains of a carcass they had obviously been feeding on for some nights.

It was with some astonishment some hours later, when the three animals had ambled on, that I left the vehicle to examine the last remaining tatters of skin and shattered bones that represented what was once an adult lioness. I had to assume it was the female three nights earlier from the waterhole. In all probability she had lost or been cast from her pride, and was, alone, no match for the opposition she faced from other innocent killers pushed to uncharacteristic extremes by pressure of the persisting drought.

At the Tsoana waterhole, some twenty kilometres to the west of Sikereti, but still just within the Kaudom border, we made contact one night with a herd of elephants, eighty or more strong. They appeared suddenly and as quietly as ghosts out of the dark to effectively surround us and our vehicle where we were just sitting down to a quick supper at the very edge of the water. The elephants concentrated their full attention on the water, plunging in up to their knees to drink noisily and urgently. All about us they revelled, some within metres of our table and chairs, where both Barbara and I sat, all but frozen with mixed feelings of total ecstasy bordering on blatant panic! It is probable, knowing the temperament of elephants generally, that all would have proceeded without further incident had I not decided to attempt a picture, by spotlight no less. The resulting stampede, of some startlingly thunderous proportions, quickly transformed the tranquil scene into one of unprecedented pandemonium as crashing, trampling, trumpeting elephants, strove to create distance between themselves and the sudden piercing light.

*Opposite page: a cheetah stands guard over its young wildebeest kill*

A later conversation with Ranger Duane Rudman revealed that when outside the borders of Kaudom, these elephants are sometimes hunted by poachers using spotlights, this especially in the northern regions where there is much conflict between these elephants and man. Naturally, the animals were to say the least, somewhat nervous of approach by spotlight!

One morning, as the dark of the night reluctantly gave way to the light of the sun, Barbara and I were awakened by the growling, yapping sounds of hyaenas and wild dogs in conflict. Hastily directing the Nissan in the general direction, we topped a rise to see ahead of us at the

*This wild dog pack has just taken a kudu victim in Bushmanland*

very edge of the Tsoana waterhole, a large pack of the elusive Namibian wild dogs, as they furiously scattered a group of four hyaenas attempting to snatch at bits from a recently killed kudu carcass. Out gunned by far, the hyaenas reluctantly retreated and we watched in awe as the pack of wild dogs devoured the remaining flesh in minutes.

We counted seventeen animals in all, nine of which were youngsters, possibly ten to twelve months old, but already approaching adult size. Having all but entirely devoured the carcass, leaving barely a skull, the dogs partially submerged themselves in the Tsoana waterhole as the fast rising sun quickly transformed the morning air into a haze of heat. A short while later the animals gathered together, threw us one last cursory glance and disappeared back into the bush, never to be seen by us again.

*Opposite page bottom: the magnificent Bengal tiger*

News of our exceptional wild dog sighting brought the biologist Flip Stander racing up from his camp some seventy kilometres south of our position. Having over the past year managed to collar a number of lions, leopard and hyaena, Flip had otherwise had little contact with wild dogs in the region, and together we patrolled for these elusive animals in the hope that one might eventually be darted and fitted with a radio collar. But of the pack, there was no sign.

Late in December, just days short of Christmas, the outdoor temperatures reached their peak, all but unbearable, while the interior of our tent was akin to an oven set to full roast! Suddenly, the horizon was black, the air humid, and the heavens burst over the scorched land. Great torrents of water fell with tremendous force, washing away our camp and submerging the surroundings in six centimetres of water, of which miraculously the following morning, there remained virtually no sign, so great was the thirst of the sandy surface of the drought stricken sandveld.

However, in the riverbeds, large pools of water were trapped from which miraculously emerged toads and bullfrogs to shatter the nights with a guttural cacophony of tremendous proportions. Insects too suddenly appeared in countless abundance, not to mention scorpions, lizards and snakes, some of which turned up regularly amongst our bedding and supplies in the tent. Before our very eyes, Kaudom transformed from brittle bushveld brown to a colourful world of almost tropical proportions. Hereafter, all big game disappeared, as temporary scattered pools of surface water removed any need for the animals to regularly visit the permanent waterholes under our surveillance.

It was at this time, while visiting a bushmen village, that we met Arnold Huber, the head guide and professional hunter for a resident safari company and the concession holders of the area. A German by birth, Arnold came to Africa to become a professional hunter. With so much of his time spent on safari in Bushmanland, Arnold later took himself a Bushman wife, whom he married firstly in traditional Bushman style, and then again in traditional European style.

Our meeting happened to coincide with a night when the fluttering rattle of millions of termite wings brought about by the rains filled the evening sky, to later crash unceremoniously minutes later about our feet. These Arnold and his wife gathered enthusiastically in a huge pot which they placed on the wood coals glowing brightly just outside the doorway of their neat, little, corrugated iron and mud abode. A drop of oil was added and minutes later Barbara and I were "treated" to a most unusual meal of lightly fried termites! Eaten like peanuts, this manna from the heavens is regarded as a delicacy by Bushmen and Arnold alike, though he confided that few of the Bushmen's traditional tastes were palatable to him.

Thankfully the next morning Arnold treated us to a breakfast of scrambled eggs, which he cooked himself over the open flame, while his disinterested wife disappeared into the bush with a spade. Minutes later she returned with a huge, bulbous root which she expertly peeled, sliced and devoured with obvious relish. A more startling and blatant example of cultural diversity I am never likely to encounter. Arnold and his wife (neither of which can speak the other's language), are an extraordinary example of two worlds bonded together in perfect harmony with each other and nature.

Working with Flip and his Bushmen trackers gave us some insight into the difficulties concerning the collaring of wild animals and thereafter the further monitoring of their movements. Telemetry makes use of a straight-line FM signal which in thick, bush country like Kaudom and surrounding Kavango and Bushmanland, generally allows for no more than two to three kilometres tracking range.

From the air however, this same signal may be audible for twenty kilometres or more. The collars that Flip was using were of American design, with transmitter and aerial snugly built into the belt itself to minimise their being snagged or damaged by the animal's activities. These cost somewhere in the region of one thousand plus American dollars each. The power sender units are expected to last at least three years over which period the animal's movements should be well established and recorded.

Flip's team of trackers consisted of three Bushmen, one of whom he had trained to drive the Land Cruiser, while Flip positioned himself on the bonnet from where instructions were relayed to the driver. This position of control was not without hazards as was apparent one day as a slight misunderstanding between the little Bushman behind the wheel and the panicked, flailing arm signals of Flip, brought about a near collision with a three metre black mamba attempting to cross the track ahead of the vehicle, a misunderstanding which rendered Flip sprawled headlong and furious in the underbrush when the little Bushman driver finally jumped on the brakes!

One evening while patrolling the western regions, we encountered a fine specimen of a lioness accompanied by her two sub-adult cubs. Staying close to these for the following two nights, we were finally rewarded by the animals successful hunting and securing of a wildebeest. The animals' preoccupation with the kill enabled us to close to within darting range, and shortly thereafter they were collared and recorded.

Anthrax occasionally surfaces in Kaudom, though not in the proportions that it does in the Etosha Game Reserve. Usually an elephant carcass, whole and with no outwardly sign of injury, is the most obvious clue to the presence of the disease. Lions, jackals and vultures feed on these carcasses, usually themselves thereafter showing no effects of the disease, though they are known to be possible carriers. Vultures, especially, bestowed with the power of flight, are capable of transporting the disease for great distances to contaminate other carcasses in other areas.

At one such anthrax-diseased elephant carcass, we watched for two days as a lone lioness painstakingly tore strip after strip of thick elephant hide from the stomach region to penetrate the softer interior. Bloated like a balloon from days of baking in the extreme temperatures, the intestines erupted pungently and noisily enough to startle both the lioness and us where we sheltered some twenty metres in the distance.

At the crack of dawn one morning our attention was attracted by a small plume of dust hovering low in the air over the dusty floor that represented the Aub Riverbed, a few kilometres west of the Kaudom boundary. Closer investigation revealed two male cheetahs having just that minute downed a sub-adult wildebeest. Flip informed us that cheetahs are not easily spotted in the region and that little was known of their movements so no accurate count of their numbers was to date available for the Kaudom and the surrounding areas.

The two located in the Aub Riverbed were obviously young and probably not long departed from their mother. It was interesting to note that due to the absence of large conglomerations of small antelope like springbuck, the cheetahs had compensated by the taking of larger animals, even going so far as to tackle sub-adult wildebeest, as opposed to the more preferable newly born. Male cheetahs are generally solitary animals, drawn to a female only for a short period for mating purposes, after which he leaves the female alone to contend with the inevitable later results. The cubs remain with the mother until old enough and capable enough to bring down prey animals, which may consist of small antelope like springbuck (in Etosha) or steenbuck (in Kaudom) or even rabbits and guinea fowl.

Camping one night close to a waterhole where we were mercilessly set upon by hordes of moths which made eating, sleeping and all other outdoor activities all but unbearable, the night was highlighted by a small pack of about six wild dogs charging in from the north in running pursuit of a steenbuck. Desperate to escape, and finding itself suddenly in the midst of our basic camp, the antelope lunged clear over our sleeping positions, closely followed by the hunting dogs which, with somewhat less dexterity, trampled us into startled wakefulness! A second later, without so much as a backward glance, the entire procession had disappeared into the surrounding bush.

Shaking from shock and excitement we clambered for our vehicles, but to no avail. Tracking fast moving wild dogs was all but impossible in the day; our chances by night, impossible. However, at dawn we were moving again through the bush at a steady pace southwards as the tracks, invisible to our eyes, led the Bushmen on a merry chase. Eight hours later saw us exhausted, hungry and battered after a day of terrible jolting and jarring our way after impossible odds. The Bushmen trackers assured us that they could quite easily continue on track, but they informed us that our progress was too slow and that the dogs were fast leaving us behind. Another close call with the wild dogs of Kaudom and another disappointment! Having experienced this again, it became ever clearer to Barbara and me just what magnitude of task confronted Flip in his attempt to collar and record the movements of the carnivores of Kaudom.

It was late January when finally the heavy rains came with such force and duration that we soon realised that all work on the carnivores must temporarily end, as the entire region became saturated, severely restricting any movement by vehicle.

Heavily loaded up with our remaining supplies and camping equipment, our vehicle was bogged down seven times on route back to the little town of Tsumkwe, where, not unexpectedly we were informed that petrol would be arriving "any week now". Fortunately we were able to scavenge enough from Flip's supply to make it back to Grootfontein, and civilisation.

The months spent in the wilds of Bushmanland and Kavango had brought a new awareness of the beauty of all wild things, and especially the plight of the ever elusive remaining wild dogs of Namibia. However, with Flip Stander and his team of Bushman trackers hard at work, there remains at least a fighting chance for the preservation of these innocent killers. Indeed, a letter later received from Flip, informed us that a number of our "personal" wild dogs had been successfully fitted with radio collars, and at last were being monitored on a regular basis. To crown it all, it was announced by the government that the lions and wild dogs of Namibia were to be declared "protected species" throughout the country! A breakthrough of some significant importance, which may turn the tide of history for these last remaining, truly free-ranging carnivores.

*Opposite page: a herd of springbuck feeding on dry Kalahari vegetation. Springbuck are able to sustain themselves without drinking through times of drought*

*Opposite page bottom: a beautifully banded Mexican king snake*

*Pciure below: the giraffe has an especially adapted prehensile tongue with which it easily extracts leaves from between the thorns on a tree*

# CHAPTER TWELVE

# The Snake

*Previous pages: an Asian green tree viper*

**T**he very word "snake" brings fear and revulsion into the minds of most. This is not surprising, seeing that man has from the earliest of times sought to blame all of the world's problems on the serpent.

*"Upon thy belly shalt thou go, and dust shalt thou eat all the days of thy life!"*

This then is the punishment prescribed for the poor snake, for what, in fact, was a fault of man, (or more correctly woman). Whatever the case may be, stories from the Bible and other works have been handed down from generation to generation, stories which in much of the world are intepreted quite literally. Thus the snake, in fact a result of millions of years of evolution, is still reputed today (amongst the less educated at least), to be the bringer of all evil. The fact that some snakes existing on the planet today are venomous, and therefore potentially dangerous to humans, does not help the creature to dispel these allegations.

It was during the Permian period, about 250 million years ago, that the

*A close view of the head of the beautiful golden eyelash viper of Costa Rica, clearly showing the raised scales above the eye from which its name derives*

first reptiles appeared on Earth. They developed after the Amphibia, (the newts, toads, frogs, etc) and became rulers of the land and sea. Many of these early reptiles were bigger and more fearsome than the ones we know today. Known as dinosaurs, these great reptiles walked the earth for some 150 million years, before mysteriously vanishing forever, leaving behind only tell-tale impressions in the earth of their ever having been. Now, 60 million years later, the snake and, indeed, all living reptiles, are evolutionary descendants of these times, with many similarities, in some cases, still quite apparent.

One existing, modern day reptile, the Tuatara Lizard of New Zealand, has survived for 200 million years with only minor evolutionary changes in its skeleton. The snake, on the other hand, has undergone a number of drastic evolutionary changes, the most immediately obvious to the naked eye being the loss of limbs. On closer inspection, however, some of the more primitive species (pythons and boas for example), still show remnants of their limbs in the form of two horny projections situated one on each side of the cloaca, and loosely attached to a rudimentary pelvis.

Of the 2,700 estimated species of snakes existing on the planet, roughly ten per cent are potentially dangerous to humans. That is to say, being in possession of a venom potent enough to cause death if an adequate dose were to be administered into the human body. This is a small percentage, and the chances of coming into contact with a highly venomous snake is therefore much slighter than, let's say for example, coming into contact with a speeding car while crossing the road. In fact, in many countries, more people are struck by lightning than are ever bitten by a venomous snake.

The snakes are the most recently evolved group of reptiles, having first appeared during the early Cretaceous period, roughly 120 million years ago, and they have today adapted to most types of habitat found on the planet. Snakes are ectothermes, (cold blooded). Thus, unable to generate their own body heat, they are totally reliant on surrounding temperature. The body of the snake is elongated and covered in a skin of scales. They possess no limbs, no external ear openings and no moveable eyelids. The internal organs, naturally, are adapted to the tubular form of the body, being elongated, with the more slender species having totally lost the use of the left lung. The tongue is long and forked, designed specifically for air molecule collection.

Snakes vary greatly in size, from 10mm threads to a weighty 10 metres. Fossorial, or burrowing snakes, have only rudimentary eyes which may, in some cases, be completely covered with scales. Most diurnal species of snakes have round pupils, while nocturnal species usually have elliptical pupils. Most snakes are considered to have poor eyesight, often not even capable of identifying stationary prey. Exceptions are the tree snakes of the genera, Dryophis and Thelotornis, which are unusual in that they possess horizontal pupils. Coupled with a slender snout, these species have a higher degree of binocular vision, a necessity when hunting agile, fast-moving lizards in the tree tops.

It is the amazing Jacobson's Organ, situated in the roof of the snake's mouth, however, that more than adequately compensates for any lack of pure vision the snake may suffer. The forked tongue, which emerges though a notch in the upper jaw, flickers and accumulates minute particles of scent scattered on the air. These it deposits accurately into the twin openings of the Jacobson's Organ, where they are analysed by the cells present, which in turn transmit the information to the brain. Thus, were the snake not able to locate its prey visually, it is in fact still able to pinpoint its exact location, within a limited range.

A further and even more specialised sense organ is to be found in species belonging to the families Boidae (boas and pythons), which have a number of heat sensitive pits along the edge of the top and bottom jaws, and the Crotalinae (pit vipers) which possess a pair of heat-pits, one situated on each side of the face, between the eye and nostril. These "pits" are sensitive to minute temperature changes and, accumulating the information from both sides, the snake is able to accurately locate the exact position of warm-blooded prey, even in the dark.

Though the skin of the snake is loosely described as "scaly", these scales form part of the skin and are not separately attached like those of a fish. The shape, texture and size of the scales vary amongst species, from large, smooth and shiny, to small, keeled and dull. Most species have large, irregular scales on the head. These become smaller down the neck and along the length of the body, roughly forming a diamond pattern as they overlap. The ventral scales, however, consist of a wide single row, reaching from below the lower jaw to the vent. Those beneath the vent may, depending on species, be paired or single. The number, shape and arrangement of scales plays an important part in the identification and classification of a species. In some species the scales are granular, as in the case of the family Acrochordidae, an aquatic family, while keeled scales (possessing a centre ridge) are present amongst many of the vipers and also the Ringhals (Hemachatus) of South Africa.

Snakes periodically shed the outer layer of their skins. This process takes place throughout the reptile's life, roughly four times per year when adult, but more often when young, as growth is more rapid. Newly hatched snakes slough their skin for the first time within days of leaving the egg, and

*The lance head viper is greatly feared and is responsible for many snake bite accidents in South and Central Amercia*

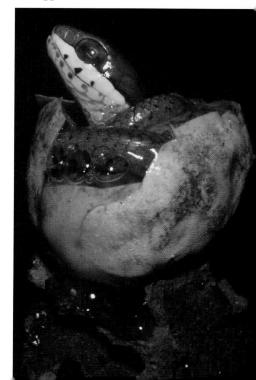

*The creation of new life - in this case a boomslang emerges from the egg*

*Centre picture: The vivid markings of a tri colour false coral snake from Costa Rica*

will continue to do so every four to six weeks if food is in plentiful supply. Gradually the rate of growth will slow down and the norm of about four sloughs per year will proceed.

The colour of a snake's skin is often an aid to blend into the surrounding environment. Desert species move from varying shades of yellow, brown, grey and dull red, depending on soil type. Arboreal species may again vary from shades of green in tropical regions, to greys, browns and black in dryer areas. Some species are perfectly colour-camouflaged to exactly simulate bark, twigs or leaves, while brightly coloured individuals are often so to deter enemies.

As with all living things, snakes too are strongly motivated to reproduce. Males are attracted to their mates by a scent trail released by a female in reproductive condition. Copulation takes place by the male twisting his tail around that of the female, that their cloacae can meet. The connection is made via one of the male's paired copulatory organs, which is inverted into the female and hooked fast. The pair may remain joined for only a few minutes, but often for a few hours. The gestation period thereafter varies amongst the species, some being ovo-viviparous and others oviparous (live bearing and egg laying). An ovo-viviparous snake is an evolutionary step ahead of the more primitive egg laying species. Here, the eggs are retained within the female's body, thus enabling her to more successfully warm and protect them, as they remain with her at all times. The tiny new-born snakes enter the world tightly coiled within a clear, membraneous sack, from which they immediately break free. The parent does not remain with the young but moves on as though nothing has happened, leaving the brood to fend for themselves.

*The Rhinoceros viper of Central Africa is amongst the most beautiful of the vipers*

Eggs are normally laid in safe places where sufficient moisture and heat is present for their development, (rotting logs, piles of decaying vegetation, grass piles etc). The majority of the egg layers take no further interest in the clutch once deposited. However, there are, as always, exceptions, the most noteworthy of these being the King cobra, which is known to construct a crude nest which it actively defends against intruders, and a number of the python species. Large pythons have been known to produce over a hundred eggs or more at one time, coiling around them until they hatch. Thereafter the female abandons the brood, and they are left to fend for themselves.

Live bearers too have been known to produce a large number of young

at one time, the record being set by a captive puff adder which delivered over fifty young in a European zoo. Average figures would, however, be fewer than half of this.

The growth rate of snakes is largely dictated by temperature and availability of food. Species living in warmer climates generally grow faster and mature earlier than those living in colder regions. The temperature will, in other words, control the amount of time during which the snake can be active and feeding. Snakes actually continue to grow throughout their lives, the process gradually slowing as they mature. Sexual maturity is reached usually when the snake is just half its eventual size, with the size of the broods increasing steadily each year until full maturity is reached, (usually after the third or fourth season).

Though some snake species are specifically evolved to eat only certain foods, (eg. the egg eating snakes of Africa, Dasypeltis) – most types feed on either rodents, amphibians or lizards. A few others are known to take fish, insects and even other snakes. Non-venomous species and some of the mildly venomous back-fanged species secure their prey by grabbing it with the mouth, before constricting it with a number of ever tightening body coils. The continued pressure prevents the prey animal from drawing breath and it quickly suffocates.

Venomous snakes are so chiefly for the purpose of immobilising their prey, and only by way of extreme provocation will this venom be expelled in self defence. The back-fanged snakes are, for the most, considered to be harmless to humans, the slightly enlarged, grooved back teeth delivering only a mild venom, which aids in the digestive process.

The venom excretion is stimulated by the chewing motion and flows feebly into the wound created by the teeth, thus entering the victim's bloodstream. The snake continues the chewing motion until the venom takes effect. Hereafter, the normal swallowing process is continued.

Two back-fanged species from the Southern African region have been known to cause deaths amongst the human population, the Boomslang (Dispholidus) and the Twig Snake (Thelotornis) while a few of the larger back-fanged species from other regions of the world are to be treated with caution, as little is known of their venoms (eg. the Mangrove Snake of South East Asia and the False Water Cobra of South America).

The back-fanged snakes are present in the Colubridae family, while the

*A puff adder giving birth to live young*

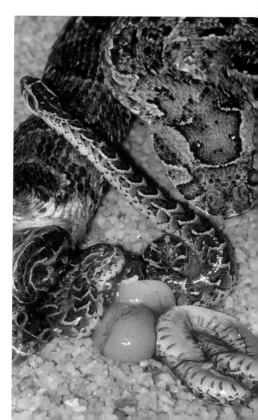

*Opposite picture: a swamp viper*

*An Indian Russell's viper*

more advanced, rigid front-fanged species are to be found in the family Elapidae. These include the mambas, cobras, kraits, coral snakes and sea snakes. All but the very smallest of this family are potentially dangerous to man. The fangs are fixed in the front of the upper jaw, are hollow and are connected directly to the venom gland by a tube. Here, venom is injected directly into the prey animal. Some of these species here will hold fast, allowing the venom to take effect, usually quite quickly, (eg. cobras). The African mambas have unusually large fangs, and prefer a fast, accurate strike at the victim, injecting a lethal load without holding on, in similar fashion to the vipers.

The vipers and adders belong to the family Viperidae, and have the most evolved venom injection apparatus of all snakes. The fangs are greatly enlarged and located at the front of the upper jaw where they are connected to a complicated system of bones which allows them to be manoeuvred forward and back, as though on a hinge. When held back against the roof of the mouth, these fangs are protected by a membraneous sheath which pulls back when the fangs are hinged erect. This system has enabled such large bodied species as the Gaboon Viper (Bitis) to grow fangs up to five centimetres in length, though an average size would be half that.

Snake venoms are of an extremely complex enzyme composition. Simply speaking, snake venom can be described as a modified digestive juice and, indeed, in the least venomous species, digestion is still its main function. The more toxic venoms are designed to immobilise and kill the prey animal as quickly as possible and they consist of a mixture of properties such as haemotoxins, neurotoxins and cytotoxins, amongst others.

*A banded sea snake*

Snakes swallow their prey whole, using the rows of tiny re-curved teeth to pull the animal into the throat by moving the right and the left sides of the jaw forward and back. The bones of the lower jaw are attached by tendons which can stretch, allowing the bones to temporarily disengage, so that prey much larger than the snake's head can be consumed. Though digestion begins immediately, it may take days or even weeks for the process to be completed, depending on species, temperature and the size of prey. Eventually the whole meal will be digested except for portions of hair or feathers. Were a snake, for some reason, unable to complete digestion, (cold, too large a prey), or were it disturbed, it is able to regurgitate the remains of its meal.

Like most wild animals, snakes prefer to avoid confrontation. This is achieved usually by concealment or flight, thus avoiding injury to themselves. However, were a snake, venomous or otherwise, to be trapped, cornered or threatened, it will not hesitate to defend itself, usually by attempting to bite the antagoniser. A number of species have developed special techniques with which they will attempt to intimidate or deter the enemy. Cobras spread the ribs of the neck to form a "hood" which makes it appear to be larger than it really is. Others inflate the throat like a balloon, while some adders will puff and blow up their entire bodies in a fierce and noisy display of warning. A rattlesnake gives clear warning and is easily identified by the buzzing sound it produces by high speed flexing of the loosely attached horny segments at the end of the tail. This movement is again sometimes imitated by some harmless species, producing a similar sound when vibrating the tail amongst dry leaves scattered on the ground. Other snakes are known to discharge a pungent smell from the anal glands when in danger.

*A New Guinea green tree python, displaying one of the many juvenile colour variations*

Feigning death is an art perfected by a few snakes, notably the European Grass Snake (Natrix), the North American hog-nosed snake (Heterodon)

*Bottled snake food in Vietnam*

and the South African Ringhals (Hemachatus). Here, the reptile may roll over and pretend to be dead as a last line of defence. Often the mouth will gape open and the tongue allowed to hang out. Should the snake be returned to its correct position, it will instinctively flip back to the "dead" posture.

In Asia and Africa are to be found species of cobra that have evolved a technique which, as far as can be ascertained, is purely designed for defence. In these species the venom canals passing through the fangs, are directed forward, and by sharp contraction of the surrounding venom gland muscle, a fine spray of venom can be discharged towards the eyes of an attacker with enough force to reach close to three metres or so. Any of this venomous spray entering the eyes will temporarily, or if not removed, permanently blind the attacker.

The potential ability of some snakes to kill humans has contributed to the persecution of all the species. Following this, the demand for an antidote for snakebite has stimulated the collecting of countless thousands of specimens each year for the purpose of extracting their venom, which plays an essential role in the manufacture of the anti snakebite serum. Unfortunately, the composition make-up of venoms varies greatly amongst species and a wide range of anti-venoms are necessary to combat venoms around the world. The number of deaths by snakebite poisoning naturally varies greatly from region to region and depends largely on human population as well as snake population in any considered area. In India, for example, there are some ten thousand plus deaths per year, the main culprits being the common cobra (Naja naja) and the Russell's Viper (Vipera russelli). However, this represents only 0.005 per cent of the population. Though Australia has an abundance of venomous snake species, only about six or seven deaths are reported yearly, the difference being that India is a largely rural community, heavily overpopulated and Australia is a vast land with less than twenty million population.

In Africa the Puff Adder (Bitis arietans) the Egyptian Cobra (Naja sp) and the Saw-scaled Viper (Echis carinatus) collectively are responsible for about one thousand deaths each year, while across the Atlantic in South America about two thousand deaths are recorded yearly, mainly blamed on the Pit viper (Bothrops atrox). In the United States the dozen or so annual deaths are blamed mainly on the common Western Diamond-backed rattlesnake (Crotalus atrox) and the larger Eastern Diamond-backed rattlesnake (Crotalus admanteus), while the Nose-horn Viper (Vipera ammodytes) is said to be responsible for most of the few recorded deaths each year in Europe.

*Bottom middle picture: a green mamba emerges from the undergrowth*

Having examined some of these figures and facts, it can be confidently stated that when comparing, for example, the annual road death figures, that mankind has by comparison, little to fear from the snake. In some way or another snakes have always been exploited. Some are eaten, some are killed for their skins. Others have body parts claimed to be effective in curing or preventing disease. In parts of the world even the venom of certain species has been claimed to cure anything from dysentery to gangrene. In North Africa and India, cobras and other species have for generation been used to entertain crowds at the market place. And in North America still today, rattlesnake "round-ups" take place where thousands of the reptiles are destroyed for no good reason.

Big business in the form of reptile dealing is flourishing in South East Asia, especially Thailand, from where thousands of reptiles are shipped, smuggled and generally distributed to the far corners of the earth. Unfortunately, there is a complete lack of concern for the well being of the reptiles, thus resulting in a high mortality rate.

Though millions of well meaning people around the world raise their voices in protest against the killing of whales, the poaching of rhino and elephant, and the steady demise of the koala and the panda to name but a few, there is relatively little protest generated for the plight of scaly reptiles with forked tongues. Reptiles are mysterious and secretive and no matter how beautifully coloured or interesting a species may be, the fact is easily overlooked in the face of the reptiles greatly exaggerated history as a bringer of evil, and even death. Yet it is the very fact that we understand so little about them and their effect on the environment, that makes their conservation as important as that of all other living species.

More recently in some countries around the world, some, and sometimes all reptiles in a given range are afforded some legal protection, poorly enforced though it may be. In certain countries legal protection is afforded to individual species, like the smooth snake (Coronella austriaca) in Britain, while in other countries, like the United States, some species are protected and others not. In other countries again however, some snakes have all but been eliminated, be it for the pet trade, the production of snakeskin artefacts or simply by the destruction of natural habitat. Extinction is a very real threat in today's world and it must be remembered that though even the simplest little beetle may be easily crushed underfoot, not all the biologists and

*A golden eyelash viper keeps a wary eye on humans paasing below its perch in the Costa Rican jungle*

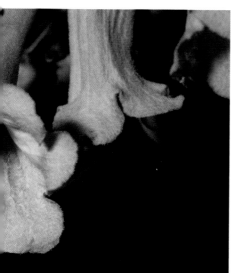

scientists in the world together, can make one. Undoubtedly, around the world, much of the snake fauna has not yet been fully investigated, and species are being exterminated without us even knowing of their existence. It is of vital importance therefore to generate a wider understanding of the effects of wholesale wilderness destruction on the planet as a whole. For though snakes may be amongst the first to go, by his own hand, man is sure to follow.

CHAPTER
THIRTEEN

# Snake Bite Poisoning

*Previous picture: an East African green mamba*

Everything in nature exists for a reason. Each plant and each creature plays a part on the planet, and survival is the ultimate aim. Some creatures prey upon others, without malice, only to survive, unknowingly performing and linking a step in the intricate chain of nature. Large creatures prey on smaller creatures and they, in turn, might prey on others still smaller. Snakes are no exception, but most people are under the impression that venomous snakes are so, solely for defence purposes. This is totally false, and from laboratory tests and recorded incidents it has been proved that a venomous snake, lashing out in self defence, often does not inject venom. On the other hand, a strike from such a reptile directed at the food animal is nearly always fatal.

Over the millions of years, snakes have evolved some very unusual methods of feeding, the venom injection being the most advanced method. But, there are still creatures that feed on snakes. The secretary bird is one; Mongoose is another; Bullfrogs eat snakes and even some snakes eat other snakes. Man seems intent on destroying snakes wherever they are encountered, yet snakes hunt down and destroy, very successfully, thousands upon thousands of man's most prolific and destructive enemies – the common rat and mouse.

What this all boils down to, is simply a general lack of knowledge on the subject, combined with an unnatural fear, which has been conveyed from generation to generation and created from incorrect facts. In many ways, instead of familiarising people with the ways of nature, today's advanced and communicative society has sidestepped nature completely, leaving the individual totally in the dark when away from the computer-city surroundings in which he has evolved.

You may wonder why some snakes possess such potent venoms. Well, the reason is simple! To secure food. To do this effectively the venom must be able to immobilise the prey very quickly to prevent the victim from escaping or harming the snake. Venom injected into the prey also aids the digestion process by breaking down body tissue and structure.

Two problems arise in the field of venom research; the availability of snake venom and the cost involved in producing it. There are, today, a number of venom-producing laboratories around the world, housing thousands of snakes which must be kept well fed and in good condition to produce top quality venom. If not housed under these perfect conditions, and venom extraction restricted to roughly once a month per snake, the reptile usually refuses food and soon dies from the constant protein drain.

*Crocodiles bred for the leather trade on one of Cambodia's many floating enclosures*

The basic principle applied for snake "milking", as it is known, is as follows: a thin plastic membrane is pulled tightly over a glass flask or beaker. The snake is then caught behind the head, (this being the most dangerous part) and then the mouth is forced over the edge of the flask, encouraging a bite. It will, of course, depend on the size of the snake as to how much venom is delivered. Sometimes it may only be a drop or two, while a five metre Asian King cobra will supply much more. The venom is then instantly freeze-dried, and converted to powder form.

In the beginning, snakes evolved teeth that were needle-like in design, curved backward and used for the capture and holding of prey animals. This arrangement, however, provided little help in the actual killing of the prey. Evolution is an ongoing process and, as time passed, some of the back teeth in the upper jaw of some species grew larger, developing grooves as they did so, along which a mildly toxic saliva was transported from the newly developing gland situated below and behind the eye. Proving to be of some worth in the immobilisation of struggling, resisting prey, these modifications continued, more quickly in some species than others, until finally, the venom apparatus of snakes had reached the standards we know today.

Most snakes have two rows of re-curved teeth on each side of the upper mouth and one along the edge of the lower jawbones. The fangs of venomous species are positioned at the front end of the upper, outer row of teeth, while the back-fanged species have a number of enlarged teeth showing in this same row, but roughly two thirds back in the mouth, below the eye. Snake fangs are attached to the jawbone by temporary deposits which make replacement possible should a fang be damaged or worn. The protecting fang sheaths help to guide the flow of venom into the fang groove (back-fanged species) or into the fang canal (front-fanged species).

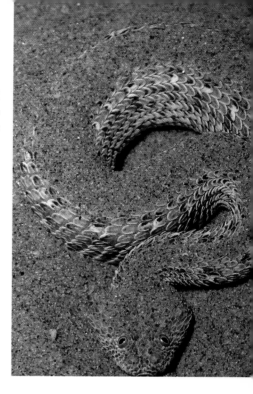

*The effective camouflage of the Namib side winding adder is perfectly shown here*

In the case of snake venom injection, the amount delivered is controlled by the snake. The venom being designed primarily for the securing of prey, the snake will inject only that amount considered necessary for the task at hand. In the case of human snakebite incidence, most bites can be considered defensive, and therefore it is likely that as little as ten per cent of the gland's contents might be delivered. However, were the serpent to feel seriously threatened, (eg. stepped on or attacked), it is likely that at least fifty per cent or more of the venom will be injected, and, of course, this factor will effect the severity of the acute symptoms.

The venom glands of a snake, having been seriously depleted, take anything from five to ten days (approximately) to replenish. The glands continuously produce venom; therefore a venomous snake is always so and is never totally "dry". Thus the amount of venom discharged is controlled by the snake and it is interesting to note that, from statistics collected around the world, figures show that in as many as fifty percent of snakebite cases, no venom is injected. This adds further strength to the theory that snakes reluctantly discharge their lethal load, storing it rather for the serious business of killing prey, their means to survival.

In the case of snakebite by one of the rigid front-fanged species, it is not uncommon that the snake holds on to the victim. Here follows a period of alternate tensing and relaxing of the surrounding venom gland muscles (eg. the cobras) and this action naturally increases the danger of the bite, as more venom is being injected. The back-fanged species too hold on, needing full penetration to induce maximum envenomation, but here a continuous chewing motion is employed to increase venom infiltration.

The fast striking, front-fanged species usually deliver one or more lightning fast strikes, often releasing a quantity of venom with each stab. However, some of these species, when attacking small, mouth size prey (such as mice), are also inclined to hold onto the animal until dead, after which the normal swallowing process will follow. But in the case of defensive snakebite, this is never the case.

Snake venoms are of an extremely complex, enzyme composition and laboratory tests have shown that only some of these factors play a part in human snakebite. In other words, certain parts of any snake venom may be designed to attack (more acutely) the body of the designed prey animal, and therefore might not be as active in the human body. Though the composition of snake venoms is extremely complex, broadly they can be described as follows: Haemotoxins, which cause a breakdown of the blood cells, leading to local brusing and internal bleeding; Cytotoxins, which cause tremendous local tissue damage, which ultimately leads to gangrene poisoning in severe cases; Neurotoxins, which effect the nervous system, acting mainly by paralysis of motor-nerve end plates; Coagulants, which cause clotting of the blood (thrombosis); and Anti-coagulants, which prevent clotting, which results in profuse bleeding throughout the body.

While it is true that snake venoms as a whole can cause human death, scientists today are probing deeper into the possibilities of snake venom fractions being used in medical advancements in such fields as cancer research. Tumours in animals, for example, shrink when injected with certain venom extractions. Haemophilia, the dreaded bleeding disease, has been controlled in laboratory tests with clotting factors taken from the venom of the Russell's viper of Asia. Drugs based on the venom of the Malaysian pit-viper can be used to relieve phlebitis. Cobra venom can be made into a non-addicting pain-killer with the strength of morphine. Scientists have discovered as many as forty different proteins present in snake venoms, so complex in nature that they are unable to duplicate them.

In experiments with, say, a cancer tumour or a nerve disease, only a certain number of these proteins are used, not the whole venom, and it is these separated proteins that are known as "fractions". By marking each protein with radioactive fluorescent dye, it can be traced and observed at work, under special laboratory conditions.

The African Boomslang is the most dangerously venomous of all the back-fanged species of snake. The dominant action of back-fanged snake venoms is haemotoxic, but the broad spectrum of boomslang envenomation is quite complex, first coagulating the fibrin in the blood to produce afibrinogenaemia, after which bleeding occurs throughout the body. Similar action has been recorded in bites from the Malayan pit-viper.

Early symptoms of boomslang, venom poisoning are deceptively mild, with slight bruising at the site of the bite, headache and lethargy. Later, nausea and vomiting will indicate the greater seriousness of the situation and sometimes a victim will require a blood infusion to compensate for large blood losses that may occur.

A specific boomslang anti-venom is manufactured in South Africa and can be effectively administered even long after the bite has occurred. This serum is, however, in limited supply and will be delivered only on request by a hospital or doctor if a serious bite has been confirmed.

Envenomation from the rigid, front-fanged species causes paralysis of the respiratory system, thus affecting the swallowing mechanism as well. The clinical effects of African and Asian species (cobras and mambas etc) are essentially the same, with the African black mamba and the Asian king cobra being considered the most dangerous because of their size, and potential ability to deliver large volumes of venom.

Symptoms of neurotoxic venom poisoning are ptosis (drooping eyelids), speech inco-ordination, difficulty in swallowing and breathing, which will later be followed with paralysis as the venom affects the motor nerve endings. Depending on a number of factors, a victim may die within minutes, or survive a number of hours after the bite (assuming no treatment is administered). Where anti-venom is available and the victim is covered against allergic effect, it is essential that it be administered as early as possible, intravenously and in large volumes.

There is in Africa and Asia, a number of cobra species able to spray their venom at an attacker. This venom, falling on the skin, is harmless and can be quickly washed off. Were the venom to land on an open sore or cut, this could be absorbed into the blood stream as if it were injected (though obviously not in a large volume). However, the main target for this spray of venom is the eyes, where it can do most damage and thus allow the snake time to escape. Fortunately, the problem is easily resolved if water or some other fluid is available with which the eyes can be washed. The venom causes immediate pain in the eyes and rubbing must be avoided at all cost, as this will inflame the capillaries and allow entrance for the venom. When the serum is available, it should be diluted with water ( one part to ten in volume) and used to bathe the eyes. Where the treatment is delayed, the optic nerve may be damaged, causing blindness, possibly permanently, depending on the severity of the case.

*Opposite picture: an African python showing a mouth full of razor sharp teeth*

In the case of adder and viper bites, there is most often pain and swelling at the sight of the punctures, usually immediate and steadily spreading along the bitten limb. The spread of adder toxins is largely through the lymphatic system and it is therefore important to immobilise both the part of the body bitten and the patient. The local effect of adder toxins can be broadly described as destruction of all tissues, especially blood vessels and their contents. Tissue destruction, coagulation and thrombosis of the blood, produces a barrier against venom spread. Bleeding then adds to the internal pressure, causing swelling, haemorrhage, blisters and necrosis. In severe cases, gangrene may follow, necessitating amputation of the limb. These symptoms are particularly evident in bites from the African puff adder, the snake responsible for about seventy to eighty percent of all reported snakebite cases on the continent. Blood loss plays a major part and often large amounts of whole blood will suffice for infusion. Plasma may also be used in certain cases. The polyvalent anti-venom available is unable to prevent the progression of tissue damage in puff adder bites.

*The hollow, needle-like hinging fangs of the puff adder are clearly exposed here*

Snake venom poisoning may vary from trivial to extremely grave. Each and every snakebite case will be unique and needs to be considered carefully and treated systematically. Considering that there are close to three hundred species of dangerously venomous snakes in the world, it is not possible here to even speculate on the number of variables that might occur amongst bites from each of these, or even amongst bites from a single species. Considering also the complexity of snake venom, one must realise that there is yet much to learn before the perfectly correct treatment can be devised for each species, or venom type.

Though the treatment of snakebite cases will vary around the world according to the species involved, there are three basic first-aid rules that apply in all cases:

1. Keep the victim calm.
2. Immobilise the victim, or at least the bitten limb.
3. Transport the victim as quickly as possible to a doctor or a hospital.

These three very basic rules are the best one can apply when otherwise uninformed on the subject of venomous snakes and their bites, and one is close to medical attention for instance. However, for those who venture into the wilds, (safari, rock climbing, hunting, caving and so forth) it is

*A green mamba is smaller and less toxic than its cousin the black mamba*

*Opposite page: a desert side-winding adder*

essential to study the subject further, as hospitalisation and treatment may be days' distant, thereby rendering your knowledge as the only hope of survival, for yourself or possibly a friend.

An anti-snakebite kit should always be included in any field trip which ventures far from civilisation and, more importantly, each person should be familiar with its contents and application.

An anti-snakebite kit should basically consist of the following:

1. Two 10cc disposable hypodermic syringes with needles, plus extra needles.
2. Two 5cc disposable hypodermic syringes with needles, plus extra needles.
3. Two 2cc disposable hypodermic syringes with needles, plus extra needles.
4. Six vials of anti snake venom serum.
5. Cortisone (for intravenous use).
6. Antihistamine (for intravenous use).
7. Adrenaline (1 in 10,000 solution).
8. Antiseptic cotton wool.
9. Antibiotic (injectable).
10. Tourniquet ( a broad crepe bandage is required here for best results).
11. A suction device.
12. An "eye-cup" (for rinsing the eye in case of a spitting snake).

A tourniquet may be a valuable first aid measure, but dangerous if misused. A tourniquet should always consist of a broad band, to avoid further disruption of tissue. In many cases it has been seen that on release of the tourniquet, swelling has subsided, showing that the constriction has been badly applied and has increased the swelling. In experiments conducted in Australia, there is evidence that the systematic spread of venom is via the lymphatics. This being so, the application of a broad, firm, crepe bandage over the bite and the entire affected limb will slow the spread of the venom, without affecting venous or arterial flow. This technique is today considered the safest and most practical. A crepe bandage can easily be carried on one's person, wherever you are travelling.

Anti-venom is the most important element in snakebite treatment. In South Africa, sterilised venoms are used to produce anti-venoms, through the bloodstream of a horse. These are then enzyme-purified and concentrated. Many anti-snakebite serums are today polyvalent, that is to say, one serum which is active against a number of snake species and venoms. This is achieved by the introduction of a collection of venom types into the bloodstream of a horse, which then produces a common antibody. For example, the South African Vaccine Producers produce a polyvalent serum which is effective in combating the venoms of all the cobra species found in the region, the ringhals, the mambas, the two, larger adder species, the gaboon viper and the puff adder. Similar polyvalent serums have been developed in many other regions of the world where a number of venomous species occur in close proximity to one another. This is a saving grace, as the need to identify the snake is no longer of primary importance, as one serum covers all (there are of course, exceptions as noted earlier, for example, with the boomslang, for which there is a specific, mono-valent serum produced).

For any snakebite, total immobilisation of the victim reduces heart action, thus minimising the spread of the venom. The application of suction at the site of the bite can be of value in extracting a certain quantity of venom from superficial bites (eg. cobras), but only if applied immediately after the bite. A crepe bandage should be applied firmly along the full length of the bitten limb.

Assuming the snake has been identified as a highly venomous species, or, if symptoms suggest this, an antihistamine should be administered, followed by 20ml of anti-venom (in the case of such species as a mamba, this dose should be at least doubled). Keep the patient calm and resting at all times! The patient must be transported quickly and calmly to the hospital. Do not incise anywhere on the victim's body! Do not rub or inject anything into the bite area!

Where no anti-venom is available, and a person has fallen victim to the bite of a rigid front-fanged snake, preparation should be made in anticipation of respiratory distress (the collapse of the muscles which control breathing). There are many reports of continued heart action after respiration has ceased. Patients can be saved by regular lung aspiration, (mouth to mouth in the field), or tracheotomy in a critical situation. Pharygeal drainage is essential from the beginning of treatment to prevent the patient from drowning in saliva because of an inability to swallow. Hospitalisation is essential for further treatment.

Suffice it to say, in the field one can only do what one can do. However, those who have taken the time to study and understand the subject more, will be capable of doing more, and this might include the saving of your own life, or the life of a friend. Snake venom poisoning is a serious matter and one would be wise to consider prevention rather than be faced with having to cure. Suitable attire in the field will play a major part in prevention. Boots and long trousers are good, as about eighty percent of all recorded snakebite cases around the world are below the knee. Only the black mamba of Africa and the king cobra of Asia appear to be capable of a high strike (tree vipers of the Americas and Asia have also been responsible for head, neck and shoulder bites). Avoid overgrown and rocky places. Do not place your hands under logs or rocks. Camps should be made on open ground. If a snake is encountered, remain still. Their eyesight is generally poor and cannot easily identify a stationary object. Sudden movement will startle the snake. Learn to recognise the snakes indiginous to your area. Needless to say, most snakebite victims are rural dwellers, wearing little clothing and often no shoes at all.

Despite the variety of venomous snakes in the world, only a few are to be feared and it is a fact that the snake fears man as much as man fears the snake. Thus the snake will avoid any confrontation with humans wherever possible, and it is up to man to behave similarly. Mankind has yet to learn that nature, in all its forms, needs only to be respected, not feared!

# CHAPTER FOURTEEN

# Reptiles on Film

*Previous picture: zebra bones lie scattered in the desert*

*Opposite picture: the large and highly venomous snouted cobra which bit Austin on the hand during filming*

The snake was enormous! Well over eight feet and in typical cobra fashion it immediately swung around to face me, its hood raised and spread in violent protest to my approach, ready to hurl itself at me. The mouth slightly agape, I could see the glistening fangs reflecting the late afternoon sunlight. This snake was ready. It did not get this big by being careless. It had got to this size through cunning and awareness, having in all probability defended itself against countless attacks by predatory animals that might consider a snake to be a potential meal. Even a highly venomous cobra is not immune to attack. There are large eagles and secretary birds to consider. Also mongoose and wild cats, and even other snakes. And, of course, most dangerous of all – humans! That was the category I represented. Whether or not the snake was aware of my exact classification was of no consequence. Random scars on its head and body told the story of a long life under harsh conditions. This snake had seen it all – and now there was me.

Behind me the film crew spread out on the run distributing themselves professionally into the best possible positions according to specific job description. To my right my peripheral vision registered two cameramen expertly slipping into unobtrusive positions of clear view, while behind me I sensed the microphone over my head. Though I could not see them, I knew the camera assistants and director were close at hand, ready to add their input should the need arise. This was not stage TV on studio set. Here was no time to call "Lights, camera, action!" This was the real thing, in wild country, with wild animals. This, the African Snouted Cobra, was one of the most venomous representatives of that department. Everything was dead quiet, as it can only be in a desert surrounding, all except the harsh, slow, powerful exhaltation of air being expelled by the giant, hooded serpent raised up before me. Everything was ready and in place. It was all up to me now and I judged the moment carefully before moving in.

Now it goes without saying that nobody in their right mind would even remotely consider approaching an angry cobra when indeed there was so much available space around in which to run from it. However, though many have claimed that I was somewhat "missing a few cups in the cupboard", it must be remembered that I have been doing this, and similar things with reptiles, for most of my life. While this does admittedly not excuse me from the category of "unbalanced", it should, at least, qualify me as experienced; and twenty years of working with venomous snakes in reptile parks and in the wild is a fair amount of experience. But, even this does not make one infallible, as was about to be clearly demonstrated on this particular day. In fact, it was just to be the first of many revelations as I openly presented myself on television for all the world to judge. As Jon Stewart of the CNN Daily Show once remarked: "The great advantage of appearing on international television is that you can disappoint the whole world at one time."

*A blue-headed rock lizard*

As I moved closer, the snake immediately lunged forward, hood raised even higher. Quickly I stepped back, just enough to be safely out of range of those fangs when the inevitable strike came. Cobras are predictable and, with experience, one can get really close to such a snake, providing you can clearly read the animal's intentions and pull back at just the right moment. While this is certainly NOT something that should be practised at home, an "expert" like myself can usually gauge the exact moment of strike and, providing you have estimated the snake's potential reach correctly, you can pull back just out of range. This technique is particularly impressive when filmed in widescreen TV, and I am even able to drop onto my knees in front of an angry hooded cobra, well within striking distance, and still hurl myself clear at the last moment. I have often demonstrated this technique with captive specimens while performing public shows at reptile parks where I have worked in the past. The whole idea now was that I would demonstrate this event on national TV.

Well, I tell you, this particular snake knew nothing about captive behaviour and cared even less about my technique and, without preamble, feigned a sway to one side and then lunged forward with an incredible extension of body, way beyond where I would normally have expected such a reptile to reach, smartly plunging a fang into my moving hand. "Oohh Lordy!!!

There I was, the supposed snake expert, well known in certain circles to be undoubtedly the world's "greatest" snake man (at least amongst some girl fans that I know!), on camera, in the Namib desert, eighty miles from the closest civilisation, with an acute case of snakebite in my right index finger, which, to add effect, was copiously squirting out blood like a fractured water main.

Now this was a new one for the film team and, like the true professionals that they were, the cameras kept rolling. Well it made sense. Here was not the usual option to "cut" and prepare for "Take 2". This was a one time happening. If indeed I was about to die, at least the event should be recorded on film, otherwise it would all be for nothing! This may not be everybody's view, but it is certainly mine. There was a whole team to assist me, one cameraman still "rolling" would not make any difference. In fact, I had discussed just such an eventuality with the team right at the beginning. Should there be an accident (not for one moment, of course, believing there would be), keep at least one camera rolling. I have experienced snakebite before in my life and was therefore better qualified to handle it. However, the shock of it still sent my mind reeling and my first thought was how I was letting the team down, and how I would be disappointing the whole world by proving myself not as capable as I had them believe I was.

The snake, meanwhile, quite rightly believing it had caused a satisfactory amount of distraction to escape, headed for the closest tangle of bushes and disappeared from sight. Gathering my composure somewhat, I barked just two orders. The first to everyone and no one in particular: "Get the medical kit!" Turning to a camera assistant, I said, "Keep your eye on the whereabouts of that snake. Stay with it!" And I took off with the others towards where our vehicles were parked a short distance away in the dry Swakop Riverbed.

Venomous snakebite is not usually the cause of much bleeding at the site, and I was puzzled by the amount of blood flowing from this wound. Once arriving at the vehicle site, the crew seated me down as comfortably as possible in the sparse shade of a motor vehicle, and I was at last able to more closely examine the bite. Gently squeezing around the wound, I was rewarded with a six inch squirt of blood straight out into the air, like a water pistol shot. That immediately cleared up any doubts. At least one fang had hit a vein! I looked around at the worried, expectant faces, waiting for me to say something, and I was not sure if I had good news or terrible news to report.

In most snakebite cases inflicted at the extremity of a limb (as this one was), with the exception of only the most quick-acting snake venoms like

that of the African Black Mamba, Cape Cobra, or the Australian Taipan, one might be expected to survive without treatment for at least some hours, this usually being time enough to get to medical attention. However, should a fang of any highly venomous, snake species penetrate and inject venom directly into a victim's vein, then these hours will certainly be reduced to just minutes! As I stared down at my bleeding finger, I knew the matter was out of my hands. The fact that a vein had been penetrated presented itself clearly in the tremendous flow of blood. In the face of this, it seemed I had no good news to deliver, but only the worst.

However, not being one to sit around and watch the world go by (or my life ebb away, which ever the case may be), I decided to proceed (immediately) with first aid treatment, futile though it may be. Quickly, I guided a team member in the wrapping of my arm with a stretch bandage in the hope of slowing down the flow of the venom up my arm towards my heart. Just minutes had passed since the actual bite took place, but I knew that if venom was at that moment being distributed throughout my body by venous route, I had less than minutes left before the effects would hit me. Next, I cracked open a 10ml. phial of anti-snakebite serum and sucked it up into a syringe. I had six of these with me, enough to control a normal snakebite case long enough to get to more. But this was not a normal bite. This was a venous bite, and my voice shook slightly as I addressed the worried people gathered around me.

"Listen carefully guys", I began and I could see the fear clearly etched into each face, "This is a venous bite, and if I have any chance of surviving it this serum must be injected directly into a vein in my arm." I lifted my unbandaged arm, turning it outward to display a good set of veins. "I know this is beyond your usual call of duty, but if I begin to feel a reaction to the venom, I want one of you to immediately push this needle into a vein and empty it slowly". They looked at me in stunned, shocked silence. "It's really not hard to do, and my veins are prominent". I tried to sound casual, but I knew that I had just dropped the biggest bombshell right into their lives. Sensing the need to reassure them a little, I added:"This serum is very effective, and it will immediately take effect. All six ampules must then be injected, whether I am conscious or not. It is important that you know this, and you will save my life".

The point was, that nobody likes to administer anti-snakebite serum unless absolutely necessary, in case complications may develop which might only be neutralised in a fully equipped, medical centre facility. So, generally, we herpetologists and doctors alike prefer to watch for symptoms before taking the plunge, in other words, when no other options present themselves. There was some small niggling doubt forming in my head. Some experienced instinct that told me to be ready, but hold back until absolutely sure. I had received anti-snakebite serum on a few occasions before in my life and had never experienced any negative reaction. But it was common knowledge that sensitivity to serum could develop at any time without warning. So I decided to wait. I knew it could only be minutes. There was nothing else that could be done. We were eighty kilometres from any proper medical facility, at least an hour's ride or more out of the desert. A few minutes would not make that much difference one way or the other.

It was the camerman, Warwick Sloss, a British member of the team, who then came forward to take the loaded syringe from my hand. Should I develop symptoms now, my life was in his hands, and I understand the courage it took for him to make the decision. No man wants to be held responsible for the life of another, especially voluntarily, and in unfamiliar

territory. I will never forget this.

So we sat there in the blazing sun of the Namib Desert, sweat pouring from our bodies, from fear as much as from heat, all eyes focused on me, expecting the worst. Fifty metres away, under my explicit order, the camera assistant reluctantly kept a watchful eye on the bush where the cobra was last seen. I did not want this snake to escape. My life was not over yet and neither was this film. Another minute ticked by. I tried to clear my head, to calm my pounding heart. I needed to know with absolute certainty the exact moment the slightest sign of envenomation symptoms might present themselves.

Another minute passed. Still no obvious physical feeling of discomfort. Once more I examined my bitten finger. The blood had congealed somewhat, but squirted out forcefully as soon as I applied any pressure. I felt this was odd and examined the finger more closely, and finally recruited the director to pour water on the wound to clear it for better inspection. It was only then, for the first time, that I became clearly aware of exactly what had happened, and suddenly there materialised in my head the almost impossible scenario of an option! There was no puncture wound as would be expected from such a snakebite. There was a cut! A quarter-inch, long, deep cut, which was being obscured by the amount of bleeding. The fang had not had time to inject venom cleanly into the vein because my hand had been moving back at speed, away from the strike and, instead, the fang had sliced through the fingertip and severed the vein. My heart leapt with hope. This meant that there was a chance that the strong flow of blood might have actually saved my life by flushing out any venom which had been deposited! This was such a slim chance, such a seemingly impossible chance, that I dared not voice my own thoughts for fear of raising hopes prematurely.

*The bronze markings of the appropriately named Copperhead from the USA*

However, after another fearful but uneventful few minutes had passed, my confidence began to grow and I declared my suspicions to the team. Really, I knew that had venom been travelling along my venous route I would have felt the effects by now. My life was not in immediate danger, and so, with the loaded syringe still close at hand, we decided to pack everything up and head towards the little desert town of Swakopmund some eighty miles away, to present myself at the hospital there for further examination and observation.

But first, I wanted confirmation that my snake would still be available on my return, because now I believed, without question, I would be returning to finish this shoot. Amidst a howl of protests from the team, and with bandaged, bleeding hand and still clutching the serum-filled syringe, I headed to the spot the snake was last seen.

The assistant cameraman on watch had done a good job and, within seconds, I spotted the cobra, sliding away quietly amongst the tangle of old flood-washed branches and other dry vegetation. There was no time to hesitate. I plunged my good hand into the tangle of branches, grabbed all the snake by the tail and jerked it out, all eight feet of it. If you want to make a snake mad, really mad, you jerk it out of a tangle of dead branches backwards by the tail. Eight feet of striking-mad cobra now focused its absolute, fullest attention on the one little problem in its life – me!

Hissing forcefully, the snake pulled up into a huge arching curve, its head almost level with the length of tail I clutched in my hand, and lunged at me with all the determination and fury of a charging bull. Again and again it did this, affording me no chance to adjust my hold and I found myself performing an amazing array of quite sophisticated, ballet techniques I never imagined possible, as I desperately attempted to avoid the glistening mouth full of teeth and fangs repeatedly lunging to get at me.

The film crew too were somewhat amazed at this unexpected, impromptu display of theatrical agility by their presenter (who just minutes before they were expecting to drop dead), and stared in open-mouthed disbelief. Soon, however, the snake tired, as I knew it must, and I stood there in the blazing sun, panting and sweating like an athlete having just run a marathon. I stood there with my left hand raised high above my head, with eight feet of dangling, squirming cobra reaching to the ground, while in my other hand, bandaged and now steadily becoming saturated crimson from the increased flow of blood due to my recent performance, I still clutched the syringe of serum, as though my life depended on it (which indeed it might have).

To top it all, I now suggested communal assistance in placing the snake into a container for later filming. This request was met with silent astonishment and an involuntary group step-backward. Like a black plague from hell, I stood there, alone in the desert, me and my wriggling cobra and my bleeding arm. This, it seemed, had silently and unanimously been decided, was definitely above and beyond the call of duty.

Re-evaluating the situation, and considering the potential risk involved in attempting to place the snake into a container with just one working hand and no assistance, I decided rather to allow the snake to re-settle itself under a nearby, cool rock overhang where I hoped it would remain in hiding until our return. This achieved with little complaint from the snake, the crew exhaled a sigh of relief and we sped off across the desert in the direction of Swakopmund and medical attention (though heaven knows, if I was not dead by this time, I was unlikely to die in the near future). Still, speaking for the whole team, the director made it clear that everybody would be happier if we checked into the hospital in case of some delayed reaction. After the performance I had just treated them to, I felt that this was the least I could do. Besides, I wanted everybody relaxed and happy again for my return.

As matters turned out, and to the dismay of the crew, after some two hours of observation and two ampules of serum introduced through a plasmalyte B drip, I declared myself fit and signed myself out of the hospital. There was no time to waste. That cobra might be heading away into the desert and my chance of finding it again, or another that size, was unlikely (I was in fact feeling a lot more shaky than I was prepared to let on, but there is this drive inside of me that I know so well, that forces me to tackle my fears head-on. I was now nervous about this snake, something I am not accustomed to, and I wanted to dispel the fear as soon as possible!).

In fact, the snake had moved away, but by some miracle of chance, I located it again some sixty yards along the riverbed. And oh boy! Was he happy to see me again! With collected fury, the snake turned to face me, this pain in the butt that just would not go away. It raised its hood and lunged at me, again and again. But this time there were no mistakes. I had learned my lesson well, and knew more about this snake now than I did before, and predicted its technique of extension. Also, the camera crew were right on it, nervously at first, then more confidently as we all learned our moves together, and I was able to deliver my piece to camera while simultaneously demonstrating the snake's behaviour and defence strategy. It was a fantastic, exciting shoot. With close strikes and

misses every second, that I knew would hold any audience spellbound, while secretly I rejoiced in my returning confidence in the face of such a magnificent and potentially dangerous adversary.

Finally, the action over, the shoot was all wrapped up, and we all breathed a sigh of relief. The snake too, by this time aware that it was obviously not in any real danger from this idiot human, got bored and headed off to the closest tangle of bush, never to be seen again. This would be a day to remember for all concerned and, lying on my bed back at home some hours later, it all suddenly hit me with a rush and I experienced a brief burst of uncontrollable shakes. The time honoured question: "Why do I do this?" surfaced briefly in my head. It was one of those questions that only materialises late at night, when one is alone and inexplicably afraid in the dark. It was a familiar question to me, but one with no simple answer.

I have lived long enough to ponder much of what life is about. If there is one thing I have learned, it is that one cannot be what one is not, and one's full potential can only be realised if you are doing what you are designed to do. And I am without question a "Snake man". Silly as that may sound, whenever I am working with, or facing a dangerous snake, it is as though I mentally depart from this world, and my whole being is focused on just that one subject and action. I hear nothing and see nothing around me at that time. My focus is complete. More importantly, this comes naturally, without any conscious thought to make it so.

Therefore, when finally I was drawn into the world of wildlife, adventure filming, I found myself suddenly faced with a dilemma. I was now expected to perform with highly venomous snakes, while at the same time delivering a running commentary to camera. This was sure to disrupt my concentration, as not all my attention could be directed to the handling of the snake alone. It is without question the most common cause leading to herpetologists the world over being bitten by venomous snakes. A split-second distraction is all it takes. Venomous snakes are always unpredictable and handling such an animal is a potentially life-threatening event every time.

I was determined not to let this deter me, because another interest that had slowly but steadily developed through my years working with reptiles, was the fascinating art of wildlife photography. It was only after some time that the realisation dawned on me that the only one other time that my mind became completely focused, to the exclusion of all else around me, was when my eye was looking through the lens of a camera. Was it not then inevitable that I would become involved in the world of reptile photography and film making?

# *Ependa*

The first time I ever encountered a Namaqua chameleon in the wild it unhesitatingly displayed its "no nonsense" disposition by biting me on the thumb and drawing blood. Shaking my hand loose with a yelp, this introductory meeting further deteriorated as the reptile thereafter pursued an attitude of total indifference and seemingly fearless disregard for my thousand-times greater size, as I attempted in vain to manipulate a natural looking position for a photograph. Huffing and puffing, and turning black, the chameleon bared its (already introduced) considerable set of teeth and lunged determinedly at my close-up camera lens. I was shocked! Chameleons don't do this? Chameleons are timid, slow moving, loveable little creatures, usually green and stuck up in a tree somewhere. Looking around, I realised that there was not a tree in sight and certainly nothing green. So that part was explainable, but the fierce, black attitude and the lunging, serrated mouth? Are chameleons susceptible to rabies I wondered?

I was in the Namib Desert, and during future travels through that amazing landscape I was to encounter more Namaqua chameleons, each seemingly with a different personality, though one trait apparent throughout the specimens I encountered – mess with me and I bite you!

It was many years later while shooting a wildlife documentary film about snakes, that my full attention was drawn to the Namaqua chameleon, when I witnessed a specimen attack and eat a desert side-winding adder. Still today I have never seen this repeated, but it was a startling enough incident to arouse my awareness to the fact that there was possibly more to these desert-evolved lizards than I had previously considered. The thought remained and I promised myself that I would one day look deeper into the matter.

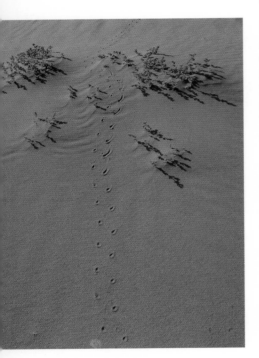

*Tracks left by a desert chameleon*

Over the following two years or so I occasionally presented my thoughts about the chameleons to people in the wildlife film business, only to receive the same negative result each time. "Chameleons? No, not interesting enough". "People want to see action, not a sluggish lizard walking across the screen." Or, "How can we fill a whole hour with a chameleon?" And so on. Somewhat dissolutioned, these comments did, however, make me realise how little was known about these particular chameleons. Basically penniless (as freelance, wildlife photographers usually are!) and knowing the cost of setting up a long term, "in the field" operation, I finally approached a well-to-do friend in Germany, hustled him with exaggerated scenarios of his name in lights, attached to the making of this first-ever look into the secret life of the desert chameleon and so forth. It was here that I discovered that if you believe in a thing strongly enough, you can get others to believe in it too. I returned to Namibia with financial backing to start my desert chameleon project.

It was not long into the project that the title for the film became obvious to me: "Dragons of the Namib", not just because of the chameleons' distinctive look, with large, bony head and powerful jaws rimmed with teeth and the row of spinal protrusions along their backs, but more because of their fearless, unrelenting, predatory attitude as they stride out confidently to feed and defend themselves in one of the world's most hostile environments. These were not just chameleons, as chameleons are known in other parts of the world, these were little predators, active hunters, which recognised no bounds, gave no quarter, and plunged headlong into the business of survival as though there was no tomorrow.

Over a period of almost a year in the field, this is how I came to know the little dragons of the Namib Desert.

Operating over a vast area, the first six weeks I achieved little. Chameleons seemed to be particularly scarce, and the few I encountered either continuously ran away from the camera, or turned black and refused to move as long as I was anywhere within sight. My fears grew. Did this mean I would have to film everything with a powerful lens from a half a kilometre away? This was not my idea at all and I realised that I was going to have to settle myself into a period of habituation. A film maker's worst nightmare is having to sit tight with one animal (or a group of animals) for so long, and under all conditions until the animal (or animals) accepted the intrusion as routine, and went about their business naturally as though the camera-toting human was not even there. There were no guarantees and not every animal was habituable. I knew of various wildlife documentary films which involved animal habituation. I had even been involved with one, but could one habituate a desert-roaming reptile?

The answer to this soon came to me in the form of a brightly mottled female chameleon as she appeared suddenly over a dune ridge and headed for my 4x4 vehicle parked a short distance from where I was attempting to film some dune beetles moving at high speed across the hot sand. Seemingly unconcerned about the unconventional shape of this object in the desert, the chameleon headed directly for my vehicle and settled herself in the shade behind a wheel. It is fortunate that I had witnessed this, or I might simply later have driven away, possibly squashing the chameleon as I did so. As matters turned out, I instinctively recognised this unusual behaviour as a potential true beginning to my project and I settled myself down, well within sight, but far enough away so as not to startle the chameleon into feeling threatened. Little did I suspect what close ties between myself and this little creature would develop over the days and nights and months ahead, as I lived, ate, slept and breathed, only to be in her company. Little did I suspect that she was to become the star of the show, to be introduced into the sitting rooms of millions of people around the world. This was to become the story of "Ependa", the brave one, (in the language of the Herero people), the story of my personal "Little Dragon of the Namib".

Those first weeks of chameleon habituation were some of the most trying of my photographic career. With mammal species, let's say lions, jackals or maybe baboons, one could usually expect a certain amount of interesting behaviour every day, enough, at least, to keep a cameraman alert and on the move. It would also generally be possible to shoot film with a powerful lens from some distance away, thereby presenting a more gradual introduction of one's presence to the subjects. In the case of the dune-dwelling chameleon, however, there were long periods of little or no movement, (I mean sometimes days at a time), while Ependa, in typical reptilian fashion, simply settled in a dollar bush as though taking the day off. As for long lens filming, I soon discovered that this simply did not capture the intimate close-up look that I envisioned for this film. There was no question about it, I had to be able to operate not just within metres of my subject, but within centimetres, if the situation so called for. I had been warned it would not be an easy film to make.

My first footage was basic and I recorded the usual facts about where and when my subject made her moves, (chameleons are not easily sexed by sight alone, and I was at this time not sure which my chameleon was). Day by day I moved myself and my camera in closer, until one day, just after a three day period of hot, sandblasting, east winds (which I was

*A desert chameleon perched on top of a Uphorbia*

149

*A desert chameleon shedding its skin*

*Main picture: the desert chameleon at sunset*

forced to tolerate huddled in my vehicle), the desert dunes suddenly came alive with hundreds of scattering, tenebrionid beetles, those black, marble-sized beetles that travel at great speed across the dunes and feed on detritus. Ependa took off like a chameleon possessed. I had never expected such speed from a chameleon. Dune sand actually kicked out from behind her feet as she charged after the fleeing beetles, her tongue striking out repeatedly.

About one in every three to five strikes was a hit, and she noisily crunched the victim up in her powerful jaws, before swallowing and immediately setting out after the next. It was the first "feeding frenzy" I had witnessed and, so excited had we both become, that neither immediately registered the fact that I was running at Ependa's side, with camera lens set on full wide and slung at ground level not thirty centimetres from her action. When it was all over, and Ependa could not force down another beetle, I dropped to my knees exhausted, as did she and we simply stared at each other. Her haunches flat on the sand, her front legs raised, I saw the gleam of the sun in her pupil, as her closer, rotating eye studied my resting form less than a metre across the burning sand from her. Be it purely because of exhaustion or something more, I'm not sure, but she made no attempt to move away, and we rested together on the dune for over an hour.

Of the footage I shot on that occasion, much was focused and centred enough to convince me further that this was the way to go; wide-lens, close-up. This meant running blind for much of the time, as it is impossible to look through the viewfinder while running with the camera held at ground level. I suspected this would result in reels of wasted footage, but I felt it was more important to be in the thick of the action when it came. So I used the technique wherever it was possible. Now, with the co-operation of my chameleon, eating scenes became much easier, and we pursued and destroyed hundreds of beetles together. Large locusts, blown from inland to the dunes, were a tougher proposition, not for the powerful jaws of my little dragon, but for me to get close up to, while she stalked

them. I am sure she sometimes became disgruntled with me as locust after locust, disturbed by my close proximity, took to the air before she could get within tongue range. It took a lot of attempts before one day I was able to place my lens down within centimetres of an exhausted locust, while Ependa stalked in for a successful kill.

So we roamed the desert dunes together, side by side, man and chameleon. A more unlikely combination I am still to hear about. Certainly, I became fond of her in an anthropomorphic way, imagining that she was happy to share my company. I knew, of course, that, like all reptiles, she was not capable of forming an attachment to a human, as some mammal species might do. However, I was content in my imaginings and, after all, I had no other company. Who is going to associate with a guy who walks around the desert talking to a chameleon? The only time I had contact with people was when I was back in town to stock up with supplies, and then I would rush back into the desert for fear that I would not find my chameleon again. This was a real fear, because I would sometimes lose her when just doing something simple like preparing a meal for myself.

On a number of occasions I was forced to search for hours, (once for days), to find her as she wandered off and blended perfectly with whatever surrounding bushes she may have entered. It is fortunate that chameleons do not roam at night. Desert chameleons simply lie down at the end of each day, wherever they are, turn pale in colour and go to sleep until dawn. Thus, my nights were free to catch up on myself and be ready to move with my subject as soon as she awakened. I did this for seven months.

*A desert chameleon hunting grasshoppers attracted by the blooming desert flowers*

*Opposite page : a desert chameleon laying its eggs*

One late afternoon I became excited as Ependa began to dig a hole at the foot of a dollar bush. Using her back legs only, she forced a basic hollow in the sand and, a short while later, she deposited five, large, soft shelled eggs. These she later covered with sand, again, using her back legs to do the work. I was ecstatic and marked the bush with a piece of dead wood and a rock. I knew I would have to watch this place in about three months' time. Ependa had obviously mated shortly before I found her. I wished I could have witnessed the happening, but was content to imagine that I might be fortunate enough to film the eggs hatching (if the desert allowed it as anything could happen in three months).

I had noticed a reluctance to feed some time before the laying, and now all became clear as Ependa's appetite returned with a vengeance and she was soon charging after everything that moved. Once she encountered a passing sand snake and the two eyed each other suspiciously, Ependa turning almost black and blowing herself up and emitting a warning hiss. I kept my distance and watched through my lens, and after a few minutes the sand snake, having possibly decided this would be a difficult meal, passed by and disappeared into a dollar bush. The event seemed to upset Ependa, and she remained huffy-puffy, bad tempered for the rest of that day. I will never know if this was due to natural instincts, or because of some earlier bad experience with a snake.

However, real trouble came a while later when Ependa encountered a large, male chameleon moving through her territory. The reaction this provoked, I was completely unprepared for. Never had I imagined such fury could be generated by this otherwise placid, little creature. Without hesitation, the little dragon charged the transgressor. With mouth open wide and hissing like a steam train, Ependa piled into the much larger male, taking him completely by surprise and literally tumbling him down a sand bank formed against a dollar bush. Gaining his footing, the bigger chameleon attempted to return the attack, his jaws fully extended in an attempt to gain domination. But little Ependa would have none of it and charged in repeatedly until finally she locked her jaws around the throat of the big male and proceeded to shake and throttle him. So fierce was the attack that the big male was capable of little but desperate retreat, only to be pursued further by the huffing Ependa, who finally drove him off the dune and onto the gravel earth below. Still bobbing and huffing and puffing, Ependa watched the beaten enemy retreat until out of sight before finally calming down and moving off. She had once again proved

*Opposite page bottom and above: a desert chameleon striking a desert viper with its tongue and then eating it - unique split second action photography never captured on film before*

herself worthy of the title "Little Dragon". I was ecstatic, because I got the whole episode on film!

There were a number of times that I feared for the safety of my little dragon, but none compared to the time she wandered up a dry watercourse, some distance out of her usual range, and came face to face with a snouted cobra. Somewhat out of its usual range itself, the one metre snake had either followed the vegetated, dry-river course in pursuit of small mammals, or had been washed down during flood periods (a number of odd snake species, including black mambas, have been recorded in such areas after flooding). Whatever the case, Ependa and the cobra met head to head in the middle of a green, succulent bush, and the snake immediately showed interest. I was not far away and, as I became aware of the situation, it occurred to me that this must surely be the end of Ependa, and also my film story. However, not allowing myself any weakness in my resolve not to interfere, I zoomed in on the camera and was just in time to see the cobra press its nose against the chameleon, like a great, white shark testing its prey and I thought it would be all over in a second.

However, once again I was treated to the unexpected fury of little Ependa. Puffed up to her full size, the little chameleon butted the snake right on the nose, causing the reptile to draw back in surprise. Taking full advantage, Ependa charged forward and bit the cobra full on the neck. Shocked, the cobra shook its head from side to side, dislodging its attacker. But to little avail, as Ependa immediately returned to strike again. Another bite to the neck. And again the cobra shook its head frantically from side to side, this time hurling the little chameleon completely out of the bush. This being the opportunity necessary for both reptiles to make a break, the snake and chameleon raced off in opposite directions, with little harm done to either, except possibly the cobra's pride. Once again the little dragon had lived up to her name, and I breathed a sigh of relief. It had all happened so fast, but I knew I had at least caught some of the action on film.

Back in the dunes I discovered that some of Ependa's eggs had been exposed by the strong winds that were prevalent at that time of year and, worse, dune beetles had penetrated some of the eggs and were eating them. Nothing to be done about it, I watched as nature took its course. Finally, after some one hundred days, two of the original five eggs began to hatch and, fitted with a super macro lens, I was able to record the event. Head first and wet from the remains of the egg, the first little chameleon emerged. Within seconds the newborn was free of the shell and staggering unsteadily across the sand, shaking its feet as if irritated by the sticking sand. The second baby hatched an hour later and was smaller than the first. Both disappeared into the relative safety of a dollar bush, where I attempted to keep an eye on them over the next few days.

It was during this period of watching the babies that I lost track of Ependa. It was simply impossible to keep track of both mother and babies at the same time and so I decided to concentrate on the baby chameleons, as they were a new element in the story. I felt confident that I would track Ependa again sooner or later, knowing her territory as well as I did.

Filming the babies was now a whole new ball game, as they were much smaller and more difficult to focus on. But at least they did not move very much, concentrating most of their feeding from a confined circle of dollar bushes where there was a plentiful supply of small insects such as moths, fish moths and flies. It soon became apparent that the one was a more aggressive feeder than the other, and the difference in size between the two became apparent within a few weeks. More confident now, the bigger specimen began exploring further each day, until suddenly disaster struck when the little chameleon came head to head with the big old male that their mother had so successfully disposed of some weeks previously.

Showing all the bravado inherited from Ependa, this tiny dragon opened its jaws and defiantly threatened the big chameleon. A brave, but foolish display, because the grumpy old male simply turned his big head, took a step closer to the threatening little chameleon and zapped it with his tongue. The crack of the baby's skull being crushed in those powerful jaws was like a gunshot across the dunes, and seconds later, Ependa's baby was all swallowed down. Bitter revenge for the grumpy old male? Or just the balance of natural things? It is the only time that I witnessed cannibalism amongst the chameleons and I was lucky to have it on film because it happened so unexpectedly.

As matters turned out, Ependa turned up one day close to where I was camping amongst the dollar bushes being hunted by the remaining baby. The two chameleons even came within a short distance of each other and, for a minute, I half feared a repeat cannibalistic performance. However, Ependa barely acknowledged the little baby and went about her hunting beetles as usual. Did she recognise her young? Or are some chameleons cannibalistically inclined while others are not? Answers to these questions I do not have and it was soon after this that Ependa disappeared completely, never to be found by me again. Deciding that it was time for me to head back to civilisation and an edit room, I packed up my desert life of some seven months and left the dunes.

In South Africa, luck was with me, as, while transferring my film into rough cut form, my footage was spotted by a member of a wildlife film distribution network who just happened to be in the building at that time and, insisted on taking an example back to England for appraisal.

About a year later, my film "Dragons of the Namib" was completed and televised on the National Geographic channel. So much for all those, "You can't make a film about a chameleon" scenarios. The wildlife documentary film business is a tough and competitive business, but I really believed in the potential interest value of my chameleon project, and only time will tell if the viewing public agree with me. I have been back to Ependa's home range a number of times, but have so far never found her again. I think of her often, alone and seemingly unafraid in that vast and hostile desert. And I like to believe that she is safe and well, and striding out in her typically, arrogant fashion against all odds, my personal little Dragon of the Namib Desert.

*A desert chameleon devouring a dune lizard*

CHAPTER
SIXTEEN

# Fingerprints of a King

I had only worked with one King Cobra in my life before. This was a twelve feet long specimen named Sheba which we housed at the park in Germany. Actually, to say I had worked with her is somewhat of an exaggeration, as whenever I entered her cage to clean, she would rear up to an impressive five feet off the ground, hiss ferociously and chase me out. Everything I had ever learned about King Cobras suggested that they were more intelligent than other snakes. Combine this with the fact that they are the largest, venomous snakes in the world (measured up to eighteen feet), and potentially hold enough venom in their giant heads to kill a hundred people, and you might just begin to comprehend my slight apprehension concerning facing one of these creatures in the wild. This was a snake that could reach me with a strike from six feet away and, as usual, to get the photography that I desired, I would have to be well within that range.

The flight to India was smooth and uneventful, and I and the team landed at Bombay (known as Mumbai) Airport in the late afternoon. Arrival, however, developed into a nightmare of chaos as our team of eight, including myself, accompanied by some twenty eight containers of filming equipment, were rigorously scrutinised, rather as though we were leaving the country instead of arriving. All baggage and containers were firstly unpacked and each item's factory number checked against the declaration list. This achieved, everything was then transported to x-ray, where once again every case was carefully scrutinised on the monitors as they passed through on the conveyor belt. This stage completed, we were now all treated to a thorough body search, after which all our personal luggage was unpacked and each item again carefully scrutinised. I tell you, by the end of this little episode there were no more secrets amongst the team. It was inevitable that a certain amount of sniggering could be detected every now and then, especially when the director's multi-coloured under-shorts boldly displayed the mantra, "Love my dick", were exposed! The girls, doubled over with laughter, were delighted at each new revelation, as their masculine co-workers stood by helplessly, our faces flushing a shade deeper red with each new secret item revealed.

This was a two way street, however, and when suddenly the attention of the customs officers was turned to that of the female department, the masculine amongst us perked up somewhat and began to show interest. This was short lived however as there came a hysterical shriek from the two girls, and all of the males amongst us were unceremoniously ushered to a distant corner under threat of death should we even dare attempt to peek.

By this time it was approaching midnight. We had been living this experience for six hours! We felt grubby, irritable, hungry and dead on our feet. In spite of the late hour the temperature was in the high nineties and the humidity was energy sapping. Of air conditioning there was no hint and the mosquitoes appeared miraculously from nowhere and everywhere. Also, there was the constant shuffle of hundreds of people around us in seemingly never-ending waves. There seemed no end to the people milling about, all loaded down with baggage and apparently with somewhere to go. Even outside, through the glass, exit doors that beckoned so tantalisingly, there were hundreds of Indians gathered around, most just hanging over metal barricades and watching the activity. It seems that watching the arrivals and departures of the passengers at the airport each day is a national pastime.

When the last item of baggage was finally cleared, our deflated spirits rose dramatically, and we heaved a collective sigh of relief and raced triumphantly towards those beckoning glass doors to freedom, only to skid to a shuddering halt as suddenly, once again, we found ourselves confronted by yet another row of x-ray machines, just yards from the final exit doors.

We were stunned! It didn't seem possible! What could possibly have changed in our luggage since the last checkpoint just fifty feet back? Was there no escape from this place? Another collective sigh. This time of defeat. There was nothing to be said, no way to argue. This was the new world of travel, adapt or die. So, with slumped shoulders, we prepared for the now all too familiar ritual. A curse on all terrorists! May their carcasses feed the scavengers in Hell.

If we thought the hullabaloo at the airport was a nightmare, it paled in comparison to what we were soon to experience on the roads of India. While we were all familiar with some or other disruptions arising at international airports, nothing was comparable to what awaited us. Nothing! Here we were introduced into a new form of chaos, unimagined by those raised in first world countries. I mean, I was born and raised in Africa, surrounded by third world activity, where the roads, vehicles and drivers alike are as antiquated as anywhere in the world, and I thought I had seen it all. In fact, compared to India, I hadn't even scratched the surface. Vast though the country is, India is populated by over a billion people, with each individual (or so it seemed), claiming a place on the road, be it on foot or in a four-wheeled motor vehicle, a three wheeled motor vehicle (rickshaw), a two wheeled motor vehicle, any number of unnamed, non-motorised vehicles such as oxcarts, or even horses, camels, donkeys and elephants. These, all packed together on every road in every part of the country, and all seemingly with somewhere to go and something urgent to do.

*The formidable king cobra*

The most noteworthy difference between Africa and India soon became apparent to me. In India there is none of the African aggression, and though the city streets and country roads are packed at all times with every imaginable form of vehicle, as horns and hooters are constantly blaring their defiance, there is no aggression. In first world conditions hooters and horns are not activated when a collision is imminent. In India, nothing is left to chance and the horn is sounded continuously as a warning of approach. On the surface this system might make fair logical sense. However, secure now in the knowledge that a noisy warning of approach is preparing the way ahead, all drivers automatically claim right of way, irrespective of traffic congestion, thus rendering the conditions on the roads little short of a Ben-Hur styled, chariot race to the finish. If it is a fact that some ten thousand Indians die of snakebite each year, I shudder to imagine what number road deaths account for.

There are no highways in India (not in the first world manner of speaking) and, for the most part, the existing main roads might best be described as a collection of potholes connected by crumbling strips of asphalt. From what I could see, it seemed that most motorised vehicles travelling these roads were older models, of which I suspect most would immediately be removed from service were they subjected to a roadworthiness test. In the city areas the traffic is congested and the exhaust fumes overpowering. However, against seemingly impossible odds, the traffic does indeed move along. In fact, it moves along quite speedily, as we discovered on that first short trip to our hotel in our rented minibus. This was akin to a high-speed chase in proportions far more daunting than any ever seen

at the movies, combined with a collection of near head-on collisions as our driver determinedly floored the accelerator in seemingly, absolute knowledge that his blaring horn would somehow miraculously clear a path through the ever present collection of assorted vehicles piled up ahead. It was an experience none of us would ever forget, and it was with some great relief that we all finally tumbled out of the bus, pale and shaken, but alive, and headed for our designated rooms.

Having described all this, at the same time I must state clearly, that from the Customs Officials, (tiresome as they may have been), to the representatives at the hotels, and even the passing throngs of public on the road sides, never before had I experienced such friendly politeness and helpfulness. No one was ever short of a smile and everyone was ever eager to help. An amazing state of affairs, I feel, considering the overpopulated chaos and poverty that is a daily reality in the lives of these people. Something else my team and I would never forget.

A night in a hotel in Mumbai, and we were off again early the next morning, this time a short flight to the Kerala District, located in the Western Ghats area of the country. The region is often referred to as the verdant paradise of India and consists of valleys, paddy fields, lagoons, mountains, and endless forests of palm trees. All the researched information we had gathered concerning king cobras in India suggested that this region, with its tropical jungle climate and protected wilderness areas, was a most likely locality for these elusive reptiles. Much of India is rural and, under the pressure of this vast human population, wild animal habitats have been invaded and overrun with the wild animals themselves, for the most part, eradicated, a situation occurring similarly in most parts of the world to varying degrees and a sad reminder that each and every problem facing the world today is either directly or indirectly connected to overpopulation by human beings.

In spite of being an internal flight, Customs regulations were as strict as when we had arrived in the country the day before. This time, however, it was not so much the camera equipment that had everyone in a frenzy, but my snake tongs! I might add, that the day before, (the same snake tongs), had been all but ignored throughout the hours of Customs "formalities". This apparatus now found itself looked upon in a new light and with some great suspicion. Endless council was called upon, and many thousands of words in a strange language commenced, accompanied by much gesticulating and still further discussion, until finally the head of security was called in and he thought to do what none of the others so far had thought to do. He asked me what the suspicious item was.

In all fairness, I must admit that if any of our equipment was to arouse suspicion at all, it should be my snake tongs. My only surprise was that there had been no comment at the airport during the previous day's performance. This snake-catching apparatus is made of aluminium, with a handle and lever arrangement at the top end, connected to the clamping arm by three feet of hollow tubing. Wrapped and taped in light cardboard as it was, the snake tongs admittedly, by some stretch of the imagination, might resemble a rifle of sorts. This apparatus travels everywhere with me when on snake business and is often the defining factor between life and death when tackling fast moving venomous snakes – such as cobras! They are the only snake-catching tongs I have. I have had them for some twenty plus years and they are not manufactured anymore. In fact, this pair of snake tongs are amongst my most treasured possessions, and so you will understand why I immediately bristled at the potential danger of confiscation I imagined was now materialising.

From past experience I have come to realise that it is wise not to declare the true purpose of the snake tongs, as few people are able to come to terms with the fact that somebody would actually go out of their way to catch venomous snakes. Such a ridiculous story aroused suspicion of obvious subterfuge and created even greater consternation, with the tongs appearing even more to be a likely hi-jack weapon.

By this time there were about a hundred people around me, a dozen or so bona fide Customs officials, and the others just casual onlookers, all seemingly interested, and each offering their own opinion on the matter that indeed was no matter of theirs at all. Over time we came to realise that this was simply the norm anywhere you travelled in India. Stop for just one minute and you are soon surrounded by smiling, curious faces, either offering help or simply just curious as to what you are about.

However, with the future of my immediate snake-catching career on the line and the hours of time spent at Customs the day before still fresh in my head, my hackles were up and I gave little thought to the consequences. "Those are my snake tongs", I stated, slowly and clearly. "I am a snake catcher and I need that apparatus to catch venomous snakes".

Suddenly all talking ceased and for ten seconds there was a stunned silence. All the hundred or more faces surrounding me turned to stare, as if I had just declared myself an alien from another planet. I thought to myself:"Oh Lordy. Now I've done it!" Instead, with the statement digested, there came a sudden, vocal applause of approval and great excitement and praise was rained upon me from a sea of smiling faces.

"You are a Snake Man!" bellowed the head Customs official, with great delight written huge all over his face. "Ooh, but that is too wonderful! It is a great honour to have a Snake Man from another continent coming to our country". This statement was met with further wild applause and much vigorous nodding of heads from the surrounding crowd that seemed now to have swelled to three times its original size.

"And for what purpose will you be catching snakes in India, Sahib?" The Customs officer's full attention was upon me now, his eyebrows lifted in question, and a hush fell over the crowd as all ears strained to hear my all important reply. "I am part of a film team and we are making a film about snakes in India". This drew another stunned silence as this latest statement was also digested, to be quickly followed by an even greater burst of applause than the first.

"Ooh, but this is too wonderful indeed!" the Head Customs Officer declared above the cacophony of excited voices, a great smile all over his face. With a flourish, he ceremoniously raised the cardboard-wrapped tongs for all to see and then proceeded to rip away all my painstakingly wrapped cardboard protection. "Such a fine instrument should not be hidden from view", he declared. Bringing his head close to my ear he added, as though a secret between just the two of us: "For fear that it be mistaken for a weapon, you understand". He paused thoughtfully, his eyes focused on mine. "You know, of course, no weapons of any kind are allowed on our flights".

I nodded vigorously, only too pleased with this unexpected turn of events. Again I was treated to a lesson in cultural difference. In Africa, snakes are generally regarded as bringers of evil and killed at every opportunity, venomous or otherwise. In India, depending on the area in question, various snake species are considered sacred and venerated as bringers

*Previous pages: the Asian king cobra which can reach lengths of up to 18 feet and raise a third of its body off the ground*

of good luck. There are even yearly celebrations in honour of the serpent and snake handlers are held in high esteem. It seemed I too fell into this celebrated bracket, a pleasant change for me.

Stripped of the offending covering now, the snake tongs were once again raised high for all to see. Thereafter a label was printed and tied to the handle and, still holding the instrument of so much attention, the Head Customs official carried it personally onto the airport tarmac and handed it to the pilot of the plane, who, in turn, placed it in the cockpit, where I was assured I could collect it upon landing at our destination. It seems that even though it had been declared an honourable item, still no one was taking any chances that it was not. Having experienced all this, I think I can safely state that, when it comes to airport security, Air India is probably the safest airline in the world!

The flight to Kerala took just two hours in what appeared to be an old DC10. Though the ageing plane shook and rattled somewhat more than one is usually accustomed to, the flight was uneventful. That is, until landing. One minute we were still gazing down at the forests of palm trees miles below us, when next, the wheels were suddenly lowered just in time to connect with a strip of red coloured sand. It was the assistant cameraman, Gerard Botha, who, with a disturbed look on his face, pointed out to me that we were still going at full speed and the runway distance indicating boards were whizzing past at a frightening speed. The palm tree forests remained visible miles below, and it became evident that we were landing on a mountain top! The passing boards flashed 60 metres, then 50, then 40 and, on 30, our bodies were suddenly hurled forward into our seatbelts as the brakes were applied and the whole plane shuddered with the strain of it. The last I remember seeing was a board with a big fat zero on it flash past, just as the plane came to a juddering, slightly askew, dead stop.

Out of the far window I could see a little shack, resembling any hundreds of shacks I was accustomed to seeing in Africa, only not as an airport terminal, which indeed is exactly what this turned out to be. Stepping out of the plane was a quiet affair, with not a word uttered by anyone, all appearing to be in varying stages of shock. This state of affairs was not improved as we viewed the end of the runway where our plane now stood. There WAS no more runway, just a half mile drop over the edge of the mountain, where, far below, we could see a collection of old rusted cars and what might easily have been scattered parts of another aeroplane.

*The flap-necked chameleon, as with all chameleons, are amongst the few species of reptiles able to change colour to blend into their surroundings*

As pleasing as it was to leave the plane, the outside temperature and humidity was stifling. This was to be an ever-present condition and we simply had to adapt or die. We had timed our expedition to arrive in India before the expected coming of the Monsoon season. Working in torrential rain is a film crew's worst nightmare: thus, choosing the lesser of the two evils, we were prepared rather to handle the high humidity and the 40C degrees heat.

For the first week or so we travelled around the state to familiarise ourselves with the country, its hundred or so dialects and its people, while, at the same time, gathering information and preparing ourselves for the expedition into king cobra territory. Everywhere we went there were people present. Every stop we made brought about great excitement and crowds, and our questions were enthusiastically answered. Everywhere there were signs of homage being paid to the serpent; from stone figures in private gardens or mounted on the walls of buildings, to whole temples dedicated entirely to the worship of this usually reviled, reptile. I was delighted. Here I felt like I was amongst friends.

In one small village we were attracted by a gathered crowd and were excited to find a snake charmer performing. This was something I had always wished to witness at first hand and, digging out my camera, and with the film crew hot on my heels, I joined the throng of excited onlookers. In the custom that I was to become familiar with during my stay in India, I was soon ushered through the circle of people by smiling faces until I was positioned right in the front. With a now unobstructed view of the proceedings, I was able to fire away roll after roll of slide film.

Quick to note the presence of "ferengi" (the common word used for Europeans), in the crowd, and noting the camera equipment being directed in his vicinity, the snake charmer pulled out all the stops and put on the show of his life. Bare foot and otherwise wrapped in nothing more than a flowing sheet of material, his head adorned similarly with a spiralling turban, the snake charmer played his flute to the hooded cobra which rose dramatically out of a wicker basket a few feet in front of him. Constructed from a hollow calabash and two thin reeds pierced with a number of holes with which to direct the flow of air, the flute emitted a harsh, screeching sound, not at all like I had imagined. Attracted by the swaying movement of his flute and body, the snake now also began to sway with the momentum, giving the appearance of dancing to the sound of music. Of course, all snakes are deaf to airborne sounds, and it is only the following of the snake charmer's movement that causes it to sway.

*Austin faces up to the mighty king cobra whilst filming in India*

My first snake catch in India was a fast-moving, rat snake that led me a merry chase through a plantation of palm trees. These large (six feet or more) snakes are non venomous and very agile and I had missed a few crossing the roads as we travelled. This time, however, I was on foot and on the lookout for just such an opportunity. As is always the case with snakes, its sudden appearance from nowhere was startling and it was with some slipping, sliding and foot spinning that I was finally up to speed and after my prey.

With the agility that only such a reptile can display, the rat snake dodged effortlessly between the closely packed palm trunks, picking up speed as it went, while I, on the other hand, seemed to develop an unexplained attraction for every trunk. It was only after some serious collisions, knocks and scrapes, culminating with a frustrated body hurl through the air, that I finally achieved my aim.

Sweating torrents of water, and panting like a mad dog, I picked myself off the ground and proudly displayed the struggling snake to the cameraman, who appeared before my eyes in triplicate - a sure sign of mild concussion. Warwick didn't look too good himself, having attempted to keep pace with me while simultaneously operating the heavy 16mm camera. A full minute passed before I could actually speak coherently, which was not a problem because Warwick himself was in no condition to steady the camera.

The next day saw us both limping slightly from aching muscles, and I sported a colourful bruise on my forehead, a reminder that one should never attempt a high speed chase after a rat snake in a palm plantation. On the bright side, and with all credit going to Warwick, the footage of the chase proved to be so exciting as to take opening slot in the final film. On another occasion the brakes were jumped on hard and our vehicle brought to a skidding halt as a five-feet manacled cobra slid effortlessly

*Austin lifting the king cobra off the ground*

across the road not five yards ahead of us. Within seconds I was out and after the reptile. It was an easy catch as the snake was exposed in the road and I grabbed its tail, seconds before it made off to the side and into the grass. This infuriated the snake and it immediately turned with raised hood to lunge at the restricting hand. This was not too much of a problem, as a cobra's lunge has none of the sped and accuracy associated with the adders and I was well familiar with the move and expected it.

Instantly releasing the tail and jumping back on my knees a few feet, I was in perfect position to work with the snake which now posed menacingly before me, its hood raised three feet off the ground. Asian cobras differ from African cobras in that they form a more rounded hood, while the African cobra hood is more slender and evenly tapered. Also, Asian cobras remain standing with raised hood more readily than African cobras and are reluctant to strike out in aggression. Unless cornered, the African species generally raise the hood for seconds only, then turn and flee. So, from a herpetologist's point of view, when it comes to performing with a cobra, the Asian species are more predictable and therefore safer to work with. Having said this, it is important to remember that all cobras are highly venomous. Armed with a powerful neurotoxic venom, a bite from such a snake would bring about death to a human being within a matter of hours. I had just a few short months earlier experienced a cobra bite and was wary, knowing that if there remained any unsurfaced fears lurking within me, they should arise now, with this snake rather than later should I eventually find the subject of my search, the much larger, and potentially more dangerous, king cobra.

By this time the film and sound crew were right on top of me, cameras and tape rolling. The cobra was magnificent, its butter coloured, smooth-scaled body glistening in the early morning sunlight. The cupped hood remained stretched to its maximum, spread so thin that the monocled pattern on the back of its neck, from which the snake derives its common name, was illuminated by the sun through the tightly stretched skin. The sight of it awoke in my memory the beautiful folk tale I had once heard concerning the origin of this monocled pattern. It was said that while travelling across the desert one day, Buddha became tired and lay down under the fierce heat of the sun to sleep. A passing cobra took note of the situation and spread its hood to shade Buddha while he slept. When Buddha awoke and saw what the snake had done, he placed his hand on the cobra's neck in blessing and the print of his thumb has remained there forever, for all the world to see. A beautiful story and inside of me, an uncontrollable urge arose to do the same.

*The cobra's head is now fully extended off the ground as Austin films*

The very most important thing when working with such a snake, and indeed any snake that is not secured behind the head, is to move very slowly. Snakes generally have poor eyesight, therefore obvious and/or sudden movements attract their attention and may entice a defensive strike. It is possible to touch a cobra behind the head, as long as the snake does not register the movement. So it is a matter of firstly attracting the snake's attention with one hand up front, while the other, very slowly, is lowered from above and behind the snake's extended hood. I did this now for the first time in my life with an Asian cobra, excited to re-enact the fable of Buddha. Doubly exciting for me was the fact that I felt in control without fear. My African cobra bite was forgotten and I was delighted to be there in India, photographing these exotic reptiles in the wild, reptiles that I had previously only worked with in cages.

Around the world, most snake species abandon their live born young or newly laid eggs immediately, the exceptions being amongst the python species. Coiling around their clutch of eggs, which in the case of a large python may number a hundred of more, these cold blooded snakes actually generate a temperature increase in their bodies by producing a continuous series of muscular contractions. Once the young have hatched, the mother leaves and they are left to fend for themselves.

*Albino Indian pythons are popular amongst snake collectors and breeders*

In similar fashion, the snake I was in search of, the king cobra, is unique amongst venomous snakes in that the female of the species not only remains with and protects her eggs, but even constructs a nest from the forest floor litter in which she lays them. This is not only a considerable feat for a creature with no limbs, it also demonstrates astonishing evidence of superior intelligence to other reptiles. This is further confirmed by the somewhat elaborate construction of the nest, which consists of two chambers, with the female comfortably housed in the upper area presiding over her eggs below. Furthermore, it has been noted that the mate of the female often remains within close proximity during the period of incubation, possibly in defence of the nest.

These are all potential signs of greater intelligence, and though the king cobra is commonly so named (cobra), scientifically it is not considered a true cobra species, but placed in a genus of its own, Opheophagus, which means "snake-eater", a descriptively accurate name as these giant snakes feed almost singularly on other snakes, venomous or otherwise.

The average length of a king cobra is usually in the region of 10 to 12 feet, though it has been known to reach an astonishing length of 18 feet. The head of the snake is as big as a human hand and, when rearing up to survey its surroundings, or face an enemy, it may raise a third of its body off the ground, while spreading the ribs in the neck to further flare the skin and give the impression of even greater size, a technique used to intimidate an enemy. As if this is not already enough to discourage an attacker, the snake emits a low growling hiss from deep within its throat, produced by tiny holes in the trachea. Combine this with the huge quantities of deadly venom housed in a large gland on each side of the head, connected via a duct to a pair of needle sharp fangs situated in the front of the upper jaw, and you have as formidable a creature as any on Earth. There I was, deep in the jungles of Kerala, searching for exactly such an animal, in the hope of getting close enough to get a photograph with a wide angle lens.

King cobras are known to frequent the cool undergrowth of rainforests, often near streams where temperature and humidity remain fairly constant, so it was in such areas that I concentrated my search. Week after week I searched, trudging through the humid forests, rivers and swamps, my crew mercilessly condemned to follow, hauling heavy camera and sound equipment as they went. Insects of every variety attacked us relentlessly, while leeches had a field day and sucked our blood whenever we crossed water or moved through wet grass. It took every bit of stamina and self-control not to just chuck it all up and go home. But we didn't, and when the day we had been imagining finally came, we were all so weary and worn, that it took us all by total surprise.

It might be more correct to say that the snake found us, rather than we found it, because if it had not so dramatically presented itself, we might simply have gone passed. It made me wonder later, as I often do when snake hunting, just how many of the reptiles had been bypassed as they lay motionless and camouflaged in the undergrowth. In this particular case it may have been that the snake was startled and opted for immediate defence tactics, or it may just have been having a bad day. Whatever the case, this snake materialised out of a bamboo thicket like a steam train out of control, charging straight at me with head raised ready to strike. I use the word 'charged' in all seriousness, as I had never before in my life experienced anything like it. Buffalos charge! Elephants and rhinos charge! Snakes don't charge? If I had not experienced it myself, I would never have believed it. This was the biggest, venomous snake I had ever seen in my life, - and all fourteen foot of it charged fearlessly, right at me! I don't mind telling you, Austin Stevens, herpetologist 'extraordinaire' almost wet himself.

The initial shock of it passed, and the great snake stopped just short of me. My heart began to slow, as natural instinct kicked in and I saw the snake in front of me for what it really was, just another innocent wild animal, without malice, defending its territory against intruders. It remained, however, the biggest venomous snake I had ever seen. And as I slowly, very slowly, lowered my camera bag from my shoulder to the ground, to free myself for easier movement, the snake did something I had never seen before with any other snake. It focused its eyes on my movement as I bent down to drop the camera bag, and it tilted its head, not forward, but to the side, at an angle, as though directing its nearest eye for a better look, much like a hawk might do when taking note of potential prey. I was astounded and, when once again the snake looked up directly into my eyes, I realised without any shadow of doubt, I was in the presence of higher intelligence. (As far as snakes were concerned, you understand).

I was awed by the presence generated by this snake. Although it had originally charged at me in fearsome fashion, it now remained completely calm, its head raised high above the ground, watchful, but with no sign of aggression. At first I just crouched there, not sure what to do next. By comparison, this was like facing an adult, where all snakes before had been children. I was unsure of the boundaries, or how far I could go. I had never felt like this before. It was a humbling experience, much like that which I experience every time I find myself confronted by a desert elephant back home in Namibia. But this was a reptile, a creature supposed to react by instinct alone, with no particularly notable intelligent will of its own. This was without doubt, the King of snakes.

Finally, with the rest of the film crew scattered to various, strategic positions behind me, I removed my camera from my bag, and began a series of experimental shots, moving slowly around the snake, firing frame after frame, moving closer and away again, continuously testing to find the limits. I was nervous, never having been in this position before, with a venomous wild snake of this magnitude, deep in the jungles of - I didn't even know exactly where by this time, and knowing full well that there was little help available if something went wrong. I forced myself to brush these thoughts away. To even consider the consequences of a bite from that deadly head was enough to get me shaking. It was unthinkable. But, though the snake watched my every move from those calculating eyes, and released a long, almost continuous rumble from its throat, it never advanced toward me.

That is, until suddenly, stupidly, while circling for a better camera angle, I tripped over a long-fallen, bamboo log, which somehow got tangled up between my feet, and sent me crashing to the ground. Startled by the sudden movement, the snake immediately reacted by lunging forward, obviously expecting attack, and the giant head loomed over me where I lay amongst the leaf litter of the forest. For the second time that day I was witness to the fact that this was no ordinary snake, but a thinking, calculating snake, because, when it realised that I was in fact not threatening it, it simply gazed down at me where I lay well within striking distance, and eyed me, with tilted head, more, it seemed, out of curiosity than anger. As I carefully raised myself up again, the great snake slowly moved back to allow me space. I have never experienced anything like it before.

By this time my film crew were frantic, and were unanimously calling for an end to the shoot, feeling, quite rightly, that we had already gathered more than enough footage of the encounter, and there remained little reason to look for trouble where trouble was not needed. In other words, let's not push our luck! While I agreed with them whole-heartedly, there was still just one more thing that I had to do. I had on many occasions demonstrated the touching of a cobra behind the hood with one extended bare hand while distracting the snake's attention with the other. However, these snakes were seldom over two metres long, raising a hood less than a metre high. Here now was the challenge. I wanted to touch this king cobra behind the head, (as Buddha might have done) but the head in question was raised up almost as high as my own standing up, which meant that to do this thing, I had to place myself directly in the striking range of this incredible snake. I was nervous as can be just thinking about it, but I knew I had to do this, for myself, if not for any other reason. If questioned later, I could always say that I did it to show once again that snakes do not attack unless threatened, but deep down inside, I knew that I needed to do this just for myself. This is not something I can explain. It is what I am about, how I am made up. It is not something I invent; it is what I need.

When finally I moved in to attempt this feat, and I allowed myself very slowly within the striking range of this giant snake, and stretched out my arm towards it, the king looked me straight in the eyes, and gently lowered its head, allowing me easier access to touch it, for just one split second, before it dropped all the way to the ground and slithered off into the jungle. When it was over I was shaking like a leaf with a mixture of reverence and awe. It was an experience that would effect my life.

I am a herpetologist, a scientist if you like, someone who searches for the natural truths in my field, truths that help dispel the myths. Scientifically speaking, in all likelihood, the king cobra in question, having long realised that I was no threat to it, had simply grown tired of my presence, and was about to lower itself anyway, that it might side-step this silly man-thing, and go about its business. Though this is almost certainly the case, -- still I like sometimes to believe, just a little, that that king cobra, greatest of all venomous snakes, paid me homage by granting me my wish, before disappearing from my life, forever.

*Both pictures on these pages: the ultimate goal is reached as Austin touches the cobra on the head, following in Buddha's footsteps*

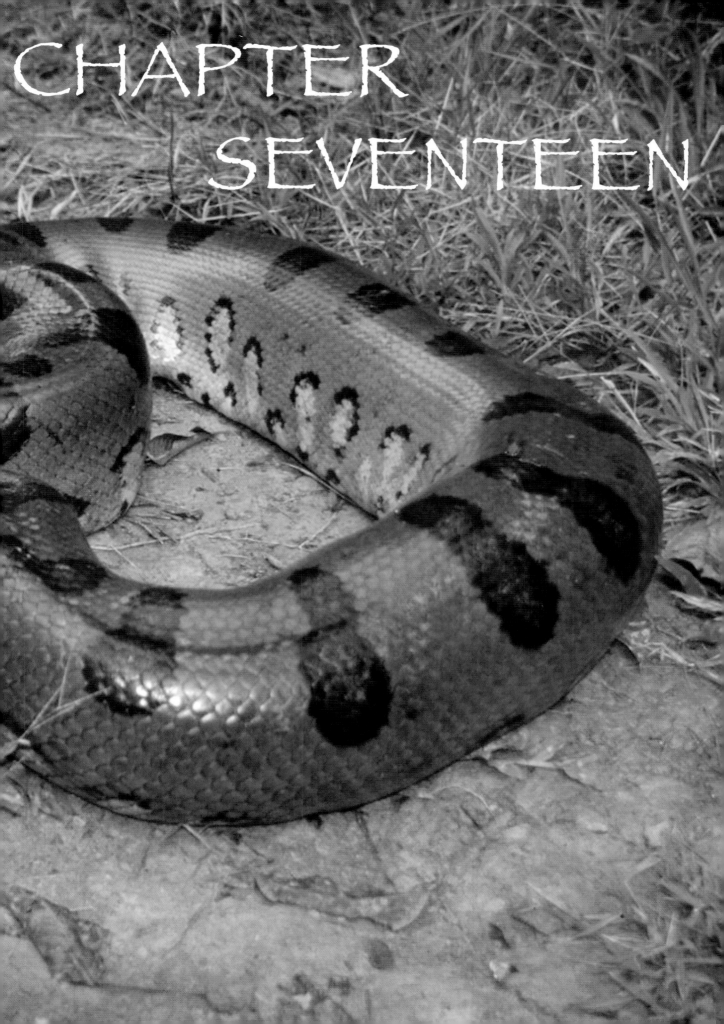

CHAPTER
SEVENTEEN

# In Search of Giants

If I were to be asked, throughout any period of my life, to name that one thing that I would most wish to do, the answer has always remained the same. To travel the Amazon River in search of the fabled, giant, green anaconda.

This is a snake like no other, with a reputation even bigger than its own remarkable size, a snake around which stories and myths abound, and of which legends become real in the minds of explorers and adventurers alike. The giant, green anaconda, is reputed to be the biggest of all living snakes, a giant amongst snakes, a fearsome killer that can effortlessly crush and swallow down the body of a large, adult man; a snake with such an appetite, that should the opportunity present itself, would attack and eat all in its path; a truly fearsome and frightening demon of the darkest jungles of South America; a snake which the early explorer and writer, Colonel Fawcett, claimed to have seen stretched out beneath his boat, so long that its tail remained on one bank of the Amazon River, while its head reached the other.

Well, having heard some of these stories, and read of such accounts, it is little wonder that when first I began to show an interest in herpetology as a young boy, that this fabled, seemingly, unreachable snake, would feature so largely in my imagination. As I grew and learned, it soon became evident that though indeed the green anaconda was to be considered a snake amongst snakes, the scientific truths about the creature differed somewhat from the myths and legends. This did little to curb my enthusiasm, and my greatest wish remained the same, to one day travel the mighty Amazon River in search of the giant, green anaconda.

When, indeed, one day, many years later, this opportunity finally presented itself, I unhesitatingly lunged at the chance. After some weeks of frantic preparations, with the help of an American herpetologist familiar with the territory, my team and I headed for Peru, not just simply to find an anaconda, but also to film the experience every step of the way. It remains today one of the most exciting times of my life.

*Austin on location in the Amazon, scouting for tree boas one hundred feet up in the rainforest canopy*

Now though it is true that the green anaconda is one of the biggest snakes in the world, when considering the seemingly endless expanse of lush, impenetrable Amazon jungle around me, as I sat with legs dangling over the bow of our river boat, El Arca, the realisation came to me that this would be like looking for the proverbial needle in a haystack, the world's biggest 'haystack' for that matter, the vast, mythical, dark and foreboding, Amazon jungle itself. In the comfort of home it was easy to imagine the excitement and adventure of patrolling the Amazon in search of my prize, like one might see in a movie, but the reality of it was something completely different. That was serious jungle out there, dark, mostly flooded and impenetrable. It would take days of hard slog to cover just a few kilometres if branching off the main river to enter the forest. Areas of dry land were few and far between, and most everything would have to be done from a boat.

The fertile Selva region of Peru, which includes the Amazon jungle, lies between the Andes Mountains and the jungles of eastern Peru. This was largely unchartered territory until as recently as the 1970's. The Amazon River, itself, actually originates in Peru, and at some points, at its widest, is measured up to 40 miles across. In the Peruvian stretch of Amazon alone, the jungle is home to some 2000 species of fish, over 4000 species of birds and at least 60 species of reptiles, and even more frogs species. Mammals include some larger species such as the jaguar, the anteater, the three toed sloth, and giant otters, as well as a variety of monkeys and many other smaller animals, with even the rare, pink, river porpoise being evident in certain stretches of the river. Insect species number in the millions, most not even studied or named as yet. These jungles have been standing as they are, hot and humid, for tens of millions of years, and are the home of an almost unbelievable diversity of life forms. I could not think of a more exciting place to be.

Our expedition in Peru began at the river port of Equitos, the main Amazon port in Peru. Here we acquired a motorised river boat with crew, big enough to house our small team and all necessary camera equipment and supplies needed for a lengthy stay on the river. Here also we were joined by William (Bill) Lamar, the American herpetologist, a man with the most remarkable brain for herpetological facts, figures, places, names and dates, I have ever encountered. We quickly became friends, and his experience acquired through earlier trips he had undertaken along the Amazon were vital to assist in my quest to find a giant, green anaconda. The Amazon was not a place to travel in blind ignorance.

However, it soon became evident that no matter the knowledge available, finding the snake in question was not going to be a simple matter. Green anacondas are elusive snakes, even more so because of their inclination to spend most of their lives submerged, where their perfectly camouflaged bodies become all but invisible, with just the tip of the snout remaining above water to take air. When feeling the need to hide, the snake can remain completely submerged for an hour or more on a single breath.

There are two species of anaconda. The smaller, yellow anaconda, seldom exceeding 3 metres in length, and the green anaconda, the subject of my quest, and by far the larger and better known of the two. Both of these species give live birth, with an adult green anaconda probably able to deliver 50 or more young at a time, each about a metre in length at birth. They are, of course, not venomous snakes, but constrictors, large specimens, capable even of crushing the life out of and swallowing such large forest creatures as black caimen and tapir. Like all snakes, anacondas have an estimated average adult length, as well as an estimated maximum length, this according to what has been observed in zoos as well as in the wild. There are no absolutes. While it is today known that the reticulated python of Asia is the longest recorded snake ever encountered, the green anaconda is undoubtably the heaviest bodied.

An average size for a green anaconda in the wild is estimated to be around the eighteen to twenty foot mark, while it is suspected, from skins collected by early explorers, that they may indeed reach a maximum length of closer to thirty feet. A snake of these proportions would be something amazing to see, but earlier published records of thirty five to forty feet are based on vague data and not considered authentic. The green anaconda occurs throughout most of the northern half of South America, but usually confined to river valleys, swamps and marshes. This now was where I had to concentrate my search.

For the first few weeks the excitement and thrill of just being on the hunt, for an exotic creature, in an exotic place, was enough and, indeed, there was no shortage of animal life. Everything was new and different and never seen by me before in the wild state. It is something to see an animal in the zoo, or to read about it in a book, but there is nothing as absolutely exciting as seeing these creatures in their wild natural habitat.

*Austin with one of the more average sized green anacondas located whilst exploring the Amazon*

*Austin with a 3 toed sloth whilst filming in the amazon*

*Opposite picture: Austin emerging from the Amazon with a green anaconda*

*The large caiman lizard of South America has specially adapted teeth to feed exclusively on hard-shelled snails*

Even at night, sparkling eyes, like illuminated jewels of red, white or green, would reflect suddenly for a few seconds in the spotlight, then move off quickly, to disappear into the dark. These gleaming eyes would appear not only from the water, but from way up in the trees as well, at every level, leaving us to speculate excitedly as to what manner of creature it might have been. And though I found, caught and filmed a variety of reptile species, including some species of small tree boas, never was there any sign of green anacondas. What sign, after all, does one search for in the watery world of the Amazon? No tracks, no droppings, no old shed skin. Everything covered or washed away by the flowing waters, no matter how big the snake. Soon I began to realise that finding such a snake might be more up to just plain, old-fashioned luck, as much as any knowledge of the creature's habits we may try to apply.

Then, just when a mood of despondency was settling over the team and crew alike, we had our first encounter. It was not a big snake, but at the time it might just as well have been the biggest in the world, so relieved were we to find something, and it generated in us new hope and enthusiasm.

We had secured the El Arca to a tree along the main stream of the Amazon River from where we canoed our way into an oxbow lake, cut off from the main stream of the Amazon River itself. This, we were assured by our boat crew, was amongst the best places to fish for piranha, those voracious, little, meat-eating fish who themselves are the subject of as many stories and myths as is the green anaconda. These fish, it seemed, were considered good eating by the natives. Indeed within minutes of dropping their hand lines and hooks overboard, garnished with bits of bloody meat, red bellied piranha were being hurled into the boat as fast as fresh bait could be placed on the hooks. Soon the bottom of the canoe was alive with jumping little fish, who snapped and chewed at anything within reach, and we were forced to keep our bare feet dangling over the edge of the canoe.

I had many times during the trip so far dived from the El Arca and swam in the Amazon waters, giving little thought to piranha attack, knowing that such stories were greatly exaggerated, and that it was only under extreme conditions that these fish would actually be grouped together for a feeding frenzy. Apparently, an oxbow lake was just such a situation, where the lake itself was isolated from the main river, and the trapped fish therein concentrated and multiplying, with food far less abundant than in the main stream. As luck would have it, right about that minute, as I was contemplating this new found-knowledge, a young green anaconda of about two metres in length, suddenly surfaced from under a huge, floating, Victoria lily leaf, not four metres away from where I sat, legs dangling over the side of the canoe. For a long second I stared uncomprehendingly, as the snake seemed to do the same, before it turned and casually swam away in the opposite direction.

'SNAKE'! I screamed, lunging up and forward out of my half sitting position, bringing my body erect in one clumsy motion and tipping the shallow canoe dangerously on edge. This brought about further confused seconds of greater unbalance as the others in the canoe swung round, startled by my shout. The sudden frantic movement of all our bodies combined finally proved too much for the little wooden canoe and we all tipped over the edge in a flurry of wind-milling arms and collapsing legs. Fortunately the second canoe, holding the camera crew and their equiptment, was some metres away to the side, and not affected by the disturbance, as some serious and frantic splashing took place by the disgorged crew, in a effort to leave the indisputably, piranha-infested water as quickly as humanly possible for the safety of the canoe, now drifting half-full of water just out of our immediate reach. Thinking back now, I suspect that any piranha close to the boat at the time of the tipping were surely themselves startled by the sudden unceremonious downpour of human bodies from above, and headed at speed for distant areas of the lake.

As unpopular as I imagine I was right then, once back in the canoe, shaky and dripping, everybody pulled together to paddle as quickly as possible in the direction the anaconda had fled. Luck was with us, because the juvenile snake had pulled itself onto another giant lily leaf, where it lay sunning itself, seemingly unperturbed. That is, until it suddenly took note of our fast approaching canoe, and made to slither hastily off the leaf and back into the water.

But I was having none of it, and dropping my paddle, I lunged out with tremendous reach to grab recklessly for the disappearing body. For the second time that day there came about some serious and frantic splashing as, once more, everybody fought desperately to leave the piranha infested water into which they had been tumbled by my enthusiasm. This included myself, but with the added burden of a two metre anaconda wrapped around one arm, a snake which quickly displayed its displeasure by sinking its rows of needle sharp teeth into my wrist, instantly drawing blood, that greatest of all elements for attracting piranha, a fact so clearly demonstrated to me just recently by the fishing effort's of the boat crew, and one that now spurred me on to super human effort, as I virtually leapt back into the canoe, as though hoisted by an invisible force from below. There I lay in a heap, with the anaconda firmly attached to my wrist, as a dripping, scowling crew, glared at me with malicious intent, or at the very least, having leanings towards mutiny. It was not my most popular day, but the camera crew from the second canoe, with wide grins all over their faces, confirmed that we did have some great footage.

Hereafter I concentrated my search in these more isolated areas, areas that would be above the water level in the dry season, but where now I was forced to walk waist deep. Here I encountered many old logs and fallen trees and various types of partially, submerged vegetation in which an anaconda could feel secure while in wait of prey. The thought did occur to me that should I be mistaken for such, I would not stand a chance, especially in deep water.

However, when first I caught sight of the rippling movement to my distant left, I was reasonably secure in water just up to my knees and quickly made my way in that direction. Getting closer, I noticed in the gloom of the forest that the movement was now somehow expanded, and moving away from me, the muddy water seeming to boil as it went. That's when I caught a first glimpse of a section of a mottled green elongated form, thick as my upper thigh, slithering silently over a submerged log. This was it! After weeks of slog, searching and enduring, I knew this was it. But right then, 'it' was fast moving away from me into irretrievable territory, so I plunged forward in frantic desperation.

Anybody who has had any experience with snakes in the wild, will appreciate their ability to disappear effortlessly into even the most meagre of vegetation, their lithe, muscular bodies propelling them with silent speed. Though this snake was many times larger than most species one might encounter on land, and therefore theoretically more visible, it was mostly submerged in muddy water, perfectly camouflaged, and with

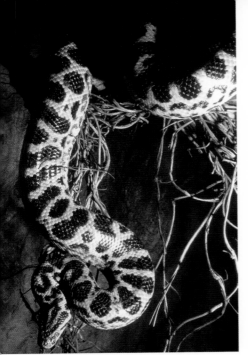

*The Amazon yellow anaconda does not grow as large as its cousin the green anaconda*

the whole Amazon jungle too at its disposal.

There was no time to hesitate. Lunging forward, the camera team hot on my heels, the water dragging at my legs, and forced to negotiate bushes, logs and whole trees protruding above the surface, and an even greater number of submerged obstacles, I recklessly forced myself forward, half running, diving, scrabbling and generally pulling out all the stops in a last ditch effort to reach out and grab at the speedily, fleeing shadow in the swamp. Desperately, with nothing to lose but everything I had struggled for throughout the past six weeks, and a lifetime of wishful thinking, I took that final, Herculean lunge, I was far too excited and spiked with adrenaline to register the fact that I was now suddenly way out of my depth, both figuratively and physically speaking, as the great, muscular body grasped between my arms effortlessly dragged me below the surface.

The minutes that followed remain only as a blur in my mind. There was terrible thrashing about, this I know, as well as a terrible drain of my physical strength, combined with lack of oxygen, and a literal, sinking feeling as my feet registered no bottom on which to stand. I was in deep water, and weighted down by a clinging, thrashing, 150 kilograms of seething snake, eighteen feet of it, as we roughly measured later. Eighteen feet of pure unadulterated muscle; I had never before felt such pressure on my body, even imagined such pressure. Although I managed to get my hands around the neck of the snake, it still managed to pull free and graze my arm with teeth exposed in its gaping jaws. And once again my blood spurted into the Amazon, only this time on a more plentiful scale.

Of course, it must be understood that the snake was at no fault here, and it is a sobering thought that even though it found itself 'under attack', (how could it suspect anything less), the great serpent still continued to try for escape rather than constrict me to death, a clear indication that snakes, even giant snakes such as this, do not consider humans as prey, rather avoiding them at all costs.

The film crew meanwhile, with cameras housed in protective waterproof splash-bags, were themselves having a nightmare of a time trying just to keep up, and rolling, with the later resulting footage revealing, unavoidable moments of sudden submersion into muddy waters, followed by startling contrasts of tree trunks reaching for the sky, and the occasional glimpse of a blue-faced and bleeding herpetologist entwined in the coils of a enormous, water snake. This was going to take some editing back at the studios.

*The Amazon - the longest river in the world*

As matters turned out, having pulled free from my grip, the snake released its coils from around my body and all but relaxed in the water, swimming slowly this way and that, as if disorientated. The relief of the pressure on my body, and the sudden ability to breach the surface for air, all but overwhelmed me, and it took a minute of gasping and panting before I was able to coherently consider my surroundings. Quickly I swam out and reached for the bulk of the snake's body, where it semi-floated, the head raised slightly above the surface away from me, and gently I pulled it into shallower water. Seemingly also somewhat winded, and not feeling any particular restricting grip on its body, the anaconda floated across with me with little resistance other than a constant, slow, undulating swimming motion. I have often marvelled at how quickly a snake adapts to human contact once it is established that the situation presents no danger. I knew, this was a wild animal, and any sudden movement or too tight a grip might convey the wrong message. Taking advantage of the reptile's temporary, more-relaxed state, I gently edged towards a raised mud bank, where I carefully, and eventually with the aid of more hands, pulled the snake out of the water, where it lay spread out in the mud.

*The greatly feared Amazon bushmaster, the longest venomous snake in the western hemisphere*

It was indeed an enormous snake, in the region of eighteen or nineteen feet at a rough estimate, a respectable adult-size by any consideration, and for the most part, as thick as my upper thigh. The snake continuously made to go back to the water, obviously feeling vulnerable and exposed. Hurriedly I set about photographing it, all the while keeping as far from the toothy end as possible, the camera crew doing the same from close behind me. Warily the anaconda kept an eye on our movements around it, and when finally it found its way back into the water, I followed suit, reluctant to so soon leave the presence of this almost, mythical creature. In the water, but unafraid now, I watched with mixed emotions as this giant amongst snakes, quietly once more headed off into the watery forest, just a shadow and a ripple in the great expanse of the Amazon jungle, never to be seen again.

While I realised, of course, that I was lucky not to be drowned by the weight and pressure of the snake wrapped around me in deep water (a slight miscalculation on my part) as it reacted naturally to my grabbing hold of its body, as it attempted to flee, I had otherwise, without doubt, proved that even these giant reptiles generally posed no threat to humans. At the same time of course, my knowledge on this subject goes only as far as what I have experienced myself, physically. Who is then to say what the case may be, should the snake in question be another ten feet longer, and another 50 or more kilograms heavier, as is almost certain they can become? Would the same rules apply? Would such a snake also opt for escape, or react instead as it might to a prey animal, crushing the life out of its victim and swallowing it down whole? I personally, having experienced only the first stages of the tremendous pressure exerted by the coils of just an average sized anaconda, surely hope that I never have to be the one to test the theory.

CHAPTER
EIGHTEEN

# The Fear Factor

I have experienced and suffered numerous physical 'accidents' to my person over the years, venomous snake bite being just one small part of it all. There have been falls from trees and rocks and numerous other places, some resulting in broken ribs, skull fractures, and torn tendons. I have also been crashed into by a speeding car, experienced my own motorbike accidents, been shot at, and attacked and stabbed five times in the back.

Then there are the diseases, especially those associated with mosquitoes and other pests, those terrible diseases that curse you with terrible sickness and then, if you are fortunate enough to survive, to some lesser or greater degree, remain in your body all the days of your life, to re-occur randomly, diseases like cerebral malaria, tick bite fever, and Ross River Fever. I know all of these. I have also been tusked by a desert elephant and lived to tell the tale.

So, it is not surprising that some have suggested that I am 'accident prone'. However, not being one to believe in fate, or any other course of direction planned other than by one's self, I suggest that it is only because I am simply out there all the time doing stuff, thus naturally exposing myself to a higher degree of possible, physical encounter with any of the above mentioned. It is no mystery. It is a risk factor, one which should be weighed up before indulging in a life style like mine. At the same time, I know it is true that, if one knew what difficulties or trauma lay ahead in any chosen field, it is unlikely that anyone would get out of bed in the morning. I do what I do with less thought to what might go wrong, as to what I might achieve to my own satisfaction, at the same time knowing full well that one could just as easily get killed by any number of means while simply living an every day life in the city.

Everyone, of course, has different abilities and capabilities, developed or learned. It cannot necessarily always be said than one is more, or less brave, than another. Some simply have talents to do things others cannot, while those others in turn might have talents in another field. Because I often work with venomous snakes, people have commented how 'brave' I am. This is, of course, false, as I am simply applying my knowledge and training to a subject to which I was at first naturally attracted to. (When I was rushed by the giant king cobra in India, I was more afraid than I had ever been of a snake before. In a similar vein, when the green anaconda in Peru was wrapped around me and I could not get my head above water, I was near panic). I have yet to decipher what the word 'brave' truly entails, but know one thing for sure, judging by the number of things that do scare me, I am no braver than the next person.

*Above picture top: a western diamondback rattlesnake filmed in New Mexico*

*Above picture bottom: the beautifully marked and seldom seen black-tailed rattlesnake with forked tongue fully extended*

There is another factor, that unexplainable fear that you have no control over, brave or otherwise, a fear so fierce and all encompassing that it can bring you to the edge of sanity; a phobia, in fact. In my case, the claustrophobia, the terror of being in small confined spaces. This is a thing that can kill through your own mind. This is the most terrible fear that haunts my life. I cannot even use a lift in a tall building for fear that it gets stuck and I cannot get out. This would kill me, or drive me insane. So I avoid lifts and climb a lot of stairs. I also avoid any other enclosed places, especially dark enclosed places, like caves. So you can just imagine my consternation and reservations when it was proposed that I make a film about hibernating rattlesnakes in their secret dens, hidden deep beneath the ground somewhere in the deserts of New Mexico, USA.

There was no way I was going to turn down the project, because naturally I was as excited about the potential adventure, as I was terrified as I had no idea what I might have to do, as is usually the case when setting out on a new expedition. You have a region marked out, a basic plan of action, and the rest takes care of itself. Never can you predict what you are going to come up against. That's what makes it an adventure. In this case, with the help of local New Mexico herpetologists, it took us just a few weeks to locate one of the secret rattlesnake, hibernating dens, large enough (at the entrance at least) to allow me access. Standing there on that day, as I contemplated going into the tunnel with camera and torchlight, I knew real fear.

The thing with claustrophobia, as I have come to know it, is that the panic can just barely be controlled as long as the knowledge is there that the way out is clear, not closed off, and that there be light. For this reason I could not have anybody follow me in, with camera or light, or anything, because the restricting width of the narrow tunnel would be closed off by another person behind me, and I would go into uncontrollable panic. Thus, the only way I could attempt to actually film these snakes in their winter den, would be to crawl along the tunnel, pushing a video camera ahead of me, using a small battery-operated headlamp for illumination. This way, if the tunnel narrowed further down the line, I could at least retreat unhindered. As I was soon to learn, there was the little additional problem of rattlesnakes present.

Needless to say, the crawl down that narrow tunnel was the longest and most frightening 'adventure' I had ever put myself through. It took every bit of restraint I could muster to force down the continuous feeling of panic rising up through my body. It was all I could do just to concentrate on what lay ahead. One wrong move on my part, one second of concentration lost, and my mind might slip into panic mode. I had to forceably keep my wits about me. This took all my concentration, and I sweated litres.

After about twelve metres, the tunnel narrowed somewhat, but fortunately just for a short distance, whereafter, thankfully, it actually began to widened slightly again, though the roof remained close above my back. The floor was dusty and coarse with loose gravel and dust, while all around me the cold touch of the rock pressed in against my body. I did not dare stop my forward motion to rest for fear of losing concentration. To stop and rest would be to think about where I was. And to think about where I was, basically wrapped up in a narrow tomb of rock somewhere below the New Mexico Desert, would have eroded my last reserves and ended it all for me. So I just kept dragging myself forward until finally the tunnel, which actually was no more than a fissure in the rock below ground, widened to twice its earlier size. Almost instantly there came to my ears a familiar sound. It was the warning sound of the rattlesnake. But not just one, many. It sounded like a buzz saw running at maximum revolutions. If there had been any doubt before, that now evaporated, as the sound grew louder with each movement I made. Somewhere ahead in the dark they waited, alerted to my presence, their backs to the wall so to speak, with nowhere to go but towards me, where I lay sprawled out, blocking their escape.

The unique structure of the rattlesnake, specifically the rattle appendage attached to the end of its tail, sets these snakes apart from all others. In adults it is an organ of loosely-attached, horny segments that strike against one another when the tail is vibrated, to produce a buzzing sound. Rattlesnakes are born with one single button attached to the end of the

*The largest turtle in the Americas, the giant Florida Alligator snapping turtle, clearly displays the powerful sharp-edged jaws with which it catches its prey*

*Austin with a giant rattlesnake in New Mexico*

tail, to which one more is added with every shedding of the skin. The older the snake therefore, the longer the rattle, and often the louder the sound produced from it. Segments of these rattles may break off periodically from wear, and so it does not necessarily confirm the age of a specimen.

Most species of rattlesnakes hibernate during the winter months in restricted spaces such as rock crevices or available underground holes. Rattlesnake dens are usually located above the frost level, situated so as not to be easily approached by larger animals. These dens may be used year after year, often by the same snakes that may frequent the surrounding territory. Usually both males and females are present, and therefore it is likely that mating may occur towards the end of the cold season. During the hibernation period, these rattlesnakes, sometimes hundreds grouped together, lie virtually motionless, until spring, when the warmer temperatures arouse them. The larger congregations of 'denning' rattlesnakes are usually found in the colder northern regions, with smaller groups located in the south. "Denning" appears to be related as much to territoriality, as to the consideration to safety in numbers and security. Most dens would be impossible to penetrate without digging and destroying them completely, thus I considered myself extremely fortunate to find one with an opening large enough to allow me access. However, I was paying the price, as this particular tunnel stretched many metres underground, and put me in a most frightening position.

My little head lamp supplied only a limited amount of light, just enough to give me a clear view of the tunnel immediately ahead, and enough to make low-light video filming possible, at close quarters. Considering my claustrophobia affliction, one might assume that to add a bunch of startled rattlesnakes to the equation would now finally throw me over the edge. On the contrary, this was just what I needed. This was my subject after all, snakes, those creatures that never ceased to excite me, no matter where I might find them. So, with my excitement now growing, and my concentration fully geared for what lay ahead, I dragged myself the last few metres into the secret cave of the rattlesnakes.

*A close up of the head of an albino western diamond back rattlesnake clearly displaying the facial heat receptor situated between the eye and the nostril*

It was an astonishing experience. I had read about such dens of course, but never imagined that I would one day actually locate and enter one. The end of the cave was rugged and crumbled, with numerous shelves of rock protruding and others long ago tumbled to the floor. Rattlesnakes were everywhere, at least two dozen or more, and they were all rattling their tails at full tilt, the sound almost deafening in the tiny enclosure. This was clearly a warning not to come too close, but it is noteworthy that there was no panic amongst the snakes, and none moved much from their positions or struck out at me. They appeared all to be Western diamond back rattlesnakes, the most common of the American rattlesnake species. It was only once I began working the video camera that I realised that there were snakes all around me, as well as ahead of me. Their heads and parts of their bodies now appeared from everywhere, almost as if re-adjusting their positions to accommodate this new presence in their midst. I experienced a moment of Déjà vu, as a flash memory of my world record snake sit-in passed through my mind. There, too, I had been the

outsider, cautiously granted space amidst a congregation of venomous snakes.

As I lay completely still, the noise from the vibrating rattles gradually slowed, then subsided altogether. However, the slightest movement from me to reposition myself, or adjust the camera in the confined space, would immediately bring about a cacophony of the nervous buzzing. After a while this became less and less until finally, after what must have been an hour in the cave, the snakes barely buzzed at me at all. One or two even changed positions, moving close to, and even across my body, as I lay frozen in position on the ground. Once more I marvelled at how quickly snakes adapt to the presence of humans, once it is established that there is no obvious threat or danger.

Lying there in the tiny cave, surrounded by these amazing snakes, I felt no fear, but actually rested myself in preparation for the difficult reverse trip back to the entrance. There was not enough space to turn around, and by backing straight out again I presented less chance of 'rattling' the rattlers. They had allowed me the privilege of visiting their winter den, and I felt it the least I could do was not disturb them more than absolutely necessary. Somewhat reluctantly I began my move back out of the cave, and chalked up another close encounter that would remain with me all the days of my life.

Looking back at some of these experiences, I know only too well that sometimes I seem to lose my professionalism and attribute actual powers of emotion shared between myself and snakes, to the point of near anthropomorphism. But I have spent so much time in close contact with snakes, really close contact, that sometimes it just feels to me as though I have some special affinity with them. At the very least, that they quickly come to realise I am not an enemy, and have no fear in my presence, while I in turn appreciate them for what they are, wild animals of nature, that harbour no malice towards human beings.

*The extreme claustrophobia of filming in a rattlesnake den in New Mexico is amply demonstrated here*

# CHAPTER NINETEEN

# Komodo

*Previous pages: the breathtaking beauty of the Komodo Isles*

As is the case with most situations, to be in control is to be secure. So it is too with the handling of, and working with, potentially dangerous reptile species. The first defence is knowledge of the species, knowing what it is exactly, and what it is potentially capable of, be it venomous or non venomous. It is fortunate that where reptiles are concerned, most are small by comparison to human size, and therefore easily distanced. In other words, should one encounter a snake or lizard in the wild, it takes no more than a step or two back to allow a safe distance between yourself and the creature in question. This would certainly be my advice to anyone unwillingly finding themselves in such a situation. It remains a fact that snakes and lizards do not attack humans for any reason other than if they themselves are threatened. The basic reason for this is simply that humans are far too large to be eaten. (Of course, technically speaking, humans would not present the ideal smell or dimensions that a reptile would usually associate with its food animal anyway) Thus humans are safe from reptile attack as long as they do not try to catch one, or step on one, or corner one.

In the case of herpetologists, there exists a whole different set of rules, as, generally, herpetologists insist upon not only approaching closely to reptiles, but even on occasion actually catching them with their bare hands, or any other means at their disposal. Or, as in my case, at least to get as close to the reptile as possible for the purpose of detailed photography. Here I have to rely strongly on my knowledge of the species in question and, where possible, my previous experience with similar specimens. In my quest for close up photography, the reptile is faced with what it interprets to be a direct frontal 'attack', having no way of knowing my true, harmless intentions. Under such circumstances all the risks are of my own design, and the reptile free of blame, whatever the final consequences.

It is fortunate that most reptiles are small enough to be approached closely with a camera, without fear of being bitten, and even those that are larger are usually controllable for photography, within a respectable distance. A good example is the cobras, which when faced head on, will raise their distinctive hood in a display of defensive aggression. These snakes are always a favourite for photography and, though it is a highly venomous species, it is predictable, and I can judge the distance of the snake's strike, and soon determine by its attitude just how often it will strike and how close I can go before placing myself in real danger of those strikes. This is not a perfect science, as was clearly displayed when I was bitten on camera by that big, old, snouted cobra in the Namib Desert. However, the decision remains mine alone. Do I stay back and get a mediocre picture, that most anybody can get, or do I crawl down low on the ground and creep my camera right up close within the cobra's striking range to get that spectacular once in a lifetime shot instead? Let me explain, for those not in the know; when a wildlife photographer has his eye jammed tight into the view finder, focused on a wild animal in action, it is like a drug, and all the surrounding world falls into the background, to be ignored until further notice.

This is where the danger lies when up close and in the face of an angered, venomous snake, because I have purposely put myself in harm's way, but at the same time must remain in control of my reflexes, and know my limitations, and totally rely on an accumulation of knowledge, experience and nerve to get me out of there again. But it is so exciting, and the

*The magisterial Komodo Dragon, the largest of all living lizards found on the planet today*

*An adult Komodo Dragon strides out with bulging stomach after devouring its share of a carcass*

picture that looms up through the lens is so dramatic, startling and close, that I know there is no other way to go, and I will do it over and over again. To compare it to other professions, I imagine it must be like hitting a hole in one on the golf course, or slamming an ace on the tennis court, or securing the final winning points by kicking that funny shaped ball through those distant poles fifty metres away. But wrap these all into one, and you only scratch the surface of what I feel when in close with a dangerous snake through the lens. To add to that, the very adventure of finding the subject in the first place makes for great experience in the outdoors. Wildlife photography is a style of life, not just a hobby or profession.

Another advantage to photographing reptiles, is that for the most part, they can be handled and relocated for a perfect shot. When photographing elephants or lions or black rhino, or any other species of mammal for that matter, one is forced to make do with the location that presents itself. Seldom is a snake located in an ideal photographic position, and because it is a creature that can quickly escape, it is an advantage to be able to catch the reptile and relocate it to a suitable surrounding. (Of course this should only be attempted by photographers with experience in herpetology) Certainly snakes, and especially lizards, do not simply oblige the photographer, but if the reptile is handled carefully, and allowed to calm down, it may well be placed to pose on a rock or log for the few seconds that is required to get the preferred picture. Some specimens, especially venomous species, may not be so tolerant and, attempting to move it into the desired location, may be too dangerous. In such a case, the photographer has to do the best possible photography on the spot.

There are some reptiles that one should not fool with at all, and if you are lucky enough to encounter one in the wild, it would be best just to shoot some film from a distance, in the name of sensible safety. Crocodiles are a good example, specifically those larger species like the Nile crocodile of Africa, or the salt water crocodile of South East Asia and Australia. There is also the black caiman found in South America, and the North American alligator. Large specimens of these reptiles are certainly capable of eating a human, and will knowingly hunt a human should the opportunity present itself. These are secretive and fierce creatures, secure in the element of water, from where they are known to attack and feast on other creatures sometimes even larger than themselves.

Also to consider are the giant snakes. The green anaconda of South America, the Indian python, and the reticulated python of Asia; these are snakes which have the ability to grow to great lengths, and possess jaws filled with rows of long, needle sharp teeth, and are capable of applying tremendous pressure in their coils, enough even to subdue the likes of large crocodilians and fair-sized, land mammals like deer and tapirs. Only a seasoned herpetologist should approach such reptiles for closer photography. I have done this, and on one occasion almost paid the ultimate price.

Though there are a number of monitor lizards that grow large enough to present problems should a human physically tackle them (long, sharp claws and powerful jaws housing rows of sharp teeth) there is really only one that is completely untouchable, and that is the Komodo Dragon of South East Asia. As the king cobra is the ultimate snake in my book, the Komodo is the lizard without equal. To be in the presence of Komodo Dragons, is like stepping back in time, like a visit to Jurassic Park. It is one of the most fascinating and frightening reptiles I have ever encountered. The Komodo Dragon is the largest lizard on Earth, reaching a length of over three metres, with some adults weighing up to one hundred and sixty kilograms. In spite of this great size, they are fast-moving creatures, known to physically run to ground wild pigs and mountain goats, and have even been known to tackle water buffalo. They do not stalk their prey; they physically chase and tackle it. They are the direct ancestors of reptiles that lived fifty million years ago, and their size, still attained today, is due to the fact that they are the top predators of the region.

These fantastic lizards were first recorded as late as 1910, on the Komodo Islands, from where their name is derived. The Komodo is one of the oldest living lizards, and may have descended from an even larger lizard which existed some thirty thousand years ago (Megalania prisca). Today they are found only on the southern Indonesian Islands of Komodo, Rinca, Flores, and Gili Motang, (an archipelago made up of over thirteen thousand islands) where they are active in the grasslands, the forested areas, swamps, and even on the beaches. They are ready scavengers and will travel great distances towards the smell of a decomposing carcass, their forked tongue and Jacobson's organ chemical analyser allowing them to detect smells an incredible ten kilometres distant. Their powerful claws and serrated teeth make short work of even the toughest animal hide, and it is not uncommon to have a number of these giant reptiles attracted to, and feeding on, a single carcass. Like most reptiles, each tooth in the mouth has multiple replacements behind it, and a Komodo Dragon may replace as many as two hundred teeth each year. These teeth are curved and serrated, with shorter teeth at the back and longer teeth towards the front, to enable a deeper cut as the Dragon pulls its head away.

There are only two species of venomous lizards in the world, the Gila monster and its close cousin, the Beaded lizard, located in the south western desert areas of USA and Mexico. These lizards have a number of grooved teeth in the lower jaw along which a salivary venom is excreted from venom glands when chewing on a prey animal. There are no other venomous lizard species. However, because of their habit of feeding on carcasses, often rotting carcasses, the bite of a Komodo Dragon is considered venomous, in as much as there is always bacteria present in their mouths. In fact, as many as 72 different strains of bacteria have been identified in the saliva of Komodo Dragons, some of which are deadly not only to animals, but to humans as well. Even when miraculously escaping the full onslaught of a Komodo Dragon attack, without treatment, death will occur later from the bacterial poisoning. And there are a number of recorded cases of human deaths by Komodo Dragon bite!

There are also accounts of local island children going missing, never to be seen again, attributed to Dragon attack. A tourist was eaten by a Komodo Dragon in the 1970's, and another in 1989, after getting lost on the island. Make no mistake, the Komodo Dragon is a top predator of fantastic proportions and capability by today's reptilian standards. It is intelligent and large enough not to fear humans. It is certainly not a creature to fool with, or take lightly. This giant lizard is a tantalising peek into the prehistoric past, and sadly, as is always the case, due to the encroachment of humans and their poaching of the island wildlife on which the dragons feed, there are today less than three thousand surviving in what is left of their natural habitat.

When the decision was taken to go shoot a film about these giant reptiles, it all seemed straight forward enough, although I did feel some uncertainty concerning close work with Komodos, as I had no experience with them at all. Everything I knew about the dragons was gleaned from books, and I had once seen a young specimen in a zoo in Australia. None the less, I always felt that the best part of a planned trip was the un-planned part. That part which takes place almost from the minute you reach your destination, and takes over for the rest of the trip. It is all fine and well to prepare everything on paper, but another entirely to follow through on a planned schedule. This is not an uncommon experience in the documentary business.

The flight to Bali was pleasant and uneventful, as was the next stage of the journey, a two hour flight to the island of Flores, where I and the film crew took a few days to acclimatise, prepare all the film and other equipment, and to familiarise ourselves with the locals and the local customs. Greater attention to the latter, we were later informed, was the root cause of what happened next. While exploring and filming in a cave on the island, I misplaced a foot amongst jagged rocks, ripped the tendons supporting the ankle, and tumbled down a steep incline onto more jagged rocks, breaking four ribs. Just two days into the project, it was a fatal blow. It took the rest of that day to get me out of the cave, which involved steep climbs with ropes and make-shift ladders, before finally I could be delicately loaded onto the passenger seat of a 120cc motorbike, the only immediately accessible vehicle capable of getting me out along the jungle track. A further day and night of agony and discomfort passed before a plane arrived, and I was shipped out to a hospital in Bali. Here I was extensively X-rayed, my ribs strapped tightly, and my foot placed in a cast and, after a few more days of attention, sent home on crutches. This effectively set the film project back by four months, and the insurance premiums associated with any future film projects virtually doubled overnight. It was a most depressing time.

However, if nothing else, I am a survivor, and four months later saw me once again in that same cave, exploring exactly the same area, this time without any mishap. The locals explained that we had failed to consult with the spiritual keepers of the caves the first time round, and therefore suffered the consequences. This time, however, they had sacrificed a chicken in my name, and had drained the luckless bird of its blood, which was then liberally smeared around the entrance of the cave, amidst much chanting and speaking of strange words. Not one to judge where I am lacking in knowledge, I thanked them heartily, and secretly hoped that the protection I was being afforded would carry through to my first encounter with the giant lizards I was ultimately in search of. As it turned out, this might exactly have been the case.

A few days later found me and my team leaving the shores of Flores, on a boat bound for the islands of Rinca and Komodo, where, so we were told, the biggest and heaviest bodied of the Komodo Dragons were to be found. My plan was not simply just to photograph the dragons in still life, but also their active feeding behaviour, and hopefully their combat behaviour, when males compete for the attentions of the females of the species, a spectacle rarely witnessed by human eyes. By all accounts, there are many more males than females present on the islands, and competition is fierce. I wanted to be right there, up close, if and when it happened. It was the month of May, roughly the right time of year to begin expecting mating behaviour. It was also the month of my birthday, which made me feel lucky.

There are a number of small fishing villages to be found scattered along the shores of the larger Islands, and we occasionally stopped off to ask about dragon sightings. Always excited to receive visitors, the villagers greeted us with great enthusiasm and fanfare, and were delighted to oblige when we asked permission to film in and around the village. On

*In a spot of bother - Austin chased up a tree by an inquisitive Komodo Dragon*

*Picture on previous pages: Austin swimming in pursuit of a Komodo Dragon*

*Picture top right: a Komodo Dragon hunting for food*

*Picture middle right: Austin with local crew on a canoe heading toward the Komodo islands*

*Picture bottom right: a Komodo Dragon emerges from the water*

hearing of our quest for large dragons, the excitement would increase, and stories of dragon sightings and happenings would pour forth. It was all our translators could do to keep up with the gathered locals, all trying to be heard at once. It was interesting to note that there were a number of stories concerning the disappearance of children from villages, some blamed on the dragons, with vivid descriptions of blood and body parts found scattered around the outskirts of a village. It is difficult to assess if all these stories are confirmed as fact, though it has been recorded that rogue dragons, attracted by human activities, can become potentially dangerous. Once familiar with humans and their villages, such a dragon, large as it is, might easily come to consider a young child as prey, especially if found to be wandering alone outside the safety of the village. However, for the most part, and in spite of this, the people revere the Komodo Dragon as a mystical ancestor, to be looked upon with respect. These are people truly at one with nature, who accept life and death as part of a greater entity.

Often we would be invited to sleep over with families, and share in their evening meal, which consisted mostly of rice and heavily-salted, dried fish. As far as I could make out, this was basically the staple diet twice a day, only rarely accompanied by some or other unrecognisable vegetable matter. Everything that sustained these villagers was either fished from the sea, or grown in small plantations around the village boundary. Other required goods were brought in by boat whenever the opportunity arose. In one village visited, this included, would you believe, a large satellite dish mounted on a rusted pole in the centre of the village, (which did not work, but was providing an excellent platform for drying freshly washed clothes) and a petrol-driven generator which operated sporadically to screen video-taped films on the one, television set mounted in a central hut, and made available to all. Had I known about this earlier, I would have brought some taped films with me, for the children especially. As is typical of less educated, poorer class people around the world, here too was an over abundance of small children, a situation that will eventually directly lead to the demise of the last remaining Komodo Dragons and, later, the human population itself. As any biologist, scientist and/or naturalist anywhere in the world knows, and what no politician will ever declare to his/her public, (with the exception of the Chinese government) -- each and every developing disaster and problem facing the planet today, is either directly or indirectly connected to overpopulation of the planet by the human species.

Our travels and explorations throughout the many islands we visited in the region did not go unrewarded, though large Komodo Dragons were proving to be elusive. I did come across a few youngsters though, which I was lucky enough to catch and examine, giving me my first encounter with these unique creatures. However, at a metre in length, they much resembled any monitor lizard found anywhere in the world, and so did not affect me with any particular excitement. I did, however, find a few snakes species that rated some enthusiasm, one being a fairly common green tree viper that, in this case was not common at all, as it was actually completely sky blue in colour, a colour variation unexplained, as far as I know, by biologists.

On another occasion, while climbing high up along a vine-entwined rocky ledge, a large reticulated python, well camouflaged amongst the greenery, struck out at me with such force that I almost lost my balance. Though only about four metres in length, (but capable of becoming more than twice that size) the reticulated python is an extremely powerful predator and, though it was certainly not intending to eat me, it had been

disturbed by my innocent approach, and was typically defending its space. (Reticulated pythons are well known amongst herpetologists for their somewhat aggressive temperament)

Finding myself suddenly dangling precariously from the vines by only one arm, I was unceremoniously invited to demonstrate my, until then, little-practised, aerial, acrobatic techniques, probably closer resembling a disjointed puppet on strings in a Punch and Judy show. I was just clumsily able to dodge a number of strikes, before, with a desperate lunge, I grabbed hold of the snake behind its huge head and gaping mouth, filled with rows of razor sharp teeth. This was not the end of the matter as the giant snake immediately proceeded to transfer its coils from the underbrush in favour of my wriggling body, with dramatic effect. Within seconds my arm and upper torso was being subjected to tremendous pressure, and I knew the snake must not under any circumstances get around my neck. With four metres of angry muscle wrapped around my body, I knew conclusively this was not a good time to be swinging on one arm like Tarzan through the jungle, however good it may look on camera.

Swinging back towards the rocky shelf with my feet, I was able to transfer myself from the vines back onto the ledge which the snake had vacated in favour of my body and, with some manoeuvring I managed to settle and stabilise myself enough to utilise both hands in my efforts not to be throttled to death. At this point, I was now able to proceed with a piece to camera. This turned out quite dramatic, as the bright red flush of my face and the bulging, swollen veins in my one arm clearly demonstrated the power of this formidable constrictor as I continued with the battle to prevent coils from getting around my neck.

Afterwards, once I had with much difficulty untangled myself from the snake and positioned it back amongst the vegetation on the rock shelf, where it continued to hiss and pose threateningly, I felt uncharacteristically depleted of energy and strength, and seemed to ache all over. At first I attributed it to the high humidity, but then realisation suddenly dawned on me. Barely four months had elapsed since my accident in the cave, not nearly enough time to fully recover. I was still experiencing limited agility from my ribs and especially the damaged leg, and was a long way from my usual fitness and, after this little tussle with the python, I felt just a little more nervous about coming face to face with a giant Komodo Dragon. Such an encounter would allow no space for error, or weakness.

Making contact one day with a group of fishermen passing by in three dug-out canoes, they informed us that they knew exactly where a number of large adult dragons were to be located. One, all but toothless and emaciated, old man demonstrated vigorously with out-stretched arms and body slithering movements, that he could take us to exactly what we wanted, and what had so far eluded us. They were in fact roughly headed in that direction and we were welcome to join them, provided we travelled in their canoes and helped with the paddling, as the canoes could get in amongst rocky coves and across shallow waters where our much larger boat could not go. When asked, the little group of fishermen unanimously assured us that the place in question was, 'not far'.

Living in Africa, and being familiar with similar deceptive descriptions from rural tribesmen, which might amount to a rough equivalent of, 'how long is a piece of string', I should have been for-warned. However, in the excitement of the pending possibilities of giant Komodo Dragons ahead, I gave no second thought to the matter. That is, until some exhausting hours of paddling later, 'not far' appeared somewhat to be the fisherman equivalent of 'not close'. To add to this, the canoes all leaked profusely, and only continuous and sometimes frantic bailing with whatever instruments available, mostly our bare hands, prevented us from going down in the middle of the Flores Sea, a frightening time for cameramen and their equipment. None the less, as my mother used to say, - 'This too shall pass', - and when it did, though tired and soaked to the skin, we found ourselves awash in shallow, turquoise water on a beautiful coral beach, surrounded by towering, mountain slopes saturated with almost luminous, green foliage, sporadically broken with towering groves of palm trees, an exact replica, I imagine, of what every person throughout their lives, throughout the western world, has been led to believe is as paradise should look. As if this were not enough, barely had we pulled the canoes onto the beach, when out of the foliage stepped a Komodo Dragon.

For a few seconds we all just stared, as though to confirm this was all real. The Komodo, a half-grown specimen, seemed more interested than afraid, and casually stepped out along the beach in typical lizard-like fashion, its massive head and shoulders swinging an arch from left to right as it strode boldly past us, not twenty metres from where we all stood transfixed. It was like suddenly being transported back in time, a time before humans, when the giant lizards ruled supreme.

But this was just the beginning, as the promise earlier so descriptively displayed to us by the old fisherman unfolded before our very eyes. With some hurried gathering of camera equipment and other necessary paraphernalia, we quickly set out after the Komodo, which soon disappeared again into the forest. Following the trail and having negotiated our way through a dense section of jungle, we stepped out onto a large expanse of dry mud-flat and, just like that, there they were. Not one, but three of the largest Komodo Dragons I could ever have imagined existed, all gathered around the carcass of what appeared to be a long- dead, mountain goat.

Their concentration fully centred on the struggle for the 'lion's share', the great lizards ripped and tore at the carcass, and occasionally at each other, as a cloud of dust rose up from their efforts. Jurassic Park 4, and I was right there to witness it, camera in hand. From around the perimeter two more smaller dragons eyed the gathering, nervously. This included the dragon who had led us there, obviously attracted by the smell, and now by the activity surrounding the smell. This was a gathering of giants around a single food item, and the smaller dragons were evidently aware that, should they approach too close, they too might end up on the menu.

Once, while working on a wildlife film with another presenter, (who was very nervous about being in close proximity with snakes) where I demonstrated some venomous snake behaviour with a vicious cobra, I was fairly startled when later he referred to me, on camera, as 'part herpetologist, part lunatic'. However, thinking back now to numerous incidents and encounters with wild animals and reptiles, and especially this approach into the midst of frenzied, feeding dragons, I can sympathise somewhat, and forgive this "desecration" of my character. One thing was certain though, after all the effort and preparation, and the travelling and the painful accident I had endured to get this far, I was not about to let the opportunity slip away.

It is one thing to get close to, and work with, a reptile that you can catch and handle if necessary. It is quite another when the reptile in question is bigger and heavier than you, can out run you, and is capable of eating you, should it so decide. While it is often possible, under ideal conditions, to approach such a potentially dangerous reptile, these Komodo Dragons infected all the time with a frenzied lust for food in the face of dangerous rival competition, did not qualify as ideal. I knew this well, all too well, but in spite of this knowledge, the urge to get closer was too great, and I knew I had to do it. This is after all what I am about, what I had come for, and I would probably never get the chance again.

With some few exceptions, reptiles rely more specifically on their sense of smell, provided by the forked tongue, collecting airborne particles to be analysed in the Jackobson's Organ in the roof of the mouth, than by any visual ability. So it is too with the Komodo Dragon, and therefore any movement might attract attention even without specific identification. When a Komodo Dragon is all fired up with the exciting aroma of food, as these dragons were now, any movement might be interpreted as food on the hoof. That is exactly what happened as I moved cautiously closer and closer, my camera raised to my eye and firing shot after shot.

Chomping and ripping and tearing at the carcass, the three giant dragons battled their way through it, spewing intestines and chunks of meat in all directions. Suddenly, one of the three lizards was literally hurled aside by raw physical force from another, which landed the creature off the carcass and clumsily turned towards me, where I was kneeling down low for ground level focus. So surprised was I by this movement, and so close was the dragon to me, that I involuntarily dropped backwards onto my elbows, and that was all it took. Seeming somewhat disorientated for a moment, the Komodo stared directly at me, then took a tentative step forward.

Now, as well as I knew that running would attract certain attention, staying where I was, half propped up on elbows and butt, just metres from this feed-crazed Komodo, left me with little choice. If I remained still, and the lizard did come at me, I would be in its jaws in seconds with not a hope in hell of convincing it that I was not actually the original prey of choice. With the option to run, I at least felt I would be attempting something productive, rather than just sit and wait for the most likely alternative scenario to materialise.

So, up and run I did, with some impressive agility to boot, thanks to a massive shot of adrenaline spontaneously pumped into my blood stream. Though I knew with some certainty that I could not outrun this lizard, I was already heading for the closest tree at the edge of the mud-flat. I was not alone as, from the very edge of my peripheral vision, I glimpsed the hunched figure of Warwick, my leading cameraman, as he kept pace from a distance, camera slung close to the ground and rolling. This was going to be some dramatic footage, the final outcome of which was yet to be determined as, from behind me, came the sound of a leviathan, reptilian body scrambling at my heels.

The tree was old, dead, and crusty with weathered bark, and I took to it with all fours, like a monkey with nowhere else to go but up. Fortunately it was not a difficult tree to climb (not that that would have made any difference at the time) and I scaled up it, ripping my hands and shirt on the rough bark. Just as the first emotions of relief began to flow through my body, I turned for the first time, and was astonished to see the Komodo Dragon, not stranded below gazing up longingly at its lost meal as I had hoped, but already in the tree and on its way up. This was a lizard with some determination. Pretty obvious it didn't get the size it was from

*A Komodo Dragon extends its long forked tongue to determine the direction of its prey*

letting prey escape from it. Quickly, I climbed higher, only to find myself stranded on the only substantial limb, which now creaked threateningly under my weight. And still the giant lizard came on, scrabbling and clawing at the bark, and making pretty good progress. Nobody had told me Komodo Dragons could climb trees, a small detail I would have to discuss with my researchers later. If there was a later!

For the second time, in a very short space of time, I found myself faced with a delicate decision. Remain where I was and wait for the brittle branch to break should the dragon reached me, or jump out now and hope for the best. The sound of approaching giant claws ripping at the bark just below me sorted that one out and, without further ado, I leaped out for the earth some four metres below. I hit the ground and rolled and was up and running, joined by Warwick, who had positioned himself not far away, camera still rolling. Like startled rabbits we covered about fifty metres through the bush before taking a chance look back, expecting to see the lizard hot on the scent. But there was no lizard behind us. It was still up in the tree, looking rather forlorn, its huge head shifting this way and that, as if attempting to assimilate where its meal had so suddenly disappeared. A minute later it turned and scrambled quickly down the tree again, unerringly heading back to the activity around the goat carcass, which the remaining two Komodos were making short work of.

The rest of the team had meanwhile collected a lot of good footage at the feeding sight, while Warwick assured me that he felt certain he had captured much of the chase up the tree. Combined, this was going to cut a pretty amazing sequence. All-in-all a good day's work, and a fascinating look into the feeding habits of the Komodo Dragons, I having narrowly missed being on the menu.

When we returned to the beach soon after, the sun had already dropped below the towering cliffs, leaving our paradise, cove bay calm and reflecting in the golden light of dusk. Too late to head back to our boat, via sinking canoes, we opted to spend the night on the beach, where we built a fire and ate dried fish and stale rice supplied to us by our friends, the fishermen. Above us the stars glittered like diamonds in the blackness, while, close by, the warm sea gently lapped the coral shore. Occasionally there would come rustling sounds from within the surrounding forest, and sometimes an unidentifiable cry of a night mammal, or bird, or gecko.

And far into that awesome night we chatted and discussed the day's events, each taking a turn to describe my scramble for the tree with the Komodo Dragon hot on my heels. Even the fisherman joined in here, flamboyantly and dramatically re-enacting the scene, until we were all but crying with laughter. Later, as the night wore on, we all became silent, listening to the tropical night and experiencing a time of absolute contentment. I felt something I had only felt before in the desert. For those few short hours we were at total peace, in need of nothing, and this world of natural beauty was ours. The towering mountain shapes in the darkened sky with the glittering stars, and the animal cries, and the lapping water, were a reminder of our insignificance in the great make-up of it all, and we would never forget it. It is, above all, the very heart of what makes wildlife filming and photography worth almost any sacrifice or risk. It is an escape to another world, a world that few people experience, a world of another dimension.